Hamish Brown has been an outdoorsman for more than sixty years. The first person to complete an uninterrupted round of Scotland's Munros, his *Hamish's Mountain Walk* is a classic of Scottish mountain literature. He is the author or editor of many books including *The Mountains Look on Marakech* (he has made fifty visits to the Atlas), the mountain poetry anthologies *Speak to the Hills* and *Poems of the Scottish Hills*. In recognition of his services to literature, he received an honorary D. Litt. from St. Andrews University in 1997 and a D. Uni in 2007. He was made an MBE in 2001.

Recent titles by Hamish Brown

The Mountains Look on Marakech
(the story of a 1000 mile, 96 day traverse of the Atlas)

The Atlas Mountains
(superbly illustrated descriptions of the best treks and climbs)

The Oldest Post Office in the World
(over ninety extraordinary places described and illustrated)

Three Man on the Way Way
(the experiences of three Fifers walking the
West Highland Way)

Canals Across Scotland
(everything about the Union and Forth & Clyde Canals;
lavishly illustrated)

As editor: Tom Weir, an anthology
(a selection of published or unpublished writing; illustrated)

Republished, with new introductions and illustrations

Hamish's Mountain Walk
(the first non-stop round of the Munros; a classic)

Hamish's Groats End Walk
(covers the English, Welsh and Irish 3000ers)

Climbing the Corbetts
(narrative of these mountains)

WALKING
the
SONG

Hamish Brown

SANDSTONEPRESS
HIGHLAND | SCOTLAND

Published in Great Britain by
Sandstone Press Ltd
Dochcarty Road
Dingwall
Ross-shire
IV15 9UG
Scotland

www.sandstonepress.com

The publisher acknowledges support from
Creative Scotland towards publication of this volume.

ISBN: 978-1-910985-58-8
ISBNe: 978-1-910985-59-5

Cover design by Raspberry Creative, Edinburgh
Typeset by Iolaire Typography Ltd, Newtonmore
Printed and bound by CPI Group (UK) Ltd, Croydon, CR0 4YY

796.522092 |BRO

*For the survivors of these years
with thanks*

CONTENTS

FOREWORD

This collection is a potpourri, mainly of articles which have appeared, or have their subject matter in events over the last fifty years. They describe *some* of the places and varied doings with which I've been involved or stories that caught my imagination. If they rather wander then I'll quote Mummery who declared 'the true mountaineer is a wanderer'. And the longer and further we wander the better. We need longer wanderings to allow the baggage we bring to fall away and, unburdened, go free. The selections have largely been left as they appeared, appealing to the forgiveness of time, and not updated though I have added notes where needed, either at the end or within square [brackets] in the text. Some are long, some brief, a few are simply snapshots, in all a very token selection with many countries and interests not mentioned. It is not an autobiography or some overview of life though, of necessity, a very personal record. It is simply a potpourri.

Chance, choice (which is chance taken) and hard work has allowed me to spend much of my life actively in mountains, at sea, and wandering the world whether professionally or with friends. Much of what is selected comes from the Sixties to the Eighties when I was most fit and far-ranging (my 'dancing days of spring') but as the Arab saying warns 'Much travel is needed before a raw man is ripened' and the writing compulsion also needs passing years to mature - or have gained experiences to draw on. The rewards always remain, as long as we can sing within the measure of our abilities, through all the ages of our activities.

I'm really quite lazy and have so many interests besides mountaineering that I *need* definite challenges to head out and up. The interests often interact: a general interest in gardening becomes a particular interest in alpine flora - because it's up there, the flowers' lure among the rocks and snow. Always, the heights pull; it is there we are most content 'Outclimbing pasture and pine / To seek beyond the mountain line / That far-sought country more divine / Where life is whole'. (D W Freshfield)

Reading about my earlier days I am struck by the confident young man I appear. Perhaps I was for those were days of hope and belief in the future. During the Japanese raids on Singapore we sang of 'love and laughter, and peace ever after tomorrow when the world is free'. At post war schoolboy camps we belted out, 'I'm riding along on the crest of a wave, and the world is mine'. And we believed it. Alas, cynicism has grown back over that young sapling's faith. ('We are a failed species on the way out'.) Those of my age and my sort of schooling in the Forties were, perforce, physically very fit and challenged but whatever confidence accrued was quite unconscious. We already knew both rough and smooth. I reckon my RAF days 'made me' with its great freedom within discipline, and any kindness I have comes from knowing the best of peoples in the Atlas Mountains.

I may have been 'below average' in many subjects at school but books, music, art, the countryside around were all part of my very being growing up in Dollar. Hobbies and enthusiasms came and went but these remained. My early interest in what was call Nature Study had me sending in so many questions to a radio programme for schools that they did a whole programme answering my questions alone. Some peers thought this excessive but I wanted to know - and I'm still that 'Curiosity Kid', only now deeply worried at what humankind is doing to our only wonder-full world. Awareness of beauty, of idealism dawns when young, losing them is to grow old. Insist on finding wonders, living with beauty, and taking challenges. As Nansen wrote, 'Try not to waste time in doing things which you know can be done equally well by others. Everyone should try to hit upon his own trail. Do not lose your opportunities, and do not allow yourselves to be carried away by the superficial rush and scramble which is modern life ...'

Memory is a strange thing, certainly for me, with a greater facility for forgetting rather than remembering. (I marvel at folk who can put a date to an incident thirty years ago!) Luckily I've always kept a mountaineering 'log' (on volume 73 now!), along with a 'Summary', big as a family Bible, with all the Who? When? Where? What? data. I need these. In 2013 when writing about the 1969 school traverse of Mont Blanc I had completely forgotten another traverse with a friend only a year before. But then, that year was rather overshadowed by what happened on the Meije. The briefest note can bring so much back from the limbo of memory. Braehead school's first week was in winter, in Glen Coe, yet months on, when the Headmaster and I wrote a script for a BBC radio based on our doings, whole chunks of original conversations returned. All this recording, at the time, is also a good check on how memory or imagination can change reality over the years, how good stories become embroidered and truths become myths. ('Essaouira Myths' shows the extremes.) I've got my personal failsafe then, and try to be accurate. Checking facts is not easy and becomes worse with the sloppy nature of the internet and so on. When I did the book on the Fife Coast the text was checked by a history professor. The only thing he queried was the date when Alexander Selkirk (model for Robinson Crusoe) died. In the publisher's office we took down four reference books and found three different dates. I had to find documents signed by the man before being sure of the spelling of our great road-builder Caulfeild.

The material has been arranged in roughly thematic sections with a few articles in each, the headings giving an idea of the subject matter. There may be some repetitions as the material has been written over such a long period. The dates of any escapade are usually clear. The book is certainly full of co-incidences, of what is often called 'wheels within wheels', how one thing leads to another. We may think we are captains of our souls but any puff of wind can set our crazy craft off on an unexpected course. Life is fascinating, simple, complex, baffling and rewarding - and so very brief. Weave a web of wonders from it; in old age look back with few regrets, and marvel at the rewards. Go places! Six hundred years ago John Donne wrote, 'To live in one land, is captivitie, / To runne all countries, a wild roguery'. This book is one rogue's attempt to have followed that advice.

My interests were too many and too varied to excel at any one: I was never a great climber, a great ornithologist, or great anything else. In some ways my niche would be more inspirational than technical, impelling others into experiences, showing that any person has a world of wonder to discover out there, up there.

When I look at all the reasons given why we climb, why we head to the mountains, or sea, or riverbank or whatever, the commonest word surfacing is 'escape'. We do it to escape from the stranglehold of everyday living to create brief heavens in those neutral worlds we imagine. There we gain respite from pressures, 'kiss the cheek of beauty', find good companions, return stronger to face the unfathomable world. It is almost a religious experience. The fact of there being thousands of religions worldwide points to an inexplicable necessity so this should not surprise. In Neil Munro's *New Road* Aeneas is girning, 'I was in a black mood all this day, reflecting on the wickedness of humankind, and sure the world was evil - ' 'So it is!' cried Ninian cheerfully, 'but man, there's blinks'. Where would we be without those 'blinks'?

Burntisland 2016

BEGINNINGS

OUR ROAD TO SINGAPORE

No one is fool enough to choose war instead of peace - in peace sons bury fathers, but in war fathers bury sons.

Herodotus

My young brother was born in Yokohama, Japan, in December 1940. I was born in Colombo, Sri Lanka (then Ceylon) in 1934, my mother was born in Thailand (then Siam) in 1904 while big brother and father were both born in Dunfermline. Father had a rough time in WWI, was wounded, recovered, sent back to the front, then captured in the big German offensive of spring 1918. Though we knew it not, being in Japan in 1940 might well have entailed a much nastier replay.

Father was a banker, with the then Chartered Bank of India, Australia and China (Standard Chartered today). Staff in those days of slow travel filled a posting for quite a few years before being given a long home leave and then posted to a new country. Mother's father had been building railways in Siam to where father was posted after WWI. (I've a photo of mother as a girl, in full highland dress, performing a sword dance for the King of Siam.)

I'd always known that big brother and grannie in Scotland

1

almost came out to Japan early in 1941 - for safety! Scotland after all was being bombed. Recently I came on a packet of letters to and from home at the time which confirmed this. Mercifully, father was then posted (January 1941) to what is now Malaysia, to a town called Klang. (The bank would become HQ for the Japanese secret police.)

I was packed off to a school in the Cameron Highlands where the climate was more wholesome. I was provided with four purply-coloured shirts, four pairs of grey shorts and all the rest of a uniform, everything with carefully sewn-on Cash's name tapes. A few months later we were fleeing for our lives.

Mother's day-to-day pocket diary mirrors this state of unreality and unpreparedness: every Tuesday was Mah Jong, Wednesday, tennis, Thursday, the Club ... There were trips to KL (Kuala Lumpur) for a perm, films (I recall *The Four Feathers*), riding, *tiffin* at the golf club (not that they played). No diary mention of Pearl Harbour (7 December 1941), then, 'Bad raid. Hamish missing', an echo of the unreality. Apparently I was most upset about bombs disturbing small brother's first birthday.

On my desk I keep a *memento mori* of those times: a piece of shattered brass door handle. Father was reaching to the handle when it disappeared, smashed off by a piece of bomb. He was often on the roof as a fire warden. The family was usually in the vaults where I built castles with rolled cylinders of coins, an excellent Lego forerunner. To this day I carry a ganglion-overgrown fragment of shrapnel in a knee. Raids were much more exciting outside - no doubt I had been 'missing' again.

Such was the speed of the Japanese advance that, after false moves, we sailed from Port Swettenham to Singapore before the year end - which was out of a small frying pan into a mighty fire. I've vivid memories of Singapore in flames, of singing in the shelters, of the frantic scurrying of terrified people. On the first of January 1942 we sailed on the crowded Dutch ship, *Mannix van St Aldergende* and duly arrived as refugees in Durban. We were in South Africa for two years before being repatriated. (Some of that period is described shortly.)

We had not seen father after Klang. He stuck to his bank duties as long as possible (an interesting story in itself) and, still lugging ledgers, only retreated to Singapore a week after we had sailed. He was 49 at the time. We never heard much from his lips but after he died (1968) we found a notebook with an account he wrote about his subsequent adventures. This was scrawled in pencil in the illegible hand of a banker and it was years before I made time to transcribe it.

Astonishingly, with Singapore in flames and the Japanese landing only two days away father was still trying to do bank business. When eventually he went to the wharf to - hopefully - join a ship (bombs falling constantly) he had his prepared suitcase packed with 'pages of the latest current account balances, rough cash book entries and the up-to-date records of Fixed Deposits and Fixed Loans'.

His ship, the *Kuala*, was joined by another sheltering off an island, Pompong (Pohm-Pohm), while a third, exposed further out, had been damaged already. Many of the men from the *Kuala* went ashore to cut greenery to further disguise the ship but Japanese reconnaissance planes found them and in a series of raids sunk all three ships, killing most of those on board, mostly women and children.

A Dutch ship picked up the wounded and the remaining women and children - but was never heard of again. Island-hopping and eventually crossing Sumatra the survivors reached Padang, the only operational port left in the country. Extraordinarily, it was neither bombed nor captured by approaching forces. Father was eventually taken off by a British destroyer, carrying all his belongings wrapped in a blue handkerchief. After a grim stay in Ceylon father landed in Durban on 27 March 1942. We were - briefly - reunited. There were the questionings of course. This is what father wrote.

'Since coming here [India, later in 1942] I have been asked many times why Singapore did not put up a better show. In the first place Singapore was not the impregnable fortress it was supposed to be. Defences to landward seemed entirely lacking and why, when it became apparent that the Japanese were coming down the peninsula, was no effort made to construct lines of defence at strategic positions. The absence of prepared positions was most noticeable on the way down from Klang to Singapore. Why was a Siamese delegation allowed to inspect Singapore's defences a few weeks before the showdown? Our intelligence seems to have been entirely misled. Why such a lack of air power? Our fighters, Brewster Buffaloes, were about 40 miles per hour slower than the Japanese bombers and it was pathetic to see how easily the enemy could get away or circle round and come up behind their pursuers. The anti-aircraft defences were good and Japanese bombers were always kept at a great height but in Klang there was no defence and the Japanese could come down over the roof tops with impunity. Why were reinforcements being landed when it must have been obvious that Singapore was doomed? Troops were actually being evacuated by the ships which brought reinforcements. There are so many *Whys* that it is impossible to cover them all but the dominant factor was the lack of resolute leadership'.

AND AFTER

Father had joined us in South Africa but as soon as he was fully fit again he was posted, in turn, to Madras, Calicut and

Karachi - where he had to cope with the horrors of the 1947 partition of India. We were only fully reunited as a family in 1949 in Scotland. He had not seen his firstborn for nine years.

STARTING IN THE OCHILS

Happiness should be the foundation of all mountaineering.
Julius Kugy: *Alpine Pilgrimage*

My first consciousness of hills (the Scots derivation includes mountains) was sitting on a windowsill looking at Fuji Yama in Japan. I was crying because my parents had gone off to climb it without me and I was crying because I couldn't see them on it (the hill was forty miles away). That was in 1941. I was seven.

After an exciting intermission we ended up as refugees in South Africa and stayed on the edge of the Valley of a Thousand Hills. With a 'best friend' I roamed the *kloofs* and *bergs* in marvellous freedom, so the clarity of the Natal air, the very scent of the landscape is with me yet and I thank whatever gods there may be for parents who gave me such freedom to roam.

When we eventually won back to Scotland it was to Dollar - in the Stirling area - with the Ochils rising above the small town with its big school. I did not particularly like my schooling: I found my peers dull conformists and most teachers hidebound and insincere. With hindsight this was an educational nadir, the staff were oldies brought out of retirement and others were war wounded, so I wasn't entirely at fault. I stubbornly followed my own interests rather than the curriculum, which led to some of my troubles. The Cross-country, for example, was a sacred cow for which everyone had to put in five practise runs. I was soon banned from taking my dog and when I insisted on wanting to know why was belted by the sports master as I wouldn't accept 'Because you're told'. After all I knew every farmer on the route and they never objected to the dog. On one run a hill farmer's wife asked if I'd take an armful of daffodils down to the church for her. I prayed I'd run into the sports master to see what he'd say about *that*. I hated the way for instance that smoking was regarded as such a heinous crime yet the master dealing out beatings for this had a nicotine yellow moustache.

From my bed I could see the steep southern scarp of the Ochils dip to the roofs of the town or tilt back to the clouds easing off King's Seat. A 'piece' shoved in an ex WD haversack, a whistle for the dog and I could be away to those tawny slopes, up by the Glen and Castle Campbell and Burn of Sorrow to Maddy Moss and Andrew Gannel and Ben Cleuch, names worthy of John Buchan, sometimes right over to Blackford or Auchterarder or, restrained by the curving cleavage of the infant Devon, descending to Tilly, Alva or Menstrie, the delightfully ungrammatical 'Hillfoots'.

In the Ochils I never got *lost*, however often I became *mislaid*. Unless going beyond the natural moat of the infant River Devon all water flowed out to the Hillfoots, the simplest of geographic assurances. The river is 34 miles long yet rises only 5.25 miles from where it spills into the maw of the Forth estuary. The early cavorting water heads east, but is turned at the aptly named Crook of Devon, before flowing west, as if to find its own start like a snake circling round to hold its own tail.

Below the river-capture of the Crook was Rumbling Bridge, a gorge as blackly dramatic as Novar or Corrie-shalloch, dizzy deep when looking over the parapet of the bridge which, oddly, sits on top of another bridge. In spate the roar is prodigious, the upstream Devil's Mill, so called because, unlike the mills of men, it never switched off on God's Sabbath. Vicar's Bridge spanned the river at one of our favourite swimming pools (now silted up; the bridge rebuilt) and one of my first researched and published articles concerned Robert Forest, vicar of Dollar who was burnt alive in 1539 for his questioning faith and charitable deeds.

The nearest cinema (bug house) was at Tillicoultry, three miles away and we often had to walk home afterwards in the dark, along a twisty road with monstrous, threatening trees which groaned and shivered, and Tait's Tomb, an abandoned, overgrown, circular graveyard, passing which we felt we could relax like Tam o' Shanter once across the bridge and safe.

If this sounds an idyllic picture then, from today's perspective, I reckon it was. Life was both Spartan and cosy. We grew vegetables, kept bees and hens (the eggs laid down in a crock of waterglass), knew the discipline of ration coupons, learned how to sew and make do and mend. I wore big brother's hand-me-downs. We were satisfied with needs, not unhappy with wants. Rationing ensured a sensible diet with issues of orange juice and cod liver oil and school milk in bottles of a third of a pint with cardboard tops (which were never resistant to attacks by blue tits). Nobody had cars. The post-war years had an earnestness to them. Life was not easy but the future was surely good.

The paths and bridges of the glen had decayed during the war years so were out of bounds officially but I knew every cranny, every pool, where what flowers grew and what birds nested. I absorbed, rather than consciously learned, about the natural world. Castle Campbell, perched above the glen, had a single mason who worked patiently on the castle's fabric for a decade and became a friend. He would tell of John Knox preaching there, of how the Campbells came into possession by a murder and a marriage, point out the chains on the hanging tree or tell how Royalists fired the place in 1654.

The whinstone quarry of Gloom Hill was out of bounds too but there I took six inch nails for pitons and applied some novel aspects of climbing. Years later I took other youngsters there to teach them to climb. (Years on others came and put up routes and claimed first ascents!) One place was avoided for part of the year as a barn owl nested in a niche.

Some of us used to walk through Glendevon to help with building the youth hostel (now closed, alas) or to go to church, feeling very like drovers or religious sectarians who in the past would do so as a matter of course. I recall a chilly bivouac with a friend, climbing to meet the sun and then, chapter about, reading right through the Gospel of St John. In the burns of the lesser Ochils beyond Glendevon we learned to guddle trout.

Dollar's golf course lay on the steep lower slopes of Dollar Hill. I preferred the golf course in winter when various sledging runs were named after the holes (we never went on the greens). The Eighteenth I recall was brutally steep and likely to land one in the Dollar Burn. Years on, my second day on skis was up 2000 ft White Wisp, which sounded appropriate. We had snow in those days. While father made the porridge I sometimes *skated* down the road for the rolls on the compacted snow of the main road. In the great snow of '47 going to the Alloa baths by bus on a Saturday morning our eyes, on the top deck, just looked out over the monster drifts through which canyons had been cut.

The Ochils taught a great deal about snow conditions, their polished steep slopes perfect for avalanches. In summer the best footwear I found were my studded cricket boots which were green-marked beyond redemption to the annoyance of cricket captains or coaches. I enjoyed both cricket and rugger (and swimming and cross-country running) but they could not compete with the lure of the outdoors. I slept out on the hills. I learned their intricacies as a shepherd does. I roamed them at night with a Tilley lamp until asked to desist. Leg movement made it look like a flashing light and the police were not too happy about 'rescuing' me!

The only adult I met on the hill and who became a gentle, wise, friend was W K Holmes, a reader for Blackies, a poet, and author of *Tramping Scottish Hills*, the most modest of books, but book and WKH would ensure an all-round enthusiasm for *everything* out there, up there, whether investigating supposed ancient copper mines, watching the weird roding woodcock above the glen, reading-up the castle's history or dreaming of adventures further afield.

When I found the books of J H B Bell, W H Murray and Tom Weir they led me to greater aspirations. When the great slot from the Long Bridge to the castle (Kemp's Score) was frozen I took the coal shed axe and cut steps up its length, an exercise the dog failed to appreciate as all the ice chips fell on him, but then the dog went everywhere, well, nearly everywhere. I wonder if that winter ascent has ever been repeated?

Nobody was interested in using the Ochils as part of school activities and I happily roamed alone till able to beguile others to come along as well. What a waste I felt even then. The headmaster's family pew and our family pew in the parish church were next to each other, the head an elder, my father treasurer as well, and the children's ages mingled. Father even persuaded the head to take up bee-keeping. Yet it was only years later I found the head was a life member of the Scottish Mountaineering Club (SMC) and at a social occasion years after he retired we had a chat and he'd obviously followed some of my doings in the Journal. He must have known of my Ochils ramblings so why never a bit of encouragement then?

Despite various family connections I, like everyone else, held the headmaster, the Bull, in awe so when a minion entered a maths class to say the headmaster wanted to see me right away I went with the eyes of the class following me speculatively. I was wondering what I had done. I didn't feel guilty. The head sat at the far end of a long boardroom table and as I neared his seat my panic deepened. 'I've been phoning your father, Brown, but can't get hold of him.' Heavens! Must be serious. 'I can't go home so you'll just have to go and sort things out. My bees have swarmed.'

Eventually I reached the dizzy heights of playing hooker for the Second Fifteen who, of course, were always at the receiving end of the First Fifteen thugs. When pitches were frozen we were sometimes made to run up King's Seat (over 2000ft) and on one such occasion the mist came down with some lads marooned on top. The gods of the First Fifteen grabbed me with a 'You know your way about these effin hills, Brown, so tell us how to get back to Dollar'. I gave them clear instructions which led them to Blackford on the other side of the range! I knew I'd be hammered at our next Tuesday afternoon meeting but it was worth it, imagining the shavers, in rugger kit, moneyless, going to the police and being loaned money to bus first to Stirling and then to Dollar, missing lunch and being very unpopular. (A version of this story was told to me decades later, the teller quite unaware he was speaking to the culprit.)

I really did fall foul of my short-tempered rugger coach (and maths teacher) on one occasion. I looked out to a brilliant spring Saturday morning and rushed off for the heights. Hours and miles away I suddenly remembered I was supposed to be playing a game that morning. I was genuinely distraught on that occasion.

There was a school CCF (Combined Cadet Force) and I was in the RAF section which was fun: at camps all we seemed to do was swim, shoot and fly - and this also ensured National Service in that cushie number rather than the army. One broiling summer's day however we were sent on an Ochils exercise with a radio set which was like an enormous heavy backpack. We had to check in from various six figure references and describe what we saw. I doubted if the teacher/officer i/c had been on top of the Ochils so we headed instead for the Out-of-Bounds glen and spent the afternoon in its cool pools. At appropriate moments I climbed up to the edge of the woods and would report in about our mythical movements - and of course could describe everything supposedly in sight. (I could do so still I reckon.) After reporting back to base and being dismissed I heard our mentor, noting our wet hair, comment on the lines, 'My, did you see the way we made them sweat'.

Sending my mates over the Ochils as recorded would be an impossible trick today for the good path they would have followed down the Broich Burn for the Kinpauch Glen and Blackford is now cut by a reservoir, one of two flooding the upper, eastern flow, of the River Devon. And there's another reservoir in Glendevon itself, edged by the road through to Glen Eagles and Crieff. If I needed any conviction about global warming I might take it from how Maddy Moss, drained by the Burn of Sorrow, has changed from being a dangerous 'moss' (bog) in those days into what is now firm rough grazing, where skylarks dance up and down the sky.

The Burn of Sorrow and the Burn of Care meet below Castle Campbell, once known as the Gloom, fitting in with the names of its moating streams. The castle served as the

Campbells' 'town house' for Edinburgh, the distance from Holyrood they no doubt felt safe enough to sleep in their own beds. The Burn of Care track goes through to Glendevon by the Maiden's Well and an older reservoir. At one stage I used to earn pocket money, and free rides (much more rewarding) by helping at stables at the Lower Mains and I recall, after having some child dropped in Glendevon, riding back through the hills. The gallop along by the Glenquey Reservoir was unforgettable. I lost my stirrups but somehow kept my seat. The Maiden's Well, passed on the way, is now largely forgotten and overgrown. WHK kept it clear in those days as we did later on. Certain traditions are lost sadly.

An ambition which we eventually fulfilled was to traverse the Ochils end-to-end over all their 2000 foot summits. There must have been about ten tops and the hike began on Sherrifmuir if a lift was arranged, or by slogging up Dumyat (*Dumb-eye-at* - the Spyglass Hill of Treasure Island some say) from the Hillfoots at Menstrie if left to our own devices. Blairdennon, Ben Ever, Ben Cleuch (the Ochils' highest), Andrew Gannel, King's Seat, Tarmangie, Whitewisp and Inner Downie are some I remember (I'm writing in the Atlas) and the day ended at or in the old Tormaukin Inn in Glendevon. If all the tops are done this is still a twenty mile tramp on the mainly firm Ochils grass with a few slaistery bits for good measure. Note Ochil Hills is tautology. Even the OS sin.

The 'Hut Man' of the BBC was one of those experts whose books were devoured and the school library had works by Ernest Thomson Seton, Grey Owl, the Kearton brothers, Jim Corbett, Seton Gordon and, of course, *Bevis* and Arthur Ransome, books which were devoured as much as G H Henty or Percy Westerman. Scottish history came from Scott's *Tales of a Grandfather* or D K Broster and, only realised recently, much historical folklore came from Seton Gordon's

Highways and Byways books. The whole family read, round a blazing fire in winter, precious LPs on father's radiogram in the background, Siamese cats on laps, dog on the hearth rug. One of the books everyone read was *The White Spider* and to my parents eternal credit, they never curtailed my onward progress to becoming a climber. After National Service, mostly in Egypt and Kenya, that education continued. (In Kenya, one morning Kilimanjaro appeared, rosy pink and unbelievably high above all clouds and I gasped 'What a hill'. My companion laughed, 'You can tell the Scot. Anyone else would call *that* a mountain'.)

My first climbing rope came in such an odd way I used to use its acquisition as a Twenty Questions topic and nobody ever got it. After National Service I was working as 'Missionary Assistant' in a Paisley parish and when the Asian flu epidemic struck I had to conduct many funerals at the crematorium. I was 20, most of the victims Oldies but each service had the bonus of a £1 fee. At last I had saved some cash and cycled up through the smog to Blacks in Glasgow to buy boots with Vibram soles and one of the new-fangled *nylon* climbing ropes.

Academically I was a failure but I took out of schooling the things I wanted and, somehow, they have been the foundation stones of the years since. Youth is a time of both hope and despair but, when one could lift eyes to the Ochils so easily, then there was great 'cumulence of comfort on high hills' (G W Young). Little did I know how I would carry their benediction with me wherever I travelled.

THE LURE OF SNOWDROPS

As mentioned my home territory as a boy was the Ochils and the whole landscape enclosed by the encircling River Devon

- an anglicisation of what Burns should have called Dowan in one of his poems. Its course in the hills has improved with the maturing of reservoirs and woodlands. The 'crook' in the river is a classic example of 'river capture' as, originally, it flowed into Loch Leven. Below the gorge with the bridge on top of bridge it pours over the Cauldron Linn. One of the area's Victorian country mansions tapped this force to make its own electricity, an energy source which has been recreated today. My western bounds of the Devon were really the Dead Waters: fields which were flooded in winter from the river to allow skating. In my youth the school had official half-holidays for when conditions were right and town and gown would flock to the site to enjoy the 'Skating Halves'. This is a forgotten joy today, such freezing a thing of the past. (Climate change? Global warming?)

One of my lifetime hobbies of 'rescuing' trees began on the River Devon. A riverbank rowan had seeded onto a mossy rock and grown into a fine small tree but its weight then toppled it from its scant hold on the rock and the victim lay thrashing in the flow, only held by a few roots. I took the tree home and planted it in our garden. It's still there, saluted every time I drive past. (When you visit Sourlies bothy or Shenaval - greet my rowans there please.)

Facing where this tree once grew is a den (dell) which was, long ago, laid out with paths from a mansion above. One path led to the Cauldron Linn, but all the paths were overgrown and the den itself almost impenetrable - which was an additional attraction for the roaming schoolboy. The roof had already been taken off the mansion when I discovered the den sometime soon after WW2. The banks below the ruin into the dell were an amazing spread of snowdrops, 'millions of them' as I reported once home and then dragged mother to 'come and see'. We took some home and they still thrive, as snowdrops do, lining the path up to the front door. We called the place Snowdrop Valley and shared its location with very few other people. It was a very special secret place.

Nosing about the half-ruined mansion at the end of one snowdrop season I found a very puzzling flower. The flower itself was rather like a snowdrop but the leaves were like big daffodil leaves, while the bulb was more like that of a hyacinth. Baffled, I took one round the village to show it to anyone who might recognise the flower. Nobody did. I was even accused on one occasion of creating a leg-pull. In despair I sent it to the Royal Botanic Garden in Edinburgh. They replied that it was a Summer Snowflake, *Leucoium aestivum*, which was once popular in Victorian gardens but had dropped out of favour. There is a smaller Spring Snowflake as well, *Leucoium vernum* and both are enjoying a renewed popularity sixty years on from my discovery.

But it was the snowdrops that became my passion and every spring I'd make a pilgrimage to Snowdrop Valley to see the spectacle. There's nothing like a woodland alight with snowdrops to make the heart lift. There is a folk story about snowdrops. When Adam and Eve were expelled from the Garden of Eden they found a world of winter desolation. Seeing Eve weeping in the snow an angel started breathing on the falling flakes so on touching the ground they became the flowers we know, ones to symbolise returning warmth and hope for the world. There is a touch of immortality about snowdrops, the way they come each year (some through tarmac in my garden!) and spread and multiply, without any need of us. Their only enemy - but also good friend - is man. Creating snowdrop woods became another lifetime hobby.

On another schoolboy visit to Snowdrop Valley I received a shock. The mansion house had been demolished and the rubble bulldozed down onto the snowdrop bank. The snow-drops were buried. I was so upset I did not go back there for about twenty years; when I did it was to receive another shock: the bank was as white as ever with snowdrops.

Investigation revealed why. The buried snowdrops had grown, and even put up white-tipped spears of flower - underground - then, instead of the plant's goodness going down into the bulb, another bulb was created an inch or so up the stem. Year by year they had fought back determinedly to reach the surface. A snowdrop miracle, take what symbolism you will from it.

WITH AUNT NELL AND I

'The last of the Raj' was the name I gave her. She was perhaps not all that gentle a person but she was indomitable and I found her fun because I refused to take her seriously. I first encountered Aunt Nell when, with mother and infant brother, we landed in Durban as refugees from Singapore on the first of January 1942 - and there she was, on duty as a nurse, bossing arrivals about.

She was father's sister and was in South Africa because her husband, an Army doctor, was stationed in Durban. Another of father's brothers, Uncle Jim, had lived in South Africa for most of his life. Their oldest was in the SAAF and was killed on a raid over Germany, their other son was in his early teens and became someone I ran wild with and admired as only 8 can worship 13. Dick would spend his life working in locust control in Africa but even then was the complete outdoor boy, typical of a country given a decent ration of sun. My abiding memory of him was on the beach at Durban where we inspected a shark which had been hauled onto the sand. Dick gave it a kick - and I was sent flying by a reflex sweep of its tail.

This family diaspora in Natal was an unexpected blessing. The ship carrying us to safety could as easily have gone to relation-free Australia, the destination only being decided on once well into the Indian Ocean. Aunt Nell spent a lot of time with us. She was tiny yet imperious, a bit like Queen Victoria I imagine. She smoked like an industrial chimney of that vintage. And I encouraged her.

Aunt Nell smoked incessantly but always with a silver-mounted ebony cigarette holder. In my teens I drew a portrait of her and without thinking had this projecting from her lips in the picture. Despite this habit she lived to a ripe old age. In her eighties her doctor told her to give up or she would soon be dead so she walked out of the surgery and never smoked again. As I said, indomitable.

Her smoking fascinated me but quickly came to mean far more. She chain smoked Navy Capstan cigarettes which came in cylindrical tins with labels showing a sailor and lifebuoy - and, important for me, included cigarette cards, at that time series on the *Flowers* and *The Birds of South Africa*. (*Ons Suid-Afrikaanse Plantegroei* and *Ons Suid-Afrikaanse Voëls*.) I collected these, and had the relevant albums into which to stick them, with the result I became interested in flowers and birds and thrilled whenever I *saw* one depicted on a card. South Africa's flora and fauna is exotic anyway. I distinctly recall seeing my first widow-bird with its long banner of a tail, and the first tree laden with hyperactive weaver birds' nests. The interest in birds and flowers would prove lifelong - and I still have those distinctive albums.

Then came a tragedy for me. We were going 'home', a place which had never been that. My Flower book was complete but I lacked a few Bird cards. I pestered Aunt Nell to increase production, vainly swopped possessions at school and even suggested I could be left behind in South Africa - I could catch up in Scotland once the cards were found.

The albums went with me on the *Andes* and the vast boys' dormitory of tiered bunks was a swoppers' market but proved fruitless. My main memory of the liner was the huge baths with great brass taps which, turned on full blast, almost shot one out the other end. I can still smell and imagine the tingle of those salt water baths. (Fresh water was rationed.) The *Andes* sailed unprotected, relying on her speed, and kept far out in the Atlantic before rounding Ireland to slip into Liverpool.

My spare Bird and Flower cards for swopping of course held no interest among my peers at school in Scotland but when I collected bird stamps later I quite often would turn to the Bird album for identifying species, and always grudged the five blank spaces. Why couldn't Aunt Nell have smoked more? She retired to Cyprus where Income Tax was sixpence in the pound and lived modestly on a doctor's war-widow's pension.

Thirty years on I was browsing in McNaughton's Bookshop at the head of Leith Walk when I spotted the familiar spines of three South African cigarette card albums on a top shelf. They were in a polybag with dozens of loose cards. There was one completed album on *Our South African National Parks/Ons Suid-Afrikaanse Nasionale Wildtuine* which presumably came out once I'd left the country, while both the Birds and Flowers books were incomplete. I paid £1 for this abandoned collection and after a rummage found the five cards I was missing! My yell of glee might have been heard in Durban. Aunt Nell, sadly, was no longer alive to inform of my triumph.

I cannot resist mentioning another - series - of schoolday coincidences. For senior rugger fixtures with Robert Gordon's in Aberdeen it was considered too far to travel, play, and return in a day so teams stayed overnight, individuals usually with their opposite number, so on this occasion the Browns had the Aberdeen hooker overnight. As we lay chatting in our beds that night a very strange story emerged. Both of our families had been living in Malaya when the Japanese arrived, both of us had escaped to South Africa, both went to the school Highbury while there, both of us travelled home on the *Andes*, both going to Scotland, both to play rugger, both to become hookers - and so we met.

I returned from South Africa covered in boils. At one stage I could almost meet my fingers round my fibula so badly had the flesh rotted away. On arrival in Scotland I could not *sit*. Embarrassing at ten years old. A doctor cousin decided I was a serious enough case to be offered a course of the new magic, *penicillin*, which at that stage of the war was reserved for military casualties. So, for what felt like weeks, Doctor Tom, stuck needles up and down my thighs every four hours. But it worked.

When retired, Aunt Nell spent as much time as was legally permitted with us in Dollar (several weeks every year) and also with her sister in Ireland. Dollar was a small village and the shopkeepers were soon shuddering when Aunt Nell appeared. Living in Cyprus much of the shopping was done by bargaining and she saw no reason why Scotland should be different. She terrified shop girls. I was lucky enough to stay with her in Cyprus while doing my National Service in Egypt's Canal Zone. She was in her sixties then and I was kindly given two weeks' compassionate leave to see 'the old dear' whom I might never see again.

Cyprus was a feast for the senses for an impressionable lad let loose. She had me riding along the sands outside Kyrenia before breakfast then all day we'd be touring the many great prehistoric sites, often with a picnic, calling on her friends, much swimming[1], dining at the Dome Hotel with a sorry-looking ex-King Farouk in the corner, or dancing eightsome reels at a dance when a naval ship, *HMS Owen*, called. In between I ranged the hills above Kyrenia, to St Hilarion Castle and the C14 monastery Bellapaise (where Lawrence Durrell was living and would write *Bitter Lemons* about Cyprus - not that I knew), and every day enjoying more birds and flowers than we ever observed by the Suez Canal. I read much about the island's history and culture[2]. A flawless holiday, but I was almost glad to return to the RAF for a rest.

Aunt Nell was still spending time with the family in Scotland following my RAF years abroad. Latterly, she needed a wheelchair for airport complexities and I was the one roped-in to push her along the passages of the then Turnhouse Airport. She had not changed much. I recall her taking her walking stick and whacking people on the bottom: 'Out the way! Out the way!' or 'Hamish, faster! Faster!' Wherever she went she knitted woollen socks, only socks, with only the one pattern and the four Brown males were still wearing these Christmas regulars for a decade after she died. We had glass extended round our bungalow in Kinghorn where we flitted once all we boys had left school and Aunt Nell had her seat on a couch and knitted interminably. (She would have made a good extra in the film of 'A Tale of Two Cities.) She was apt to clatter her dentures while knitting, which she emphatically denied, till I tape recorded her doing so. That did not go down well. She was also supposedly deaf.

Several fellow-teachers had called and a lively conversation on international affairs was under way when someone made a statement that had the needles stop their clicking, so everyone looked at the deaf old dear, who snorted, 'Nobody's going to tell me to call those [censored] people brother' - the conversation guillotined. I could only laugh at the discomfiture of my friends, not at her arrogant racist remark, which was not something our family would tolerate. We'd had enough of that in South Africa.

In South Africa I'd been given a small Hornby train set while living beside a place as beautiful as its name, the Valley of a Thousand Hills. We had a rondavel (a round chalet) to ourselves in the hotel grounds. My 'best friend' was a Zulu boy from down in what was a 'native reserve' where 'whites' were not allowed to go, or vice versa. When the hotel owner came in and saw us playing with the trains he literally kicked my 'black' friend round and round the room and out of the door. In Durban my mother flew at a hulking brute who took a backhand swipe at a black girl with a baby on her back because she did not step into the gutter for his passing. To this day I can hear the sound of that baby's head hitting the ground[3]. I found all this bewildering. Of course, living in the East, we always had servants but they were people who mattered. (Just after World War Two, in Dollar, we had a happy visit from a man who had been the family cook in Ceylon, in 1934!) In South Africa we then lived in a bigger house with a large garden where there were mulberry trees, so I bred silkworms and spun silk from their cocoons. (I've a cocoon on the windowsill beside me as I write.) We also had a formicary to study the wonderful world of ants. The black gardener I regarded simply as a friend. (I helped him by chasing after the headless hens when he'd 'executed' them.) My baby brother was watched over by a black girl who was all tears when we left. I went off to a posh school Highbury and I've still two of its magazines which are filled with lists of former pupils who had been killed in the war going on in that far-away Europe. Talk about the 'end of innocence'.

Aunt Nell again. My big brother also visited her in Cyprus,

in much more troubled times[4], and we three 'boys' were to be her executors when she died. In her nineties by then, she died while staying with her sister in Ireland, her ancient will we eventually found in Dunfermline, her 'estate' was in Cyprus and the Turks had just invaded the island, landing on her beach, and the first thing they blew up was her cottage. A next door expat's cottage was called 'Iona Cottage' (pun intended) but Aunt Nell's was rented. She, luckily, knew none of this. You can imagine how long it took to untangle that lot, which was pathetically little anyway. While visiting her in Cyprus and knowing my interest in books she said I could have her modest collection. This included a huge leather-bound set of the works of Voltaire of all people. She also had a small framed pen and brown wash sketch by Gainsborough and its loss I did regret. Two years passed before the lawyers in three countries had taken their whack and we were able to say *fini*. A few days later an envelope with Cyprus stamps came through the door. We groaned. What now? The letter however was from Aunt Nell's former venerable maid, the charming Cristalla, whom we knew. We had rather assumed she had died in the Turkish invasion so, good news, she was alive and well and, er, could she please have her back wages?

---

1 On one expedition we intended to swim at the beach where the goddess Aphrodite (think Botticelli) drifted ashore on a scallop shell. What we came on were four very plump, very naked middle-aged ladies disporting in the sea. In Aunt Nell's opinion much more Rubens than Botticelli.

2 An article I wrote about Cyprus while in the Zone was one of the very first I would see published. A play about St Mamas (one of the many Cyprus saints) had reached the stage of being read with a view to performing it at RAF Deversoir when the station began to run down. Just as well, maybe, there would have been a challenge having the saint, 'Enter right, riding a lion'. Aunt Nell gave my article on Cyprus five out of ten.

3 Apartheid being learned, not instinctive, the pair of us playing with my train set were innocents. I'd simply gone off and found friends where I could. Our main activity in the Valley of a Thousand Hills seemed to be following streams to their source (something I'd do all my life) and hunting for snakes or finding chameleons. My friend was a chief's son and we became blood brothers (the scar is still clear on my wrist) and I've often wondered what his future held. We were obviously typical boys for the only Zulu words I can remember were often enough yelled at our gang by irate adults for me to remember, the equivalent of 'Bugger off!'

4 Calls for *Enosis* (union with Greece) had started from about 1952 and the situation would explode in December 1954, not long after my visit. A State of Emergency was declared in 1955 then the inevitable independence came in 1959. In 1964 a UN peace force was set up to keep Greek and Turkish fanatics apart. The latter invaded in 1974 and have held the northern half of the island ever since - the part of it I had enjoyed so much.

ON SCOTTISH HILLS

A WET FUN DAY IN THE CLACHAIG

Who bothers with this big drain today? Maybe those who still read W H Murray's classic *Mountaineering in Scotland* where he describes its first ascent in the spring of 1938. For fifty years (Collie in 1894) it had repulsed attempts, this 'longest gully in Scotland' at 1700+ feet. Murray had failed earlier at the Great Cave but returned on the last day of April: Murray, MacAlpine, Marskell and Dunn. They met another party also after this 'plum' but the rival party eventually retreated. 'Exploratory rock climbing is the best of all' his account ends - which is why they took nine hours yet, a year later went up in five hours. And here were we, a bunch of tyros, having a fun day. But we knew our Murray. Today's guidebook gives it as '520m. Severe ***. One of the great Scottish gully climbs; not to be underestimated.'

So, Sunday 30, June 1963, five of us set off for the Clachaig Gully: Joe and Mike, former pupils of mine and Robert, John and Hugh who were student friends. Ah, the enthusiasm of youth. We had intended starting at 7am but it '*Glencoed*' (ie poured down all night as only it can in Glen Coe). When it stopped there was much humming and hawing, but we decided to 'have a look' - that magic phrase that leads to so many days that end with 'served you right'. These are just my logbook jottings of the day, scribbled in my teacher's lunch break the next day. Some of us had to go to *work*.

We set off at 11.00 and had it 'dry' as far as Jericho Wall and then four hours of downpour. But as Mike said, 'We were not to be put off by a few thousand gallons of water'. We roped up above the first waterfall: Joe and I, John and Mike, Robert and Hugh. I never liked the greasy slabs there and the corner was disintegrating, mud having to be scooped from the niches which passed as holds. Typical of the day, we were hemmed in by sheer walls, jungly growth pressing down to the strip of water-purged rock, today often below the flush of water. Only beyond tree level did it become 'bare and stern' (Murray).

I was very unfit and retreated from the Great Cave Pitch with legs a-tremble but Joe floated up (as he always did), and belayed from the tree. The others were well behind as Hugh had been dangling. Not really the best place to try the climbing game. This had been Murray's 'most perplexing of barriers' but, with the passage of time and human feet, it had become something of an easy day for a laddie.

Joe and I went up our awkward 30 foot shelf unroped. ('In a mossy corner near the top I was pounded for five minutes to the joyful surprise of the party below' - Murray.) We then brought up Hugh before going on to Jericho Wall. Water fell with renewed Glen Coe dedication and we would end soaked in every part of clothes and skin. Joe went up fast and shouted in glee at what was a good pitch. This woke me up so enjoyment flooded back on the steep, sharp holds of the wall. The belay had to be away up on a tree, preferred to the lip of the fall where an old sling hung - and would see any slip ending in a nasty pendulum. We brought up Mike and left the rest to push on. Robert then escorted Hugh out of the gully, a spot we'd found for a retreat previously, then abseiled back down.

'A wee chimney, no more than 15 feet, proved the most awkward pitch of the day.' Then came the real waterfall pitches, not mentioned in the guides, presumably because the writers hadn't been there in our monsoon conditions. Fun in its way, clean rock and fast climbing, roping and unroping. Joe was halfway up the Red Chimney before realising it. We roped and he carried on up and then stepped across into the gutter above the cave. The belay was on a flake *in* a cauldron of water'.

Here, or somewhere, Mike, already soaked, sat in a gutter to belay with the water building up behind him, then stood up to release the sudden spate onto Robert struggling below, not that this made Robert any wetter. He'd obviously read his Murray description of a second 'jammed half-way up ... icy jets poured down the open neck of his shirt. His breeches bulged and quivered round the accumulating volume, which at last spurted under pressure from the knees'. The released water 'surged down like a tidal wave'.

'The last pitch came all too soon, good holds up cracks and slabs. We met some walkers on the rim, ('There's joost a great big ole down ere, luv.'), and suggested they took an alternative route down. We pitied them as the heavens opened again. The river was threatening the tents on the Clachaig Green*. Our aquatic ascent had taken eight hours. We headed south on the A82 at 9.30pm and I put out my Fife bedside light out at 03.30. I feel sorry for my Monday morning classes.

---

* Camping on the Green was too popular and the Green was closed because of the sanitation worries. On one occasion we were camping there for a week and during that time saw no sign of life at one particular tent, which was worrying enough for us to report our concern. When the police checked they found a man inside who had been struck dead - by a bolt of lightning!

Then and Now on the Loch Maree Hills

Loch Maree's only possible rivals are Loch Lomond and Loch Awe, neither of which has a mountain with so powerful a presence as Slioch.
W. H. Murray: *Companion Guide to the West Highlands*

I almost let out a whoop of delight on coming on an interesting description of the Loch Maree hills in John Macculloch's *Highlands and Islands of Scotland* 1824, four tomes which he'd written as letters to his friend Walter Scott. Macculloch is described as not a very pleasant person but the wandering geologist was one of the earliest to report on our remoter mountains and did so with a mix of practicalities and the romantic for which I was prepared to forgive the rest.

Macculloch (1773-1835) was actually quite a whizz kid. Born in Guernsey of Scottish descent he graduated as a doctor at Edinburgh when only twenty. He then took up chemistry and was appointed to the Board of the Ordnance Survey aged thirty and in 1814 became geologist to the Trigonometrical Survey. He became President of the Geological Society and was a Fellow of the Royal Society and the Linnean, he prepared the first geological map of Scotland and one of his many scientific papers first described the puzzling Parallel Roads of Glen Roy. He only married in 1835 but was thrown from a horse soon after and died following the amputation of a leg. He made long expeditions in the Highlands and Islands from 1811-21 (and 1826-32) so must have visited Loch Maree in this period. Expedition is the word. There were no roads at that period and the mails went by runner along the north shore of the loch - wild walking even today. He had a ship's boat loaded onto a cart and dragged from sea to loch by a dozen men. If a bit long-winded, he is worth quoting.

'Loch Maree's mountains present a greater diversity of form and character than any of the Scottish lakes. Ben Lair is the principal feature. The middle ground is splendid and wild: rock and wood, silvery clouds and the sun shedding a flood of light over the lake. Even the dark firs and cold grey cliffs of Ben Lair seemed to rejoice in the bright sunshine while the warm brown and purple of heath tinged the nearer hills with a richness of colour only known to these mountainous regions. Every summit assumed a blue tone till the last peaks emulated the misty azure of the sky into which they melted.'

This was being written before the upsurge in Romanticism. As he corresponded with Scott might he not have influenced that greatest influence of all? He continues with a nice touch that also brings us down to the reality: 'It was a scene, as the Emperor Charles said of Florence, too beautiful to be looked at except on holidays. But such days are indeed the holidays of the Highlands, rare and precious, and compensating for many previous ones of mist and rain, of weariness and disappointment'. He knew those more testing times too, once complaining about an ascent of Ben More in Mull when his summit champagne had frozen.

I knew the hills from Torridon and north through the country beyond Loch Maree to Ullapool far better in winter conditions from our Hogmanay meets or house parties in the area and they certainly were times of wild, wet and the woeful - and, whiles, the wonderful, as on one first of January when Slioch looked like meringue and Beinn Airigh Charr appeared as *chantilly*. This summer visit saw me on the west coast, working northwards, Munro/Corbett-bagging by canoe, and Loch Maree was to be the start of a long summer heatwave that followed me up Ben Hee, Foinaven and Arkle,

Cranstackie and Quinag. I would later describe it as 'blundering into the Sahara'.

I launched onto Loch Maree at 7.30 in the evening and it was still monstrous hot, as pitiless as impersonal. (I pitied Macculloch's poor crew who rowed him up the loch and back again.) An oily swell led out to the choke of fifty or so islands and some interesting navigation followed through their jungly, chunky sandstone chaos as my maps disagreed with each other and with the reality. A startled deer on one island careered off along its shore and went right round to come back almost on top of me again. After going north about Eilean Subhainn I headed for Isle Maree, accompanied by a noisy red-throated diver. Eilean Subhainn (*everlasting isle*) is the largest and a real jigsaw piece in shape. Isle Maree looked like a green tea cosy.

The name Maree comes from Maelrubha, a saint of this name coming to settle for some years in Applecross in 673 before moving on to the island that bears his name, no doubt establishing his Christian site on an older pagan spot. Nothing remains today and the old walled graveyard has all but vanished too, the few old stones weathered beyond reading. St Maelrubha's Well, scene of ancient bull sacrifices and many hoped-for cures for insanity, had also disappeared but the 'penny tree' was obvious. The original tree had died (copper poisoning?) and chunks of it lay embedded with coins like fossil armadillos in a deep litter of coins. Queen Victoria no less had a penny hammered into the tree in 1877. Tree after tree sees the superstition carried up to date for though the well has gone and, no doubt, much of faith, 'for luck' remains. Every visitor it seems adds a coin. And a dire curse waits on any who would take away a coin. The well reputedly went dry after someone tried to cure a mad dog in its waters.

The midges rather curtailed my explorations and I headed for the north shore. Macculloch again: 'The northern margin presents rocky, wooded bays and creeks rising into noble cliffs and mountains. Sleugach [Slioch, *the spear*] is perhaps more striking than any mountain in Scotland. Where the skirts of Ben Lair descend into the water the remains of forest produce a landscape that might be expected in the Alps rather than the tamer arrangements of Scottish mountains'. He and his no doubt weary crew had fun navigating the islands in the gloaming back to the west (Tollie) end of the loch. Even at midnight he recorded over 70°F (21°C).

I dragged my canoe up on a bracken bank and camped on a knoll two hundred feet up among oak, birch, alder and holly. Camping was just lying stickily inside a sheet bag on top of my rucksack in the cushioning heather, aware of the subdued scents of a warm earth. There were lots of wee beasties making scratchy noises and a roding woodcock went round and round on clockwork flight. I was granted Macculloch's end of day: 'The long shadows of evening gave a repose so that even the liquid sound which followed the dip of the oars seemed an intrusion on the hush of nature. The last crimson at last vanished from the summits and all became wrapped in one gentle hue of tranquil grey marking the twilight of a northern July'.

He continues: 'Ben Lair will well repay the toil to its summit. The height exceeds 3000 feet [it is 2821 feet, a notable Corbett] and though it produces few alpine plants there is perhaps the greatest variety of quartz, from jet black to snow white. The great attraction is the view and chiefly to the north over the wildest mountains of Ross. It is usual to speak of rocks and precipices, whether present or not, but here they exist with no need of exaggeration. Here the mountains show the very skeleton of the earth. Everything is gigantic and fearsome, wild and strange and new'.

Sir Hugh Munro of *Munro's Tables* fame wrote much later (1905), 'Beinn Lair is a long flat but broken ridge presenting on its Loch Maree side no outstanding features. To the north however, for a distance of two miles it throws down what is possibly the grandest inland line of cliffs to be found in Scotland'. That brought the climbers. The Scottish Mountaineering Club duo of Ling and Glover came in 1909.

Not much had changed since the time of Macculloch. Ling and Glover hired a charabanc at Achnasheen and were a bit taken aback at a fifteen seater for the pair of them. To stop the risk of bouncing off the track into the loch some bags of corn were loaded to act as ballast. They walked half the length of Loch Maree then climbed over the Bealach Mheinnidh (490m/1607ft) to reach the north side, climbed a gully to the summit, came back down, had a snack overlooking Isle Maree and continued along the loch out to Poolewe - a day's activity which I'm sure few would care to copy today.

The next day a keeper led them round to the north side of Beinn Airigh Charr, Ben Lair's western neighbour (791m/2595ft). The great tower, north of the summit, is locally known as Martha's Peak. 'Martha was a legendary heroine who took her goats to pasture on the mountain and was reputed to have made the first and only traverse of the tower. Unfortunately she dropped her distaff and, in endeavouring to recover it, fell and was killed.' Ling and Glover's day on Martha's Peak was exciting enough that they were back again the following year with some other climbers and several new routes were climbed.

At 6.30am I was off for Beinn Airigh Charr, teasing my way up the steep mix of crag and trees which is so typical of this shore of Loch Maree. Slioch had an edging of golden light which soon faded as the world once more pulsed and shimmered in heat haze. The Torridon peaks stood on their heads in the loch below, reflection and reality identical.

Macculloch was lucky enough to spot a sea eagle. I didn't though they are now back in the area. The shady gorge of a torrent led to grassier slopes and my devil's halo of flies slowly faded. The flora was quite varied I found with quiet banks of aven and campion and louder shouts of tormentil, and thyme. A wild rose had glowed in ghostly exuberance against the dark trees where I'd landed the night before.

It was too hot to botanise with a brain scrambled by sun. I didn't perspire so much as ran salty water. Long before the top, my shorts were as wet as if I'd been swimming. Approaching along Meall a' Choire Ghlais I set off some goats (the descendants of Martha's flock perhaps?) but the deer lay comatose with the heat and simply watched as I passed. The view vanished into haze so when I finally stepped onto the summit of Beinn Airigh Charr the dizzy drop on the north jolted with the shock. I perched on a knoll and finished off all the water I'd carried. Another score of goats lay on the ridge out to Martha's Peak. Far down, among the map-like array of water and land, a tiny tent gave scale to the empty quarter leading away up to An Teallach, country I'd tramped through and over many times and still regard as hard to beat in Scotland for sheer wildness.

Eventually I went on, down to the Strathan Buidhe pass and up intervening Meall Mheinnidh, 722m/2370ft. A rabbit bobbed away; a mutual surprise. A brief photo stop and down again to the Bealach Mheinnidh where a short traverse led to a burn and the brewing and downing of two pints of tea. Angling up Beinn Lair seemed endless but led to a notch above the great cliffs, then a cairn with the summit beyond. Gleann Tulacha, between these arrayed ridges of Beinn Lair and those of A' Mhaighdean, which some claim as 'remotest Munro', can have no rival for dramatic grandeur; superlatives are superfluous in such elemental simplicity, in such an aloneness from all the world's distractions.

The summit cairn (860m/2821ft) was reached at 11am. When a small breeze tried to blow it was like opening an oven door. I descended on a long, steady-angled traverse line that bisected the paths over the Bealach Mheinnidh and Strathan Buidhe, duly collected a new buzz of flies and fled the land as quickly as I could. I paddled past Isle Maree and on to complete the circumnavigation of Eilean Subhainn, dipping into a fish scale glitter of water below an abstract blaze of sun, and landing at my launching spot by the A832 at 3pm. I've never sweated so much canoeing so took myself and a bar of soap into the shallows of the loch, to the amusement of a passing coach-load of tourists.

Let Macculloch have the last word. 'It is not only that nature gives us a keener enjoyment of those gleams of happiness which break through the dreary atmosphere of life but, as if in compensation of the savage aspect of the mountains derived from bad weather, its hours of sunshine are hours which can be found nowhere else. No one can know the full value of summer who has not known it in a land of mountains, no one can feel, who has not felt it among the hills, the joy which can fill the mind, the sense of beauty, the bounding, exuberant happiness . . .'

A HILL FOR JILL

Hillman's legs have restless feet, one called memory, one called hope.

The summit of Sgurr a' Mhaim is 1098m so it does not feel overshadowed by Ben Nevis (1344m) next door. There is no gentle way up, the direct route from Glen Nevis giving an unrelenting haul of 1000 metres, the ridge connecting the

Munro to the rest of the Mamores being the Devil's Ridge, hardly an encouraging name. Big, bold and beautiful might summarise the peak's characteristics. There is a classic view of Sgurr a' Mhaim looking *up* Glen Nevis. And this was the summit a friend recently kept to be her 'last Munro'; last in the sense of completing all 284 of them rather than intending any retirement from the hills.

Some wondered at her even taking up Munro-ing late in life - a granny septuagenarian, diabetic, with nine toes in her medical boots and one leg held together with what looks like scaffolding! But there she was, running through a long archway of walking poles to stand on top of the quartz cairn with a grin that stretched from Ben Hope to Ben Lomond.

I've been on several of these celebratory 'last Munro' days and, without exception, they have been days of wet and storm with people cringing by summit cairns, unrecognisable in hooded waterproofs, shivering with cold, and hands holding plastic cups, the argument whether the bubbly should be served chilled or at room temperature rendered academic. Jill had things much better organised.

Just as well, for not a few of the fifty-strong party were 'creaking old' and/or inexperienced while curtailed vision, replaced joints, arthritis and various other ailments had their representatives too. This is the great thing about the hills of course: they are a joy and a reward for everyone. Nobody would have chosen to have been anywhere else in the world that day. Some present had been to many places in the world, that year alone to the Alps, Baffin Island and Arctic Norway - but that day Sgurr a' Mhaim was Everest and Scotland everyone's Paradise.

Of course there were plenty of old hands (and old feet!) present, several had completed the Munros: Charles had driven up from Sheffield for the big day. Staff from the

Mountaineering Council of Scotland were present. But more noteworthy, perhaps, were the members of over-fifties groups who, in trepidation, made it along the Devil's Ridge, to find the euphoria of being stretched which is one of the blessings of the ancient hills. You don't, can't, dumb-down the Munros. Munros are good for you whatever your capacity.

Many threads wove together the patchwork group that day. Well represented was the Perth Hillwalkers' Club, the Mid-Week Mountaineering Club, Kinross and Scone fifty-plus groups, several who had shared Hogmanay house parties over the decades, those who had metric-Munroed in the Atlas, family (brother from Ullapool, Jill's children), and hospital staff. It was as diverse a gaggle as could be seen outside a supermarket any day of the week. Off the hill the common link would have been impossible to guess - the bountiful bens, the benison of friendships bubbling from that secret source, as sharp and fresh as the waters of Mamore burns.

We were glad of the burns that day. The oven had been set at high and, until the doors were opened on the heights, we grilled. There was no hurry however and people stopped and started, chatted from person to person, and group to group, over the steady haul up by the Allt Coire a' Mhusgain. Success was almost certain on such a day and the kind old sun created a jovial mood. My great memory was the joyousness: a whole day passed in blessed, happy harmony, hills and people, people and hills.

The colours were sharp and crisp, slopes vivid green and crags purply black against the sun. Tiny dots moved on distant skylines. The eye was led downwards, too, for the glen merges with Glen Nevis to form a deep corridor lying between the kissing ranges and led the eye on to the dwindling tones of the west. Some of the slower, older walkers had set off early, some of the super fit had romped off to take in Stob Ban as well, but there was a general gathering at the lochan tucked in below Sgorr an Iubhair at the head of the glen.

This acted as a reflecting pool for Stob Ban, a hill of cathedral-like presence. At over 700m the lochan must be one of the highest and best paddling pools in the land. We paddled. Water bottles were topped up at its chilly inflow.

Ahead lay Jacob's Ladder, a zigzag of stalkers' path (of which the Mamores are liberally endowed) leading up the encircling slopes to gain the green Sgorr an Iubhair - Sgurr a' Mhaim saddle. Fair weather cumulus drifted over the blue fields of the sky like stray sheep to give blessed coolness as the route onwards beckoned. Jill really had organised things perfectly. Others completing should invite her along.

The Devil's Ridge is a narrow crest which waves along with several highs and lows and, in one of the latter, like a reef showing its teeth at the withdrawing of a wave, is the crux: a rocky jumble of rocks only a metre wide and nasty to cross. Crampon scratches pointed to winter thrills. But the difficulties can be side-stepped, though the outflanking made one very aware of the steepness of the slopes and how far down they went. The crest for the rest is grass, coming to an apex which has been worn into a path by passing feet. That is certainly narrow by any reckoning, giving a good touch of exposure. The speedier had to wait two hours on the last shoulder for the tail to catch up. Not that this inferred slowness. Fifty passing any one spot takes time. Climbing 284 summits also takes time.

Impatient for photographs I wandered round the sacred summit to admire the view. There wouldn't be much time for that when the fifty stravaigers arrived. I laughed aloud at the incongruity of this. Jill, and lots of the hill regulars are frequently out alone, the perquisite and necessary demand in the making of a mountaineer ('Never go alone' is nanny-speak) and normally we'd never enjoy being in such a mob. But, of course, this summit cocktail party was different. So was the view. There was a view.

There was almost too big a panorama to work it out in the time, but the eye could range from the Paps of Jura to Skye to Torridon, and from the Cairngorms to Ben More and Stobinian. There were bold bens such as Bidean or the Vair pair or Resipol. Eastwards the rest of the Mamores peered over each other's shoulders to watch our show while Ben Nevis, the usual grumpy neighbour, seemed to nod benevolently.

The surge arrived, to the utter bewilderment of a group who just happened to be there. Will they expect champagne on every Munro now? Jill reached her ultimate cairn by running through that archway of raised trekking poles and scrambled up onto the quartz pile while the cameras clicked.

The jollity that followed then and later in the evening can be left to the imagination. Next day I was with Jill, Charles (who would drive back to Sheffield that night), Lorraine (who does much with blind walkers) for a day on the hills between Loch Linnhe and Loch Leven. They were not Munros, not even Corbetts, but they too, gave a glorious day of blue distances and dreams ahead.

This is the last blessing of the hills: who or whatever we are, we carry them off (big or small, in fair or foul) in the rucksack of memory. Hillgoers are people who put legs to their dreams. There's everything right in having 284 memories, and in Jill's case a display at home of 284 wee stones from her summits.

TALES OF AN TEALLACH

*The yearning to explore hills was born in myself in 1934,
when I, a confirmed pavement-dweller, overheard a mountaineer describe a weekend visit to An Teallach ...*
W H Murray: *Undiscovered Scotland*

Many years ago I did a survey to find which Scottish hills
were regarded as our finest. Two came well ahead: Liathach
and An Teallach, with An Teallach just taking top place.

Like Liathach, An Teallach is more than just a simple
hill. Both enjoy the status of having two Munros with
a great deal of excitement in between. An Teallach's
highest point, Bidean a' Ghlais Thuill (*peak of the greeny
hollow*), 1062 metres, just overtops Liathach's 1055
metres. An Teallach's second Munro, Sgurr Fionn (*white
peak*) is 1060 metres. The hill's fame is not in its statistics
however. Adjectives are heaped on An Teallach like scree:
majestic, spectacular, imposing, lordly and all accurate
enough. And who, driving across the Dirrie Mor on the
A832 doesn't gasp at the revelational rising of An Teallach's battlements in the west? (I've also seen it described
as 'an architectural monstrosity with Gaudi leanings'
and to C18 travellers like Pennant it was merely 'naked,
rugged and dreary'.)

My first visit to An Teallach is an early memory. With
a young friend we worked north from Kinlochewe, camped
by Loch an Nid, discovered the then unrestored bothy of
Shenavall, climbed Beinn Dearg Mor and made the traverse
of An Teallach from a camp by Lochan Toll an Lochain;
often the corrie is claimed as the most dramatic in Scotland.
Buttresses and gullies tower up, to a crest of weathered,
stepped pyramids such as no pharaoh ever imagined. That

sortie ended by going over by the strange double-topped Beinn Ghobhlach and the ferry from Altnaharrie to Ullapool.

Bidean a' Ghlas Thuill and Sgurr Fiona are only a rocky kilometre arc apart with no real difficulty traversing between them but after Sgurr Fiona, sweeping round above the Toll an Lothian, lies the array of pinnacles that makes An Teallach special. One, Lord Berkeley's Seat, sticks out like a thumb, overhanging the cliffs below, on Corrag Bhuidhe the ridge is no wider than a table top; all this gives delightful scrambling on rock W H Murray described as 'piled pancake formation'.

There's also a long, easy crest running north west which drops then rises to the fine viewpoint of Sail Mhor (767m), above Ardessie on Little Loch Broom. A stream drains this well-named encircled Coire Mor an Teallach on the 'wrong side' of the mountain and tumbles to the sea in a whole succession of falls.

That 'wrong side' of An Teallach witnessed a story both tragic and heroic. I knew the hero, Iain Ogilvie, who of course scorned that accolade, saying he only did what any climber would have done. The other two involved were a 'Tommy' Handley, a member of the Alpine Club and Peter Francis, being initiated to winter climbing but a good rock climber. Another friend of mine, Charlie Gorrie, had been with them for two days on the Fannichs but missed this day because he slept in. I can recall one newspaper giving his story the cringe-making headline, 'The Man Who Cheated Death'.

Conditions were perfect with the snow hard. The technical, more difficult traverse of the great ridge went happily and a contented party snacked on Sgurr Fiona some time after noon. Iain then scampered off to add the nearby 'top' on that NW ridge but was horrified to look back and see the other two sliding out of control down the north face of Sgurr

Fiona. They fell a considerable way over the icy slopes and rocky drops before the rope snagged on a tiny rock spike and there they dangled, unconscious, unmoving.

Iain carefully traversed across the face to reach them. Both were obviously seriously injured. Iain had a rope but below them lay a rock band so he had to pull them sideways to where snow ran down instead before he could attempt any lowering. The technicalities of this were complex, too complex to detail, but meant endless rope manoeuvres and tricky lowers, one from Iain's own ice axe stuck in the snow as no other belay was possible. He was left with a piton hammer in lieu of ice axe - and almost fell himself. Remember all this was on a steep face with only his own skills and stamina to draw on. Eventually safer snow was reached and Handley was lodged on a ledge Iain cut in the snow. When Francis was lowered (assumed dead) Iain did trip and went flying down the face, crashing over rocks and snow for hundreds of feet. Shocked and injured (a dislocated disc in the neck, a leg wound and multiple cuts), he then set off on the five mile descent out of the rough, boggy, rocky Coire Mor to reach Ardessie - in itself an epic feat.

He went to a croft house but it had no telephone so the lad of the house cycled along to someone who had, who collected Iain by car and he was then able to contact Dr Tom Patey at Ullapool who set rescue procedures in motion and arrived himself to head up into the darkening mountains. Neither casualty had survived. It is worth finding a copy of I D S Thomson's *The Black Cloud* to read the full complex story. Tom, himself one of Scotland's best climbers, in his report to the procurator fiscal, called Iain's activities 'superhuman' (Iain was awarded an MBE). Iain was kindly looked after for a couple of days at the croft and then simply went home. Contrast that with one other incident. As there was no phone at the croft when he'd arrived a car had been flagged down but the driver, finding his likely passenger was injured and bleeding, drove off.

One of the earliest ascents of An Teallach was made by the exotic figure of Dr John Macculloch FRS, whom we met in the Loch Maree description. 'I continued along the giddy ridge, in the hope of seeing its termination; but all continued vacant, desolate, silent, dazzling and boundless . . . its apparent altitude greater than of any single mountain in Scotland, excepting perhaps Ben Nevis.'

His zest and enjoyment was a contrast to the usual traveller's ideas and descriptions. Pennant again (on his 1772 'tour') wrote, 'West, a view where the awful, or rather the horrible predominates - peaks with sides dark, deep and precipitous; with snowy glaciers lodged in the shaded apertures . . . here Aeolus may be said to make his residence - fabricating blasts, squalls and hurricanes'.

Perhaps my most memorable day on An Teallach involved a fellow teacher Ann, with pupils Kay, Bill, Tom and Billy, memorable from both what we experienced on the hill and the aftermath. We nearly didn't go at all that last day of September and procrastinated at a low level all too aware of the clouds shrieking across the slopes above.

We eventually set off up Glas Mheall Liath, the rocks and scree as grey as the name implied. The wind became stronger and stronger and eventually we decided Ann would take Kay and wee Billy back down and I'd go on with the older, tougher Bill and Tom. (Tom had traversed the Cuillin ridge a few months earlier.)

After the spur of Glas Mheall Liath there is an intriguing moment where the grey quartz turns into rufous sandstone with such a sharp demarcation that you can stand with a foot on each. We had a hilarious time watching Bill trying to do this, for every time he lifted a foot he was blown aside. On the final slopes among red pinnacles the wind was so ferocious that we roped up and reached the summit on hands and knees. Conversation was impossible but big grins said it all. We cringed in a nook to shove in some food, the dog receiving his share. Reading my log of that day, the dog was never mentioned, and he seemed hardly ever to have been bothered by the wind. But we made the summit. Don't say summits do not matter. Success is wildly rewarding and 'nearly' or 'down' doesn't ring the same.

We had arranged with Ann that we'd descend the far, easy side direct to Dundonnell and meet in the hotel. Our descent was made in driving rain so we arrived at the hotel completely soaked. We collected dry garments from the car and, one by one, made a complete change in the gents. We then sprawled by a fire in a small inner room, a trayful of afternoon tea before us.

I leaned forward to pass round the tiered cake stand and my wrist accidentally touched the metal hot water jug; in an uncontrolled reflex jerk I sent the stand of sandwiches, scones and cakes across the room. Ann, who had stood to pour the tea, brought her hands up to grab the stand but simply lifted the brass table top so everything else flew off. The dog made for a sandwich on the floor and thereby put up a cat we had not noticed. The dog turned to say hello to the cat. Ann tripped over the dog and fell flat on top of the wreckage.

Shell-shocked would describe our state. In a panic we grabbed our wet garments to wipe tea and milk off walls and furnishings, gathered everything together (by some miracle nothing was actually broken), threw the food scraps in the fire and collapsed into our seats again. The serving lass looked in. 'Everything all right?' We nodded then Ann calmly asked,

'Do you think we could have another afternoon tea please?'
The girl collected the tray. 'My, you have been quick'. Later,
replete, glowing from hill and hotel exertions, we were
sitting quietly when the door was opened by a little old lady.
She turned to a companion, 'I think we could come in here,
dear, it's nice and cosy and peaceful'.

In the Past

The Secret Prisoner of St Kilda

When taking part in a National Trust of Scotland work-party on St Kilda our group was shown an old building outwith the village row which was known as 'Lady Grange's House'. On hearing her story the general feeling was 'poor Lady Grange'. The story is both bad and sad as was Scotland in the early part of the C18.

This was the time of the various Jacobite risings, the Union of parliaments, the coming of the Hanoverians, Marlborough battling through Europe, Tory and Whig at each others' throats - and very little of this would have meant anything to the folk of St Kilda. After Culloden for instance rumour had it that the Pretender had fled to St Kilda so a military party was dispatched to Hirta. When a few men were discovered (most of the population hid at the sight of a strange ship) and interviewed they had never even heard of a Charles Edward Stewart let alone that there was a King George! That there was a book about St Kilda titled *Island on the Edge of the World* suggests you could not have found a better place to hide away the abducted Lady Grange.

Lady Grange was born Rachel Chiesly, her father Chiesly of Dalry. He had deserted his wife and family and when the courts demanded he paid alimony of £93 for their support, this so enraged him that he assassinated the Lord President.

Robert Chambers *Traditions of Edinburgh* reported (I've abbreviated):

'The Lord President was walking home from church when Chiesly came behind, just as he entered the close, and shot him in the back. The ball had gone through the body, and out at the right breast. He was taken into his house, laid down upon two chairs, and almost immediately was a dead man. Some gentlemen seized the murderer, who readily owned he had done the deed, which he said was 'to learn the President to do justice'. When informed that his victim had expired, he boasted, 'he was not used to do things by halves'.

'The wretched man was tried and sentenced to be carried on a hurdle to the Cross, and there hanged, with the fatal pistol hung from his neck. His body was to be suspended in chains at the Gallow Lee on Leith Walk, and his right hand affixed to the West Port. The body was stolen from the gallows and it was never known what had become of it till more than a century after, when, in removing the hearthstone of a cottage in Dalry Park, near Edinburgh, a human skeleton was found, with the remains of a pistol near the neck. No doubt these were the remains of Chiesly, huddled into this place for concealment . . .'

James Erskine (1679-1754), a Law Lord with the title Lord Grange fell for the beautiful Rachel but, getting her pregnant, refused to marry her - so she confronted him with marriage lines in one hand and a cocked pistol, in the other, hardly the start to a happy union.

James Erskine was the young brother of John, who was the Earl of Mar, political 'Bobbing John', a ringleader in the 1707 Union, and the ineffective leader of the 1715 Jacobite Rising. After the Battle of Sherrifmuir he made for the continent, had his estate forfeited, and died in exile in 1732.

James, however, was seen as a staunch Calvinistic Presbyterian but in private life was quite otherwise, as indicated by his treatment of Rachel Chiesly. In 1705 he had returned from studying law on the continent and was admitted to the Faculty of Advocates. Mar was Secretary of State so in a few years James was a Law Lord, taking the title Lord Grange; thus Rachel became Lady Grange.

Under the Tories Grange was made Lord Justice Clerk (1710) but when Walpole came to power on the death of Queen Anne he lost the position. He distanced himself from the 1715 that saw his brother the Earl of Mar lead that messy episode. Walpole was a vindictive enemy and had a bill put through parliament to deny it the presence of Scottish Law Lords. Grange promptly resigned and had himself elected as an MP (Stirling Burgh). At Westminster he started badly with a wordy speech on witchcraft (he owned a large library on the topic, housed in a garden pavilion) and somehow became entangled with the lady caring for his brother's deranged wife - who was a friend of Walpole. He returned to Scotland and practiced as an advocate, ironically before the court where he had been a judge. So, what of his wife, Rachel?

She was thought to be dead. A funeral was held at Greyfriar's kirk after all. 'They were a right pair' in local parlance for she was unstable, loud, physical and often inebriated. Nevertheless they had eight children in the twenty years before separating. She was sent off to the country but returned to Edinburgh to cause trouble which soon took a dangerous turn. Cutting through the myths (she hid under a sofa to eavesdrop a gathering of conspirators) she began rather too publically to denounce her husband as a secret Jacobite activist. Whatever the truth, in 1732 Lord Lovat, the sneakiest of Jacobites, had his men abduct her. She put up a fight but was bound and gagged and carried off in a sedan chair for six months of close confinement at Polmaise. Her disappearance did not cause much comment as it was put about she had gone to London and later was pronounced dead.

She was shunted around Macdonald country in the west and then spent two years on desolate Heisker, one of the Monach Islands off the western seaboard of the Outer Hebrides before ending on MacLeod of MacLeod's St Kilda, forty miles out in the Atlantic where she endured seven or eight years of misery, among a people who spoke another language, lodged in a one-roomed cell (no better than a large *cleit*), with no books, no companion and minimal comforts. She apparently wrote various letters pleading for help (one of these pathetic pleas has survived). Her lawyer, aware of the Edinburgh gossip, was not convinced of her death and took up the matter only to be warned-off by Lovat. When, eight years later, a letter from Lady Grange got through (perhaps smuggled out in one of the rolls of tweed which the islanders exported on the annual factor's visit), this tenacious man again acted, was warned off from above but went ahead, chartered a brig and sailed to Hirta, only to find that Lady Grange had been moved. By then she was almost out of her mind. The SOS letter that arrived in 1740 had been written two years earlier. The whole matter became lost in the furore of the 1745-1746 Jacobite Rising. Lovat lost his head on Tower Hill in 1747 and Grange went steadily downwards to end living in London on a meager pension, dying aged 75 in 1754.

What befell Lady Grange is not altogether clear. She seems to have been moved about in Harris and Skye and perhaps Assynt and died in Skye, completely insane. A public funeral was held at Duirinish, the coffin full of stones, while she was secretly buried at Trumpan church in Waternish. The bill for her funeral survives, an unexpectedly, unexplained £30, a lot of money. Why this weird duplicity? 'Poor Lady Grange' indeed and all her sad monument today is that cell on distant St Kilda, where the myth-makers would have her still roaming the stormy nights bewailing her lot. Her portrait, attributed to Medina, can be seen in the Scottish National Portrait Gallery. Ironically she died in 1745 the very year of the Jacobites' last disastrous fling.

THE RANNOCH MOOR FIASCO

The story of this crazy escapade was originally told in *Blackwoods Magazine* in 1927 and retold in two issues of the *Scottish Mountaineering Club Journal* in 1936 and 1937. The latter's resonant introduction explained it was the 'tale of a little band of seven determined men, with plenty of confidence in themselves, a lamentable contempt for the conditions, and a sublime disregard of the weather, who set out to cross the desolate Rannoch Moor and, as happens even to the unwisely bold, achieved their object'. The events took place at the end of January 1889.

There were three Forman & McCall engineers: Charles Forman (40), the surveyor James Bulloch (33) and a young assistant Harrison (28), Robert (later Sir Robert) McAlpine (41, the contractor and head of the famous firm), Major Martin of Kilmartin (40, factor of the Poltalloch Estates), John Bett (60, factor of the Breadalbane estates) and N.B. McKenzie (42), a Fort William solicitor, agent for the railway company.

They left Spean Bridge by coach and reached Inverlair Lodge mid morning, then walked almost an hour to the end of Loch Treig. The landowner Lord Abinger had organised a boat to row them to the shooting lodge, at the south end of the loch, where they would spend the night. There was no sign of boat or boatman and when eventually he turned up (in time to stop them breaking down the boathouse door) their craft proved a tarred antique. Night and sleet fell on the party. Forman was unfit (he died of TB later) and all were clothed for town rather than country conditions. The younger gentlemen helped to row, others bailed the leaking water with their boots while cringing below umbrellas. Investigating a light they grounded and two had to go into the water to free the craft. Eventually they were rescued by local keepers in their boat which took them to Craiguaineach Lodge. By then it was midnight. Neither food nor beds were ready, the messenger, sent by the Lairig Leacach, not having arrived, and after eating as best they could, they passed the night under blankets while rain, hail and sleet blattered down, dawn bringing no improvement to the storm.

Unbelievably, they continued: ferried over the first river as the bridge had been swept off, then facing a toilsome ascent to the edge of Rannoch Moor, beyond which lay 23 miles of 'weary-looking desert' as Robert Louis Stevenson called the moor's mix of heather, bouldery hummocks, bogs and lochans. The lodge's keeper, having taken them up to the moor, pointed into the wilds, and left them to it. Bulloch, was the only one present who had any knowledge of the moor. After four hours of squelching through the bogs and trudging the braes in the rain and sleet showers they reached the River Gaur where, equally unbelievably, they had a planned noon business meeting with Sir Robert Menzies of Rannoch Lodge to discuss minor alignment problems of the route. Menzies, more sanely, sent his head keeper and invited them to Rannoch Lodge, at the west end of Loch Rannoch, for the night. Ahead, there still lay

14 miles to Inveroran with only one cottage eight miles off between, and three hours of daylight remaining. They decided to carry on!

They were ferried over the River Gaur near its outflow from Loch Laidon at 1.30pm. The Gaur is the main eastward drainage of the Moor, well-described as the 'birthplace of many waters'. The weather remained wild and wet. They straggled on, each choosing his own line.

Towards dusk they realised their mistake. They were floundering, unable to pick out details, falling full length at times, becoming tired, soaked, cold and depressed, Bett and McKenzie being helped by the fitter members of the party. Eventually Bett could go no further. The major and Harris stayed with him, their shelter the old man's umbrella, Forman and McKenzie struggled on but soon sought shelter in the lee of a boulder, while McAlpine and Bulloch took separate ways onwards, the former aiming for Inveroran, the latter hoping to strike Gorton where he knew of a cottage from a previous survey.

Bulloch, several hours later, collapsed over a fence and lay stunned for four hours then, recovering, groped his way along the fence, found a track - and reached Gorton. Out on the moor Bett had fallen unconscious and the other two only kept warm by running in circles. At one stage they lost sight of Bett so marked his position by tying a white handkerchief to his brolly, before continuing their athletic circlings.

About 2.30am they noticed lights and lit matches which were spotted by the two Gorton shepherds dispatched by Bulloch. They and their dog then found Forman and McKenzie and half carrying, half dragging Bett, they headed for a wooden hut two miles off, on the Avon Dubh. There was an old stove and some peats inside and they managed to light a fire only to be nearly asphyxiated, till one of the shepherds removed a peat which had been placed over the top of the chimney. The stove became red hot. The shepherds then returned to Gorton and were back at daybreak with food and drinks. By 10.30am the railway party was recovered enough to set out again and reached Gorton at noon. Their anxiety about McAlpine was eased and the search party stood down when a messenger brought word that he was safe in a cottage three miles down the Tulla. He'd arrived soaked to the skin and covered in mud after fourteen hours floundering alone on the moor.

Using a cart for Bett they moved on, collecting McAlpine on the way, and eventually reached Inveroran nine miles to the west. The snow was already falling and that night a blizzard raged; had it come the night before there would have been a certain tragedy. Next day they had to struggle through huge drifts to make Tyndrum for the Callander & Oban train.

Their line was built however and opened in 1894. Storms often overwhelmed traffic between Loch Treig and Gorton in the years ahead. Gorton had an old passenger coach used as a school, with eleven children attending at one stage. Serious proposals were also made for running a railway line up to the summit of Ben Nevis. After all the Forth Bridge had been opened in 1890. One can only wonder at the self-confidence of the Victorians.

An Arran Murder

A murder on the Scottish hills sounds like some melodramatic fiction but for years I kept hearing snippets about just such a happening in Arran but only recently did I learn the full story. The facts were stranger than the myths. What did happen on Goatfell back in 1889?

On Friday 12 July 1889 a 32 year old Brixton builder's clerk Edwin Rose sailed on the *Ivanhoe* from Rothesay to Brodick. On Thursday 18 July his brother went to meet him at the station in London. No Edwin Rose. The brother rang the Rev. Goodman, son of Rose's employer, who was staying at the same Glenburn Hydro from which Rose had left for Arran. No trace of Rose. On Saturday 27th the brother and the Chief Constable for Bute landed at Brodick. On Sunday 4 August Rose's body was discovered by a Corrie fisherman high on the Glen Sannox side of Goatfell.

Three search parties (over 200 people) were on the hill that day as they had been for a week. Following the call a police sergeant, the brother and others went to the spot, a large boulder against which boulders and heather had been heaped but in which part of an arm could be seen. The smell can be imagined. Dr Gilmour from Linlithgow, on holiday at Corrie, was sent for. The head and face had been 'fearfully and terribly smashed' and the left shoulder blade fractured, otherwise there were no injuries. But to take things in order.

Rose was a fit, active person, perhaps a bit bumptious to use a good Scots term but outgoing and friendly. On the steamer to Arran he grew pally with another young man, Annandale, and while the steamer went on to Whiting Bay during the hour ashore they decided to come back and lodge at Brodick. Being the Glasgow Fair accommodation was difficult to find. A Mrs Walker however said Annandale could have a small one bed annexe on the Monday which they could both share, he eating there, Rose at the village teashop. They sailed back to Rothesay and went to Rose's Hydro.

Two friends, Mickel and Thom, were heading for the weekend at Brodick and they met up with Rose and Annandale on the *Ivanhoe*. Unable to find rooms they slept on a friend's yacht. The four had a touristy weekend but Mickel didn't care for Annandale and urged Rose to get rid of him.

Rose and Annandale saw Mickel and Thom off from the pier on the Monday afternoon after which they were observed both on the way up and then on the summit of Goatfell. Mid-morning on Tuesday the landlady found the annexe empty, a few belongings left behind, and nobody thereafter returned. No doubt she shrugged at the loss of the rent. There was no point reporting the incident. However, within days, everything changed. Annandale had been seen catching the early boat on the Tuesday. He had Rose's black bag with him.

One wonders what today's advanced forensic expertise would have made of the case. The slope above where the body was found was a mix of granite slabs, heather and grit with a small stream in a gully and some crags, typically Arran and not presenting any real problem in descent. On that slope were found Rose's walking stick, his waterproof (ripped in two, stuffed in a dub), knife, pencil, a button and cap (folded in four and held down by a stone). The Lamlash doctor joined the Linlithgow holidaymaker for another examination before Rose was buried at Corrie. Later the body was exhumed for further study. Rose was buried at Corrie and someone - anonymously - placed a memorial granite boulder on the grave, enclosed in iron railings. The inscription simply says 'In Loving Memory of Edwin Rose, who died on Goatfell, 15 July 1889'.

On the mountain they'd seen that all Rose's belongings had been taken: watch, money and his return ticket to London. By co-incidence Mickel and Thom had introduced Rose and Annandale to another friend, Gilmour during their weekend and Gilmour travelled Brodick to Ardrossan with Annandale on the *Scotia*, noting several things which were later shown to be Rose's.

Annandale returned to digs at Rothesay but skipped without paying on Saturday 20th. A friend Aitken who knew Annandale at work in Glasgow had had Rose pointed out by Annandale earlier and now wondered why he had Rose's yachting cap. To Aitkin his workmate as patternmaker at the Springburn Works was known as John Laurie. Annandale was an assumed name. Meeting Laurie/Annandale on the street on 31 July Aitken asked what he knew of the Arran Mystery the papers were full of. 'Wasn't Rose the chap you went to Brodick with?' They agreed to meet later but Laurie/Annandale never showed. Four days later Rose's body was found and Aitken went to the police.

Laurie had taken his wages, sold his tools, and gone. On 6 August he took lodgings in Liverpool but on the 8th left. (The Liverpool papers that day had the Laurie-Annandale-Rose connection writ large.) He left some Rose property behind. On the 10th he'd written an anguished letter to a Glasgow paper proclaiming his innocence. He said he'd left Rose on top of Goatfell with two other men. This just stirred the pot and a second letter followed, its Aberdeen postmark taken as a blind. He'd returned to Scotland however and on 3rd September entered a small station near Hamilton, encountered a policeman, was recognised and chased by the constable and local colliery workmen. He was caught in a wood, an open razor beside him and a superficial throat wound. Being charged, he admitted robbery but not murder.

Two thousand people tried to gain entry to the November trial in the High Court of Edinburgh according to the *Scotsman*. Those legally involved read like a *Who's Who* of the judiciary. He was accused of murder, of battering Rose to death. The defence claimed there was no evidence for this. Rose could have fallen and rolled. The complete lack of other wounds or even abrasions makes this unlikely, as any modern Mountain Rescue Team would vouch. But this was 1889. And somebody had thereafter taken time to pile 42 stones on the body in an effort to hide it - yet left other belongings scattered about. Why?

Those met on the summit were off the mountain by 8.30pm. Laurie was seen in Corrie at 10pm, taking refreshment before walking back to Brodick - then scarpered. But there was no direct evidence of murder. At Corrie Laurie did not appear unusual, he never disguised himself when among friends later, even with Rose's belongings in evidence. Nothing from Rose's person was found on Laurie, and his counsel declared Laurie's admitted robbery was simply of belongings found at the digs. But why did Laurie not raise alarm at Rose failing to join him at the digs and then just sneak off? Did he simply panic? Or take the opportunity to steal what he could? An assumed name usually indicates some ill plan afoot.

The jury took forty minutes and returned a verdict of 'Guilty, by a majority', which was 8 voting for 'Guilty' and 7 for 'Not Proven'. Nobody voted 'Not guilty'. The Lord Justice - Clark pronounced the death sentence, to be carried out on November 30 at Greenock.

Greenock was outraged. Since 1675 only four people had been executed there, none since 1834. Two days before the execution date Laurie was found to be of unsound mind and the sentence commuted. In Peterhead prison he showed no sympathy about Rose and made leading comments that Rose had had little enough money. He escaped a work party in a fog but was recaptured. He died in Perth Criminal Asylum in 1930.

Greenock may have been spared, their borrowed scaffold was returned to Glasgow, Laurie removed but the Greenock magistrates were left to pay the bill.

An odd footnote. At the trial the Arran police were very

unhappy answering questions about what had happened to Rose's boots which had disappeared somewhere sometime. The sergeant said he did not know where the boots would be by then. To a direct demand an admission was then made that they had been buried on the beach above the high tide line. The Chief Constable had been present. It was believed in Arran that a murdered man's ghost would walk again unless his boots were so buried. In 1889? You can see why this whole story has taken on the gloss of folklore.

The story is covered in great detail in one of William Ronghead's *Famous Trials* series.

CYCLE TOURING - IN KNICKERBOCKERS

Throughout my teens and for years afterwards I cycled extensively in Scotland. It was the only way possible to get about at the time, very few people possessed cars and it was some time after Hitler's war before facilities became other than rudimentary. Fortunately many of the practicalities were helped by the then extensive coverage of youth hostels, cheap ex-wartime ration packs, and a very different attitude to rationing in the Highlands.

I can still recall the shock of surprise and admiration on reading a small paperback *Cycle, Camp and Camera in the Highlands* published in 1905 (priced one shilling) which I had found in a junk shop - for sixpence! Theirs were exactly the same sort of activities I was having fifty years on [and it is now over a hundred years later].

What changes and yet how much remains the same. The resinous scent of Scots pine smoke as I drummed-up on Loch Lomondside would have been the same for Messrs

Henderson, Walker and their friends, it rained as much then and the midges were just as hungry.

Henderson and Walker and their companions obviously were middle class enjoying eccentric adventurousness rather than the poorer necessities of gangrels either side of World War Two. However, I feel they, Borthwick, Weir and Broon could have sat by a fire by the Bonnie Banks in contented fellowship. The two Edwardian gentlemen met by chance at Invergarry in the Great Glen, Henderson from Glasgow, Walker from Edinburgh and they recount their wanderings in turn in the book.

Almost as interesting as the storytelling and illustrations are the advertisements clustered at front and back. There are eighteen pages of these and twelve have adverts for alcohol, including brands of whisky like Glen Leven, Lord of the Isles, MD, Auld Scottie, Bennett's Three Star, Five Castles, Canteen and Grafton Blends, this last 'sold in cases and sent, safely packed, by Road, Steamboat, or Rail'. How many of those names exist today?

Adverts included several for Jewellers (one of the companions was a jeweller), Tea Merchant, shop for Artists' Materials, Chemist and Druggist, Photographic Dealer, Bagpipe maker and Pawnbroker. There are adverts for Cycles and Accessories and they sound familiar: bells, lamps, toe clips, repair outfits, etc but what about a 'Claremont special bike with BSA Fittings and Palmer tyres, from £11-10-0'? Then there are Bromides or 'Green embrocation for sprains and bruises, giving tone to tired muscles', sold at 1/1½ per bottle, post free. What, though, are 'S.C.P.'s and 'self-toning P.O.P's? There's a full page map of Scotland showing the sixteen sheets of maps by W. & A.K. Johnston. 'Price, in cloth case, 1/- . . . Mounted, cut to fold in Patent Transparent Celluloid case, 2/6'.

Their cycles, perhaps surprisingly, look very little different to the sort of heavyweight I had as a boy. Considering the advance in technology these pioneers went no more burdened than today's tourists with their panniers flanking both wheels, huge saddle bag and bar bag. (As a boy I frequently managed with only a saddle bag.) Pictures show the writers neatly dressed in tweeds, cap, jacket and 'knickers', collar and tie - and they sport trim white beards.

Their equipment is home-made yet still very 'with it'. The tent was originally little more than a canvas sheet strung between trees, with a groundsheet and a rug each. But a lack of trees when required and a need to keep out driving wet and foraging midges led to creating a proper tent. Starting with army canvas they ended using the lightest yachting sail material, the ultimate weight of a tent four pounds. Most cooking was done on wood fires but E.E.H. designed what is basically a form of the meths-burning *Trangia*. Various waterproof boxes and bags carried food and belongings on their panniers. They seldom carried as much as 30lbs weight. J.W. however had a bag hanging from the cross bar for his photographic plates, the tripod across handlebars and camera on his back. (Nothing digital then!)

The book fascinated with comparisons and contrasts, noting the familiar as well as the differences. I'll summarise Henderson's first ventures then add some of Walker's unusual experiences. The spellings of place names are theirs.

The first tour began up Loch Lomond, two of the party crossing the Renfrew Ferry the day before and pitching at a spot near Tarbet and, finding in the morning, to their distress, they were in a nettle patch. On one of my tours, brewing up here, I was suddenly receiving a shower of pots and pans on my head. A lorry with girders had touched a caravan so one side sprung off - and the contents came tumbling down.

Two others joined them for breakfast then on they went
for Glen Falloch and Crianlarich 'where the *Callander and
Oban* and *West Highland Railway* cross each other'. Duncan
Ban country follows, along by Loch Tulla to Inveroran before
a 'long and weary tramp over the interminable hills' of the
Blackmount. They pitched in the dark facing the Buachaille
and a kind shepherd brought them peat and wood and his
wife a jug of milk and a dozen eggs. Glen Coe gave snow
showers - in June - and they reached Ballachulish soaked
so didn't visit the great slate quarries but crossed a ferry to
Onich and pushed on to Invergarry to camp by the ruined
castle, a 53 mile day.

Early rising saw them in Ft Augustus, cold and wet, so
took the chance to sail up Loch Ness on the steamer. A 20
minutes halt was made at Foyers to let tourists see the falls.
Leaving the loch they passed the 'beautiful' cemetery of
Tomnahurich. I wonder if they knew of an earlier traveller
who, seeing this place, declared it so beautiful that 'That is
where I will be buried - if I'm spared'.

They stayed with friends and then had their hardest,
longest day, 66½ miles, to Ullapool, the Dirrie More ('Dreary
Moor') giving them the storm of storms. Many cyclist readers
will sympathise. They stayed with an exciseman brother
who somehow produced clothes for them, one of them in kilt
and red coat 'which fitted like an orange skin on a pigeon's
egg'. The steamer could not sail for Stornoway in the gale so
they back-tracked, blown across this time and looking at the
300 foot 'fearsome rent' of the Measach Falls on the way. A
gravel pit gave a sheltered camp near Lochluichart.

From Achnasheen they followed the *Dingwall and Skye
Railway* route through Glen Carron to Stromeferry and the
steep braes beyond for the Airds ferry at Dornie and a last
crossing of Loch Duich to Totaig. In Glen Shiel a tyre burst

and an hour was spent below a bridge repairing it while the rain poured down. They camped at Cluny and then over the hills to Tomdoun to end staying at Bunchaolie Lodge, a family pad, a return to being gentlemen. Stalking over, they cycled to Spean Bridge and the train home to 'the black city of smoke' (Glasgow).

Equipment was refined and next year a start was made by two of them at Fort William, camping in Glen Nevis and climbing the Ben. At the halfway house they had to pay a shilling each, a toll to help maintain the path. At the cloudy summit they spent 'most of the time casting stones over the precipice' and telegraphed home that they were having 'a high old time' at the Hotel and Observatory.

They headed on to Glenfinnan then walked the steep uphills to camp by Loch Eilt for two nights. A picture shows a woman milking a cow in the open near their camp. Stones 'large as a fist' made some road unrideable but they pushed on to Mallaig and took the sheep-laden *Clansman* to Glenelg where they were taken ashore in an overladen small boat. That night they set up camp *inside* the walls of one of the Glenelg brochs. 'Stiff work' took them on to Arnisdale where, in the herring season, the bay was filled with fishing boats. They were rowed up to Lochhourn-Head, passing the 'little fishing village of Skeary' on the way. Another 'stiff bit of work' took them up to Corrieshubh and so to Bunchaoile Lodge, the family summer home.

The next season Henderson took along his wife and a 'lady friend' but they demanded a roof each night which really caused them more hardship than camping would have done. The start was Ft William again and a couple of days were spent exploring Glencoe, the ladies based at Ballachulish, Henderson with a friend (a keeper?) at a remote house two miles up a side glen from the Clachaig which he reached afoot in the dark after something of an epic up the trackless glen. They cycled on to Mallaig and took the mail boat to Kyle of Lochalsh where his father met them and so on by train to Kinlochluichart. The Dirrie Mor played up again (when doesn't it?) and at Loch Droma the ladies and their cycles were taken onto the mail coach. He arrived at Ullapool 'feeling very much done up', the road dangerous from rain and the many carts encountered. The grip of 'the Sabbath' is graphically described but next day they crossed Loch Broom to Clachnaharrie and the hill road to Dundonnell. There is a photo of them on this stiff brae, the female cycling garb being ground-length skirts!

The party struggled to make Aultbea that night, soaked through by torrential rain the whole way, walking much of it because of impossible winds in their faces: 'cold, tiresome, miserable' conditions. A lonely house at Gruinard gave them tea and directions, their only break. Aultbea Hotel was reached at midnight. Bouncing back, the next day they sailed Loch Maree on the steamer *Mabel* from Tollie to Kinlochewe, wended up Glen Docherty then took the train from Achnasheen to Kyle and crossed to Kyle Akin. The next night was at Cluny and then over the hills to Bunchaoile Lodge again.

I can recall almost identical itineraries on my youthful tours and I'm sure touring today still is a mix of grind and glory. That road from Cluanie to Tomdoun was cut by the creation of Loch Loyne in my day and I'd welcomed new roads such as Shieldaig to Applecross or Glen Lochy to Glen Lyon. Most roads were unsurfaced in 1905, some still were for me. In the early Thirties my father hired a car to drive over the 'New Road' to Glencoe. Their 1905 route over the Blackmount would be considered mountain bike terrain now.

John Walker (JW) began his explorations following the opening of the Ft William railway in 1894. He then 'had just learned to mount and ride though as yet I only dismount by falling off', but for seven years the Edinburgh trade holidays saw him off to the Highlands, 'bike n' hike' as I called my similar tours. Ben Nevis, Ben More, Stobinian (from the south), Ben Lomond (from the east), Cruachan (winter conditions) and hills above Loch Hourn were climbed and those of Sutherland admired and photographed.

The camera of course was a huge plate camera, for which he would have to change plates at night or hiding below the tent thrown over the tripod. There were often problems. At Loch Eriboll the gale blew the camera over. On Ben Nevis when the tripod broke he just telegraphed for a new one and picked it up next day at Glenfinnan. Photographing Streap was abandoned as they found themselves standing in 'a nest of snakes' - which proved slow worms, not adders.

The railways were frequently used to start tours, several from Dalnaspidal. He recalled a snowstorm in March 1881 which completely buried a train on Drumochter. It took five days for 200 men, five engines and a thaw to free the train. On Rannoch Moor a platelayers' hut gave shelter from midges as they trundled their cycles along the line from Rannoch Station. They left the line at Gorton siding for a track to Loch Tulla and concluded that tour by catching a train home at Aberfeldy.

Walker's last tours were all to the far north and north-west as he considered nowhere could equal Sutherland, so his shortcut to start/finish was often by sea: from Leith to Cromarty on the *Earnholm*, Invergordon or Wick to Edinburgh on the *St Clair* (Wick harbour crowded with the herring fleet). The lochs in the north had ferries, such as over the Kyle of Tongue. The Kylesku ferry was crossed along with a horse and dog cart carrying a rich honeymoon couple from America - the Vanderbilts. When I was at the Kylesku ferry the roadmen (surfacing the road) were crowding into a tinker-style tent to escape the midges. At Braemore they noticed the lodge/estate of John Fowler, chief engineer of the 'new' Forth Bridge.

Another millionaire's residence was noted: 'Across the Firth was Skibo Castle, residence of the well-known Mr Carnegie... I could not help contrasting him with myself, both Fifers, one of us sleeping like a tramp in a dark, dripping wood'. Camped by a road in Sutherland on a solo tour he was hailed by a roadman who thought he might be a stonebreaker looking for work. By Loch Awe they had pitched in trees by the Free Kirk in the dark and next day had the police onto them, the assumption being they were tinkers.

A journey round Loch Katrine had been interesting as they found 'a strong force of navvies making a new road at higher level', the loch being raised and tapped to provide Glasgow's water supply. They expounded at length about the Parallel Roads in Glen Roy because, after years of speculation, their cause was at last understood. New geological knowledge fascinated. And they knew their history - which enticed them over the Corryairack, perhaps the first cyclists recorded doing so.

I laughed when I read how at one stage, they pitched their tent inside a shed to escape ferocious weather. We had done just that once on the Dirrie More, a stone building slightly bigger, the guy lines threaded through the walls and pegged outside. They once woke to find their kettle of water frozen, not at all a rare event even now.

Accidents happened. At Ballachulish a chain snapped (on top of trouble with crank bearings) so a blacksmith removed a link but then the chain would not go back on. So? Walk 17 miles back to Ft William or 24 to Bridge of Orchy? (The Ballachulish railway only came two years later.) They chose to walk to Bridge of Orchy. ('Rub on dry soap when feet become tender'.) Another time a collision at the west end of Loch Laggan saw a wheel badly damaged so, with one camp on the way, they walked on to Dalwhinnie station, just 21 miles.

In the Preface they hope their adventures will encourage others to follow their example and enjoy 'a holiday, which, for healthy exercise, abundance of fresh air, freedom, and enjoyment of Nature, cannot be obtained by any other means, and at a cost so trifling ... The poorest city clerk, the apprentice mechanic, or the struggling student, can enjoy wandering by lake and river, mountain and valley, storing up health for the struggles and studies of another season, at a less cost than a weekend to the coast or at a popular Hydropathic ... Nearly all the young men from the Boer War whom we have met are enthusiastic in their praise of outdoor life'. And so are we, their fortunate successors.

Cycle, Camp and Camera in the Highlands by E E Henderson & John Walker. 1905. (John Corsar, Govan.) Profusely illustrated with pen and ink sketches by T C F Brotchie and photographs by the authors.

Times and Places

A Day of Glory Given

Only a hill; but all of life to me,
up there, between the sunset and the sea.

Geoffrey Winthrop Young

A step onto the terrace at seven o'clock revealed Venus brightest among the frosted stars and only a cuticle of moon. Beyond the placid sheen of sea the light on Scalpay winked its friendly presence. Everything pointed to respite from a riotous week of dead-of-winter storms. And it was Christmas Day in the Hebrides.

Setting off an hour later from Reinigeadal (Renigidal) Todun was just visible, as if the big hill shied from meeting the new day. The summit loomed ghostly white with fresh snow - as if the storms had been stopped in their tracks and forced to precipitate and now had no evil left in them. I drove, cannily, up the steep hairpins, but all was wet below the snowline and the road had been treated. A dozen years ago there had been no road to Reinigeadal and the hamlet was dying. People reached it by sea or by a footpath from Tarbert over a thousand foot pass in the hills and a dizzy drop to sea level again to follow the cliffs round Loch Trolamaraig. The postie had to walk the path regularly.

'Driving the road to Reinigeadal rather makes you appreciate walking' was the expressed feelings of a Spanish lad, Enrique, who with a Czech girl, Ivana, had taken the chance of a cosy hostel Christmas away from work in Inverness. Even if it was the worst time of year for a journey they had travelled by bus to Ullapool, crossed in the ferry *Isle of Lewis* to Stornoway, hired a car and driven south and arrived, not a moment too soon, in the smothering dark of late night at what they felt was the end of the world. The Reinigeadal road starts where the arterial A859 circles An Cliseam, the highest summit - the only Corbett - in the Outer Isles and plunges down to sea level to run along Loch Maraig before rising brutally to the pass by Todun, a crossing with steep inclines and hairpins both fore and aft. Heading out in winter there's always a feeling of relief on reaching the A859.

The A859 is the main road, the only road, from Stornoway to Tarbert and on to South Harris and ferries to the gentler southern islands. Heading north from our junction the road still swoops and climbs with some exuberance, passes through the biggest wood on the island (nature trails), touches the headwaters of Loch Seaforth and Loch Erisort, and runs through the three mile straggle of Baile Alein (Balalan), where I stopped.

I had drawn in on reaching the A859 hoping Enrique and Ivana would soon follow and I could watch their car's headlights wander against the jet-black landscape. Instead, I saw day come up over the hills, tentatively tinting and toning the sky in subtleties too difficult to describe but surely drawn from a subdued palette of pearl, citrine, topaz, beryl, jade, coral, amber, saffron, turquoise...

Nearing the woods a hind and her calf of the year stood

silhouetted on a rise and, thrice, snipe rose, ricocheting off, from the ditches. A sea eagle came at me along the road, alarmingly like some attacking aircraft, and then casually lifted over the van. When I drew in at Balalan geese went flying off in echoes of their own laughter. The world was awake. Of humans, there was one dog walker being towed along the road.

From An Cliseam the highest hills of Harris line up westwards to end with an island hill on Scarp; another line of bulky rather than beautiful hills are lined left of the road I'd travelled and the most northerly of these is Roineabhal (Roineval). Only a modest 281 metres it has an isolated prominence and catches the eye when seen from afar, a good objective for Christmas at the end of a weary winter.

A cold start I had of it, the puddles on the initial farm track feathering over with ice as I walked and my toes soon pinched with cold in my wee wellies. Turning off all too soon I splashed over the well-named Allt Dubh and faced several kilometres of moor to reach the upthrust of hill. To start I followed a fence line, with one side heathery, the other starved grassland, the russet and the tired tawny. *No hay camino, se hace camino al andar* - there is no road; the road is made by walking.

My fence line led along to a cropped grassy knoll above the outflow of Loch Stranndabhat, oddly the only loch I would pass near on my pilgrimage. The loch's south end, two kilometres off, lay by the A859 and often the buzz of a vehicle on the road came like an annoying insect and then vanished again. The loch waters lay unruffled in metallic tints with sharp-cut reflections. Nothing stirred. Three silent sheep wandered up and stood eyeing me speculatively but, receiving nothing, turned and went their way. On setting off a grouse exploded at my feet. Had it kept 'cooried doon' I would not have noticed it. Grouse and conversational ravens now and then were the birds of those moorland flanks, an undulating, worn-out landscape, interrupted by the hollows of three running streams I'd have to cross. By the lochside would be too boggy, higher too heathery, so the middle way was the way I would go. I like this decision-making, this choosing, based as it is now on a lifetime of mountains big and small, home and away, reducing complexities to simplicities, at ease in the joy of going - and mindful of the Arab saying, 'Hurry is the devil'. Not that hurrying was possible, that was denied by both the landscape and eighty-year-old joints. Our great Scottish explorer Joseph Thomson took as his motto an Italian aphorism, 'He who goes carefully goes safely and he who goes safely goes far'.

The ground was sour and saturated (hence the wellies), smelling of vegetation's decay, with orange-tinted grasses, mosses, heather, black peat, slimy pools. Every step needed care. Heather stems were lethally slippery. Progress however was helped by innumerable sheep trods which, from above, patterned the tweedy landscape in parallel lines. (There was an irony in the very beasts who caused this soggy desert providing the easiest way through it.) Here and there were green knolls and, invariably, they bore the rickles of grey stones pointing to the brave people of the past. The map noted the sites as *airidh* or *shieling*. But the people have gone, by demand or desire, and only the occasional ATV track indicates any working of the land today. How many generations of women and children had passed their summers up here, herding, making butter and cheese, the slopes echoing to songs and children's voices? The ground would have been sweet-scented then.

I passed small parcels of sheep all day. (On the descent of the rockier heights I would laugh aloud on seeing an old ewe posing presumptuously on a boulder like a Landseer stag.) Walking had warmed me, not the sun, which lay behind horizon-anchored cumulus. Golden rays occasionally escaped to shoot up in to the sky, a sky the delicate blue of a blackbird egg. Down in a trough I was then ambushed by one of nature's miracles, an experience overwhelmingly vital, yet of the almost impossible: silence, complete, total, unbroken silence, a sort of crystal clarity, enveloping all the senses, to leave the heart throbbing, standing transfixed in case the aura shattered, an experience quite wonderful and really ineffable. I have met the effect several times in the deserts south of the Atlas Mountains. With a group I once became aware of its presence and bade everyone stand still and be completely quiet, but someone moved a sandal, someone's breathing could be heard, and there was no magic, no nothingness. They strained for what they never knew and which I couldn't describe. You have to be alone and very still for this natural miracle. On Roineabhal when eventually I moved *I* became noise and broke the bubble of the experience. The passing of a silent raven overhead (Odin's bird) wasn't silence at all. I could hear the flurry of its wingbeats. Usually, however quiet, faint and far, wind makes noise, water makes noise, man makes noise - which is why one goes alone, to enjoy the talk-free companionship of the wild, to relish a respite from the inanities of life.

Height was gained slowly. The going became steeper and more heathery and the trods tended, as they do, to head along rather than up. The sun at last looked as if it was going to break out of prison so I scrambled up onto the spur, Cnoc Foinaval, a sort of base buttress of Roineabhal, and there met its flooding light. My pullover soon came off as I headed up, the ground now broken with slabs of rock, deeper heather and a skin of bog. I enjoyed picking a way through the mix, trying to keep my steps in that rhythm that appears from a distance just to glide. A short barrier of crag girdled the hill and gave a brief scramble then it was all much steeper and rockier. I kept my eyes on my feet, partly of necessity, and partly to hold back the big view for a summit surprise. Soon, just ahead, was some quite substantial walling and I wondered who could have built what, when, in such a spot. It proved a summit shelter, a horseshoe dyke with its back to the west. I'd arrived - and was duly astounded.

World on world seemed to open in the vast lightness of Hebridean distances. South, the big hills were alpine white in the brilliance, their names a rumble like distant thunder: An Cliseam, Uisgneabhal, Oireabhal, Tirga Mor, Huiseabhal - a mini Oberland - the night's blizzard having singled them out in a linear painting that had left the rest of Harris and Lewis untouched. The far west group of Mealaisbhal, Tahabhal, Cracabhal, Griomabhal were faint, grey-blue against the western merging of sea and sky. South east rose the jumble of hills in the trackless heart of Pairc which those hungry for land had once hoped to tame (a stark monument to the land-raiders stands by the A859 just south of Baile Alein). But it was north and north east that truly astonished; between my stance and the road over to Calanais (Callanish) lay a crazy world woven on a warp of water and a weft of rock. A single loch, as complex in shape as a piece in a jigsaw, could reach into a dozen kilometre grid squares on the map, or a single grid square could hold a dozen lochs. Creator as Rothko. Far to the north in Lewis's emptiest quarter were the projecting cones and whalebacks of Muirneag, Beinn Bhragair and Beinn Mholach, the last prefaced with a row of wind turbines, arms at rest. The naming of the hills was comforting for this sad, harsh world, shrouded into the mists of prehistory, fable and recent history, has known peoples much misused whose only desire was to be themselves.

The myriad waters all lay still. Only on the very summit was there a faint breeze, courteous enough to cool but not chill, Heart-happy, I sat to demolish pieces with egg and tomato and a scone with heather honey, fully conscious of the grace of such a day of glory given when we - so small - are possessed by landscape.

Christmas is often the worst time of the year but, over decades, a gang of us aimed to climb a hill every Christmas Day (and, a harder discipline, New Year's Day) but this tradition had rather 'weed awa'. Old men are only young for so long. (Ah, but I was young on Roineabhal!) I recalled some of those days back in the years when it knew how to snow: Beinn Eighe by the round of Coire Mhic Fearchair; Beinn a' Ghlo's trio of Munros when we watched an otter tobogganing in the snow on its tummy over and over for the fun of it; Fionn Bheinn, where we found a lost collie by the cairn; Beinn Liath Mhor, climbed from a high camp by Lochain Uaine; Conival and Ben More Assynt, gained from my first camper van; Fuar Tholl by a challenging ridge route; Slioch on another day of glory given. There were a few gaps: once recovering from taking part in a night rescue, or preparing for the first (of an unimaginable 53) visits to winter in the Atlas, or a family gathering after our father died, or sailing up Lake Malawi on the *Ilala* during a Cape to Kenya peak-bagging sabbatical.

The sun, past noon, was already lowering its head, the cold sharpening. Time to descend. To a new year of who knows what? 'Everybody needs beauty as well as bread, places to play and pray in, where nature may heal and give strength to body and soul alike'. That's John Muir. Robert Louis Stevenson, travelling with his donkey, wrote of the 'Bastille of civilisation'. How lucky we are to have these safety valves, how easy to escape, to satisfy the insatiable itch of wanderlust, of wonder lust, be it an hour on Duncarrow, a day on Roineabhal, or months on great ranges.

Descending, I made something of a right-flanker to avoid the rock band and came down to a heathery shelf. Though concentrating fully my foot went through into a hidden hole and momentum felled me like a tree onto heather, luckily a surface soft as a duvet, but it reminded me of the uncontrolled chances of just being. Life *is* risky, if less so on the hills than on city streets. I circled round and down to more or less follow my upward route, at one stage being surprised by a boot-print in the mud, until I printed one the same beside it. I walked with a long shadow, trying to keep on the sunny side of any rise.

My mind ran on about the hill names I'd ticked off on the summit and those of Christmases past. What Gaelic I recognise is largely hill and map related though my first ever remembrance of speech is of a person who used to kiss me goodnight with a gentle, 'Oidhche mhath'. Making the names of places in duplicate everywhere I find questionable. Baile Alein followed by Balalan is sensible, and helpful, for the anglicisation at least hints at pronunciation, but home in Lowland Burntisland, to see An t-Ailean Loisgte added is daft, this used neither in Fife nor in the Hebrides. Language is quite capable of sorting itself out, and does so, quite happily absorbing words from other languages or through inventive necessity. A word like *pixels* must have invaded nearly every language on earth. Reminds me of a programme years ago when a rather pompous Englishman was being very dismissive of Gaelic, pointing out its constant interjection of non-Gaelic words. 'What, for instance,' he blurted out, 'is the Gaelic word for *banana*?' The gentle Gaelic speaker's reply was, 'Just so, and what is the English word for *banana*?'

Two hours from the summit saw me back at the van. There were noisy geese once more, oysterpipers (as I thought them as a boy) flew over the road for Loch Eireasort, and a half-heard chorus came from a blowing cloud of distant gulls. And the same ancient dog walker I'd seen at the start passed, once again being towed by his shaggy mut. The plummeting temperature made the icing over of the puddles visible again, fronds and fingers suddenly appearing and spreading, quite freaky, but then wonders are found through eyes to the heart. The drive along the A859 was far more dangerous than my ascent of Roineabhal or Ivana and Enrique's romp up the Clisham. The sun constantly blinded me with its dazzle through the windscreen. Winter sunlight however is often shortchanged; as soon as the Clisham and Todun were gained their bulk threw the world into curdling shadow. It was like having a curtain drawn down on the day. I sped the ups and downs and ins and outs back to the more temperate hideaway of Reinigeadal.

The hamlet has about ten scattered houses and above the road-end is the white-gleaming cottage which is the Gatliff Trust hostel. There are three Gatliff Trust hostels, the other two both being traditional old thatched-roof cottages, one on Berneray, one on South Uist (Howmore), all are renovated and comfortable and all have the pull of indefinable character. They were the inspiration of an eccentric Whitehall civil servant who saw the value of outdoor experience and threw himself into promoting bodies like the then new youth hostels' movement. The Hebrides were special and had special treatment. The hostels are always open, inexpensive, and sit kindly within the community. Julius Kugy wrote that, 'happiness should be the foundation stone of all mountaineering' and Reinigeadal, Berneray and Howmore have given that glow to the happiness of many. Our Christmas day had registered high on the scale of fulfillment. We were all sad to leave.

My departing drive out was through snow showers and rainbows, escaping not a moment too soon. As the *Hebrides* left Tarbert the loch was arched over by a brilliant bow, but behind it, a wall to wall of dirty cloud was rushing in. Before we had passed Scalpay everything was blotted out in a major snowstorm. Reinigeadal would be isolated. The storm blew through and, looking back past our wake as we neared Uig on Skye, the whole Hebridean horizon was dazzling snow down to tide level. Once home in Fife I'd meet or hear from many friends who all enthused about that one magical, Christmas, day and praised God, gods or reality for a day of glory given.

THE UPS AND DOWNS OF HOGMANAY

Adventure is nowadays the province of the determined, the curious and idiosyncratic.
Salman Rushdie: *Imaginary Homelands*

On returning from Mull after this Hogmanay I was told there wasn't much I'd be writing about. We had hardly left the comfort of our rented cottage yet in a strange way relished relaxing so completely: the television was never even switched on, many books were read, meals created and one evening passed with an infuriating but intriguing jigsaw: a 1:50,000 Ordnance Survey map centred on Perth, where the owner lived. Given a six figure reference a made-to-measure puzzle can be produced for any location. Guess what all our friends and relatives are having for next Christmas?

Someone had suggested Hogmanay in Mull was bound to

be bit 'iffy' weatherwise. But, let's face it, Scotland's weather is on the erratic side of reliable. But at Hogmanay there are no midges! On one Mull Hogmanay we had two extra days on the island because no ferry could operate on the wild seas. On the other hand when I began the trip over the Munros in a single walk on Mull the girl in our party ascended Ben More in a bikini, in April.

So if there isn't much to write about Mull's 'Hogmanay Past' there have been many good ones over the decades, and these we recalled as we lounged, well wined and dined, cosy in the candlelight (the power had failed) while the disorderly storm sloshed the world outside. Even the names of venues are a litany: Torridon, Inveralligin, Sligachan, Tarbet (L. Lomond), Ullapool, Overscaig...

The Hogmanay hill habit goes back over many decades: winter routes in Glen Coe, the Sixties a school party camping in Glen Carron, then there were years of running winter courses in the same glen, till I decided I could be had under the Trades Description Act: winters weren't. Our Braes o' Fife Mountaineering Club maintained an MBA bothy so we used it for some years but it was too accessible and over-often others arrived intent on booze-filled nights rather than hill days. We visited other bothies but then tried a cottage in Torridon. The comfort I must say appealed: coming down soaked and tired, not to a cramped tent in a saturated field or a raw chilled bothy, to cook over a Primus, but to a dry, warm building, with a full kitchen - and a bath or shower. Roughing it is the art of maximum comfort from minimal effort after all. We had a decade in Torridon before deciding we really should ring the changes so, subsequently have ranged from Sutherland to south of the Atlas. (The last to escape the ballyhoo of the Millennium.) The variety certainly spiced up the seasons.

On those winter courses over Christmas - Hogmanay I met clients off the train at Achnashallach station. The lights switched on for a period before and to just after the train time but as the train always ran late this led to people invariably arriving in the dark. Once I found the party one short and, the train pulling away, we were about to go when we heard a thrashing among the rhododendrons beyond the platform. A head-torch picked out a figure pinned down by his rucksack, arms and legs waving like a demented tortoise. Innocent Londoner, he had assumed station platforms were always longer than trains.

Our Glencarron school camp was blessed with plenteous snow and great hill days. At the end, having an early train to catch, we packed the frozen tents the night before and slept in the tiny waiting room of Glencarron Halt. In the black of morning someone noticed the signal lamp was dead so it was brought down, filled from a Primus, and set to red. Quite the do-it-yourself station we thought. As we scrambled on board the last boy was given a yell by the driver to go and turn the signal to green. The station was in fact closed down. When the lamp ran out of fuel it would never be refilled.

Our bothy years were enjoyed. Suardalin was hidden away 'between Beinn Sgritheal and the Saddle' as one lad put it, 'Upglens from Glenelg'. The risk there was having Mam Ratagan snowed up and impassable, but that excuse for turning up to work late after the break was never called into play. The Mam, though was a serious start or end to hill days other than those in the immediate vicinity so, with all the Glen Shiel hills climbed and nearer Beinn Sgritheal and Sgurr Mhic Bharraich done several times we decided to move on. (Beinn Sgritheal was regarded by Munro as a favourite among the lower hills he listed.)

We thought Nest of Fannich [sadly no more] would be

remote enough not to attract anyone else but the Corrie-mulzie Club was having a reunion meet and we ended up with about thirty people in two rooms. In the lower room eightsome reels were danced by rotation (the piper closed in the scullery) and a minute after the New Year had been traditionally welcomed one member, in his undies, raced off into the blowing snow to maintain his 'first swim of the year' tradition. He left at 00.05. He was back at 00.06.

One year just two of us went in over Am Faochagach to Glenbeg bothy, then added Carn Ban to reach Coire Mor to see in the New Year at that remotest of remote spots. Conditions were certainly wintry enough and in a concrete cell, which is all the place was, with no fuel or heating, once we'd fed we retreated into sleeping bags with our drams. In the end we set the alarm for 23.55 and cooried doon completely. Apart from a chilly nose and hoar gathering at the breathing hole I was snug and happy and when the alarm went off almost prayed Dave would not hear it. He didn't stir. The long night passed comfortably enough while the snow blew steadily outside. The kip and a good breakfast would be needed to face the long slog out. Over the first brew in bed Dave confessed he had heard the alarm but, if I didn't stir, he wasn't going to. So that was the Hogmanay we didn't see in. We made our exit over Seana Braigh, Clach Geala and Ceapraichean.

Nights could pass perfectly happily without stone walls and a roof. My most memorable winter night 'howffing it' found me in one of the most dramatic landscapes in Scotland, where a boulder on a col was all the shelter on offer. (I'd spotted it previously in summer.) I started from Strath na Sealga and traversed that great skyline of Beinn a' Chlaidheimh, Sgurr Ban, Mullach Coire Mhic Fhearchair, Beinn Tarsuinn and Ruadh Stac Mor, then headed down to my howff. I settled in under the boulder, cooked a good meal and had brought a book to read by the dancing candlelight. The sky was black and threatening. The howff might well be tested. I put on dry socks and long johns, got into my sleeping bag and with the dog for hot water bottle really did enjoy roughing it.

I woke once in the night to see the moon skipping through the clouds and to find it had snowed heavily and, as if to prove the efficacy of my shelter, the snow tide line was safe inches away while, beyond, lay a shimmering sea of white. I recognised one of those moments when life is ambushed by the exquisite arrows of painful joy. Beauty manifest. I eventually drifted back into sweet dreams.

Eventually we started hiring a cottage for Hogmanay, beginning with the one at Annat by Loch Torridon for some years. Immediately after the hour struck we would hurry outside to see, or rather hear, the local Torridon tradition of someone - literally - shooting the moon. One evening the smoker in our party went out to indulge only to race in and yell, 'Come out, everyone!' We were given a glorious display of the Northern Lights. Christmas lights back home were never like that!

There were years when we never saw our accommodation in daylight; if conditions were good we'd be away in starlight and not back till after dark, if bad we'd not be outside. Every precious hour of winter daylight was needed for climbs in Applecross, or An Teallach, a traverse of Liathach or bagging Slioch. At the end of one meet I even did A' Mhaighdean out and back from Kinlochewe in the day, one that was greatly assisted by being able to walk along a frozen Lochan Fada.

We were equally happy to enjoy new, lower, hills. An Ruadh-mheallan gave a great day in itself and with superlative views of the Torridon giants around. Ben Shieldaig was another stunning viewpoint and between Torridon and Glen Carron the Corbetts are superior to many Munros. Size isn't everything.

There was one mild Hogmanay when the Torridon hills were quite snowless. We were in the village when we met a party tramping along (at midday) with their rucksacks jangling with ice axes and crampons, wearing full winter gear, mitts, gaiters, the lot. As we were in shirt sleeves it was weird but became ridiculous when they told us they were off to traverse Liathach.

Sgurr Dubh, overlooking Loch Clair, was climbed several times: another 'dubh with a view' and with its fascinating skirt of hundreds of moraine humps along from the Ling Hut. (One day, straggling over to the Ling Hut a school lad came out with 'Ah well, at least the path's flowing downhill now.') What caught our eye on Sgurr Dubh one visit was evidence of a lightning strike. There was a sizeable hole with boulders tossed aside then a furrow down the hill to another hole where presumably the strike went to earth.

An earlier Christmas Day came wetly behind several of the same so we took the chance of practising river crossings in the swollen River Carron. Several of the party were heading for Arctic Norway later where river-crossings can be serious (as on p. 240). Being quite warm we simply wore waterproof jacket and trousers on top of underwear, and our boots of course. We had an interesting time, practising various techniques, with or without ropes. I'd a pair of waterproof trousers which I'd cut up the side and added Velcro fastening so I could put them on and off over my boots. At one moment, when I was waist deep, on the verge of being swept off by the force of water, there was a strange flapping about my legs and I found the trousers had split. Not the Velcro, it held, but the actual seams had been ripped apart by the strength of the water flow.

A warning here. Ropes should not be used unless with a technically *au fait* person present. Van der Post's *Venture to the Interior* contains a classic example of a fatality by someone tying onto the end of a rope as a presumed aid to cross a rapid, and one of my best friends was swept off a fixed rope and drowned in the Allt Coire na Ciche in Knoydart one Hogmanay.

Perhaps the most superlative day ever on the Hogmanay hills was Beinn Dearg Mor across from An Teallach which we climbed from Shenavall bothy. This entailed four river-crossings. A long-time alpine climbing partner, a doctor in the Himalayas, took two more experienced lads up a gully and gave them an unforgettable day. ('Never been so frightened for so long' one admitted after their return in darkness.) I had several novices who learned quite a lot about deep powder and its ambushing presence on ice. My log noted 'Keep to edge of rocks as big snow slopes had slabby feel and could have produced avalanches. One nice bit of zigzagging up ledges, then up a corner where a wide step round to get out. Icy slopes to a gully. Up it. Continuation goes OK and led to easier ground. Soon yelling our glee on top of the Top. Echoes round the corrie. Eat and a photo spree then a flog of tracking down and up deep snow to the summit. Blue skies and blaze of white; really moving. An Teallach was completely white, an array of icy wedding cakes. Name everything in sight then along to break down . . .'

The next day was as fine. We added Beinn a' Chlaidheimh (the cover view). 'The usual boulder-hopping spots too tricky and go halfway to Achnegie with no chance so decide to wade! D off first to break the ice. It, and his language, break under the strain. Dipper goes off laughing. Knee deep, with ice to break and much ice on the bottom too. Nobody fell in but T, having paddled, goes back and refuses to come so he got equally cold with nothing to show for his pains. I used the old trick of peeing on my toes to warm them. We made T throw over the oatcakes and cheese for lunch. J went up further and tried boulders so of course fell in. Brown's Law says that at any water hazard in a party of four or more at least one will have a mishap'.

During our Skye Hogmanay we made a visit to Raasay to climb Dun Caan, only 443 metres but so recognisable with its sliced off summit. We found the final cone of frozen turf, so solid we could not kick even tiny nicks in it. One of the party happened to have his crampons in his rucksack. He put them on gratefully which must have made his ascent a 'first' of some kind. On Johnson and Boswell's tour of the Hebrides the latter danced on the summit with some of the local lassies.

Overscaig gave a proper winter too, almost too much as it froze the water supply and we had to carry all water used from the burn up the road. Ben Stack, that dominating wedge that draws the eye from so many northern places gave a traverse that had the feel of an alpine day. We went north-south which meant quite a few miles back to my van at the start but some of us just reached the road as the post bus came along. The tail of the party wondered at our disappearance but were happy enough when the van appeared so soon.

Tarbet is mostly remembered from the panic of losing my spectacles. I turned rucksack, van and cottage upside down without finding them so I must have dropped them on Cruach nam Mult. So, while everyone else set off for a hill I made the drive back to the top of Hell's Glen - and, greatly relieved, found my specs beside the tyre marks where we'd parked. I'd laid them on top of the car to put on my pullover and, senior moment, driven off.

At Overscaig we had some correspondence with the hiring company (we had an unexpected refund for there being no water!) in which we were told the owner of the house had just died. Next year, following our Tarbet visit when we thought of using it again we were informed its owner had died. We were somewhat relieved when the following Hogmanay passed without any fatal consequences to the owner.

The biggest concern involving a new place each year was finding suitable premises for a party of about eight. To show our lack of nationalistic bias one of our best Hogmanay meets explored the delectable country between Hereford and Shropshire in England. Apart from the Millennium blip of 2000 I have to go back to 1971-72 for the last foreign Hogmanay and that was spent on a train from Dar-es-Salaam, heading to Moshi for Kilimanjaro.

Mull last Hogmanay was violently wet and windy together, the ground was utterly saturated, the bigger hills were never glimpsed and at that time of year there is not much open for alternative interests. One discovery however, in Tobermory, was a letter box with an ER VIII monogram on it. Can't be many of them[1]. We kept indoors much of the time though most people went off once or twice out of desperation, and were duly punished. Jill and I however had one enjoyable last day sortie by choosing a small hill (275m), on Dawson's list, not far from a road: Tom nam Fitheach in Glen Ballart. Others had done this hill by flanking along opposite ends to reach it - and reported ill of their routes - but we found a tame forestry break that went straight up. A steep finish gained the high moorland where the cloud was tearing across mere feet above us yet a wee crag made a perfect shelter to have a break. We could see showers sweeping near but were untouched. Having reeled about in the gale to find the vague summit we descended along a bit and found we could amble down, out of the wind, *in* the spruce. Not often one blesses spruce. A stag crossed our path in the trees and on the way up I'd nearly stepped on a woodcock. Brewing at the car we were delighted at our one hour raid[2]. It then rained all the way back to base. And I've written something after all about last Hogmanay.

---

[1] Tobermory has the only two known EVIII post boxes: one by the ferry pier, one up on Beadalbane Street.

[2] I was working on a small guidebook to Mull's hills - the one Munro, one Corbett, 7 Grahams and 18 others listed in Dawson's *Relative Hills of Britain*. This was published by Brown and Whittaker, Tobermory, and is on sale in Mull shops. Proceeds from sales go to Tobermory's small museum.

HANDA ISLAND

A right little, tight little island.

Thos Dibdin

Handa (Sandy Isle) lies about 20 minutes south of Cape Wrath as the gull flies, off that northern, scoured, watered landscape of grey rock with Loch Laxford to the north and Scourie round a headland to the south. West, over the sea, lie the sunset lands terminating at the Butt of Lewis.

Handa is a bird island now, a reserve managed jointly by the Scottish Wildlife Trust and Scourie Estate. From April to September it is wardened. While not an island of bird rarities it shocks with numbers instead. The red sandstone sweeps up gently from machair-edged silver sands facing the port of Tarbet on the mainland then suddenly finishes on the sea-sliced precipices facing the Minch. Here there is an urban bedlam of birds, an ornithological tenement-life, with the

Great Stack the high rise of them all. Nobody can fail to be impressed by the Great Stack. It stands in the mouth of one of the many *geos* with the highest point of the islands not far off (406 feet), a bold ledge-banded monolith of rock, riddled with sea-level tunnels, capped with rank, gull-manured vegetation and, in season, every ledge crowded with guillemots, razorbills, gannets, puffins and shags. Ten thousand or so of these at a time is a memorable sight, sound, and smell.

A lassie and I were lucky to spend a month on Handa as voluntary wardens, the last month of its 1983 'open' season of April to mid-September. From Tarbet, Robert MacLeod, one of the hamlet's crofter-fishermen took us the mile and a bitty across to land on the sands of Traigh an Teampaill. (One of our tasks was clearing those beaches of the international garbage deposited by the tides.) This beach is one of several arcs of white shell sand backed by dunes and machair, but there was no sign of a chapel (*teampaill*).

Beside this spot, built on the site of an old fishermen's bothy there is a day shelter for visitors with displays and information about the island wildlife. One of us would usually welcome any boatful of visitors and give them a map of the 3 hour circular walk that has been laid out.

Visitors are asked to keep to the marked route, partly because the centre is featureless and they can become disorientated easily, but mainly to protect nesting birds. If eggs, or young, are left exposed at all the robber skuas are there in a flash. The skuas are one of the more unusual birds (with the attributes of stukas) and there are both great and arctic skuas breeding. They accept people on the path and so can easily be seen, but if anyone strays they will be vigorously attacked. The sound of the querulous arctics was one of the background sounds to life in the wardens' bothy.

This is a one-time shepherd's cottage lying up behind

'fank' and walled 'park', where 'the desert and the sown' once met. There's a wind-seared stand of lodgepole protecting a planting of native trees: alder, birch, willows, rowan, sallow, hazel and holly. I brought out two dozen birch to plant. Handa, in some ways, is a microcosm of Sutherland history.

James Wilson in his book *A Voyage Round the Coasts of Scotland* (1842) found the island tenanted by 12 families 'who though forming a loyal people, have curiously enough combined to establish a queen of their own in the person of the oldest widow'. Subsistence, he noted, was partly fishing, sea-fowl and eggs. They also exported feathers. But the decline had started.

Victorian laird, Evander Maciver of Scourie wrote 'When I came here in 1845 I found Handa occupied by seven crofter tenants, with a queen amongst them. They lived comfortably, and grew large crops of potatoes on its sandy soil, when top dressed with seaweed. When the potato disease broke out in 1847 the crop failed in Handa completely; the people's source of support was gone. They said they were willing to emigrate to America if the Duke of Sutherland would pay the expense of sending them there. The result was that not only were the tenants of Handa, but a very large number from Assynt and Eddrachillis sent to Canada and Nova Scotia during the next two years - in all exceeding 500 people'. They were all native Gaelic speakers but no doubt their marching orders came in Queen's English.

In 1848 the 'sportsman' Charles St John (who contributed so much to the clearing of Highland birds, including Sutherland's last Osprey) visited Handa, not long after the evacuation, and described their croft houses lying desolate and overrun by starlings. On the rocks a large white cat sat 'looking wistfully towards the mainland'. One of the boatmen commented, 'She is wanting the ferry'.

John Ridgway visited the island several times while we were there (his Ardmore Outdoor Centre is just up the coast) and we waved to *English Rose IV* as he and Andy Briggs set off on their round the world non-stop trip. That remarkable feat, which knocked about two months off the record, is told in their book *Round the World Non-Stop*. A sad and ironic footnote though was a postcard from John, once back, to say that Robert, the canny boatman, had been drowned in Handa Sound, while they, sticking their necks out for months on end, had returned home hale and hearty.

We were lucky to visit the Great Stack with Robert. We chugged off, east-about, along the coast. The cliffs steadily grew in scale, *geos* and caves honeycombed the coast and we dodged flat islets, bases of long-fallen stacks. The north reach of coast is a massive 400 foot blank 'curtain wall' which has resisted the attacks of the sea. At its west end the attack had been more successful with a chaos of broken pillars and crags. The Great Stack so fills the mouth of its *geo* it cannot visually be separated from the land. With necks craning up at the whitewashed ledges (empty with the lateness of season) we passed its outer bastion. Robert turned the bows in towards what seemed no more than a doorway in the rock, a doorway that reached to the sky. Shags crashed out about us as we chugged through the gloomy corridor while the sea surged and gurgled in and out of the many holes and tunnels. The Great Stack is a huge tooth with rotten roots. We shook our heads in wonder that this 'impregnable' tower had been climbed. Climbed is used loosely. The techniques were slightly unusual.

We are constantly told in historical works that rock-climbing in Britain began with this or that English ascent in the 19th century but this is quite wrong. In 1876 the men of Lewis 'raided' Handa and 'conquered' the Great Stack, an event paralleling *Sassenach* on the Ben, except the players were obscure peasants and the event only just recorded! But their *forebears* were the first British climbers - with cliff-scaling deeds on Sula Sgeir, North Rona, St Kilda or Handa recorded long ago. The men who led the first ascent of Stac Lee (St Kilda) may have had ulterior motives (the capture of birds) but it was a rock climb of some skill. This was Britain's first recorded rock-climbing.

Some would detract by saying these climbs were not done for sport but that is misleading. The main objective was food gathering but young men are young men and climbs were also done purely for fun and kudos - just as first ascents today. Nor did they carry pitons and chalkbags, and I doubt if their horse-hair ropes would appeal to our jangling heroes today. To prove their worthiness as prospective husbands, lads on St Kilda would show off their climbing skills. All males climbed and some climbed better than others - human nature has not changed. The ascent of Handa's Great Stack was the result of just such a bit of showing-off. Climbing on St Kilda is mentioned in the C17.

The men of Noss (in Lewis) regularly culled the birds of North Rona. They do so to this day, by a special clause in Bird Protection Acts, though they no longer *row* there (North Rona is 45 miles north of the Butt of Lewis and can just be seen from Cape Wrath on a clear day.) They had no *need* to head for Handa to collect birds - but it was a good excuse. It had probably been planned and talked about for long enough.

There was a certain confusion about the first climb, but it is now clearly seen to have been by this party of skilled Lewis men. They were thoroughly familiar with cliffs and rope-handling. An ascent from sea-level was rather discouraged by the bird-crowded ledges, a fact re-discovered by

Tom Patey long after, but they won their summit by a piece of bold simplicity - lateral thinking! They walked the ends of a long rope out both arms of the *geo* until its central length between came to rest on the Great Stack!

The rope was then tied or anchored firmly and 'ace climber' Donald Macdonald swarmed along the rope: a feat, simple perhaps, but of staggering boldness for there was no security as he swung along 400 feet above a crashing sea and with birds shrieking round. A sort of pulley system was then rigged up and the birds were culled. Stakes, stuck in the middle of the green cap of the Stack, remained visible till after World War Two - as challenging a sign as a peg in the middle of a big face.

On the first of July 1967 Tom Patey, with henchmen Chris Bonington and Ian MacNaught Davies repeated the Lewismen's raid on the Stack but even with all the aids of modern mountaineering found it no easy task. Nylon rope stretches more than natural fibre so as soon as the fixed line bore Tom's weight, it sagged. He was sitting in a harness, suspended from *jumars,* and these proved frustrating and exhausting for Tom's parabolic route. Birds cannoned into the rope and Tom noted, while dangling like a spider that a guillemot 'was pecking thoughtfully at the taut rope' where it crossed its territory. A few days later this gang was off for the Orkney Isles and the tele-spectacular of the Old Man of Hoy. (Tom Patey, alas, was killed in 1971 when abseiling off another sea stack in Loch Eriboll.) The Great Stack was finally climbed from sea-level by Hamish MacInnes, G N Hunter and D F Lang on the first of August 1969. They also climbed the obvious Stack in the bay (Puffin Bay) where the path across the island reaches the cliff edge. There are many other unclimbed stacks and cliffs. My eye of faith noted several as we returned from our circumnavigation, a happy exercise as there was never any possibility of having to attempt any. [More recently the crossing to the Great Stack had a TV re-enactment.]

Handa, for me, was a marvellous return to nature, to a way of life ruled by weather rather than worksheets. It was hard work but to a purpose. You saw the results. And you could lift eyes to the hills at any time. There were always the sounds of sanity: divers flying overhead, the cat-crying arctic skuas, running water, the chug-chug of an outboard, the heart-beat of the sea, the impatient wind winding over the island.

The Alpine Journal of 1913 has a fascinating article by Richard Barrington concerning a visit to St Kilda in 1883 when he joined locals in catching puffins on the cliffs and then took part in a show-off raid to climb Stac Biorach. He had to prove himself before being allowed to join the local 'aces', who obviously regarded climbing as a sport as well as a necessity. Ironically, he had partly gone there to assess *their* climbing skills and compare them with alpine guides. (In 1882 he had climbed the Schreckhorn, Finsteraarhorn, Jungfrau and Matterhorn all in ten days, in a stated rivalry with his brother who had earlier first ascended the Eiger. Nothing changes!) He was duly impressed. Landing from the sea was exciting and the climb as hard as the hardest an alpinist of the day would tackle. At one stage a lasso was used and at a hand traverse *he* came off and was held by the two to whom he was roped. (I've also read of a local man in later Victorian times who soloed up the stack for a wager simply to win a pouch of tobacco off a tourist.)

These activities deserve greater prominence in any history of climbing; they are seldom acknowledged. Tom Patey's succinct judgment was that 'no mountaineering amateur of that era would have committed himself to such an undertaking [as the Handa climb]'. W H Murray visited the son of the Lewismen's lead climber, a hard working crofter-fisherman, who pointed out how his father often would go off to the cliffs round Ness just to enjoy the climbing, or simply for a spot of bird watching.

NAME DROPPINGS OF A BOOKWORM

The book that most caught my imagination while still at school was Tom Weir's *Highland Days** (1948), his first book telling of his youthful exploring the Scotland he would come to know so well. Little did I know how he would come in and out of my life over the years. At the other end of his life, *Weir's World, An Autobiography of Sorts*, written in his eighties, is one of the most readable such accounts.

I think my first meeting with Tom was with a school party near the west end of Loch Monar, about as remote a spot as you can find. If we were surprised to come on someone, he was even more astonished to come on a group of enthusiastic fourteen year olds, lads who could talk birds and flowers and pitched tents and did things with practical skills. He once made one of his TV programmes on rock climbing with some of my Braehead lads, using the quarry on Gloom Hill above Dollar. I remember one boy being directed to show a hand groping at a sharp edge for a hold and doing this by lying on the ground to grasp a convenient stone block. End of his belief in TV veracity.

Tom was a perfectionist where work was concerned. I once heard him called, 'A thrawn b . . .' and so he was (but so are most SMC members) but he had more right to be so than most. One interest in putting together a Tom Weir anthology was gaining insights into his life. I just wished we'd had more days out, and arguments in, together.

The Weir anthology came my way as a direct result of the two anthologies I had done from the 27 book Seton Gordon *oeuvre*: *Seton Gordon's Scotland**; *Seton Gordon's Cairngorms**. I never met Gordon but had written to him with some questions about Svalbard (Spitzbergen) where I was bound and where he had been in 1921. He replied fully without notes to check on and also told a story of how to save money on telegrams there was a code based on bird names: 'Curlew' meant they had arrived safely, 'Eider' meant they were off exploring northwards, and such like. Seton Gordon as naturalist, writer and photographer was to influence a whole generation of field workers: Adam Watson, Tom Weir, Desmond Nethersole-Thomson, Morton Boyd, David Stephen, Mike Tomkies, Don and Bridget Macaskill, Jim Crumley.

A fellow teacher and SMC member at Braehead was Charlie Gorrie, a friend of Jimmy Bell so we met this character. I recall one school gang invited into Jimmy's house in Clachmannan and being given an idiosyncratic Bell soup that was mostly water in which floated diced, near-raw vegetables. The boys were polite and munched through it. Taking two of these lads up Tower Ridge I noted climbers on what I pointed out was a 1928 Bell route. One queried 'You mean the Bell we met?' When I said yes, he gasped, 'But, sur, he's history!' Bell only began his Munros aged seventy. ('Got to give the effin hills a chance.')

Charlie told me of a climb he did with Bell soon after WW2. They were heading for the Posts on Creag Meagaidh, after having had a dook in the loch. Charlie, still recovering from a war wound was struggling and before tackling the crux demanded to know if Bell had a good belay. 'Of course I've got a good effin belay.' When Charlie eventually reached Bell he found the leader with the rope being held between his teeth, busy pulling on his trousers.

To many of us post-WW2, J H B Bell's *A Progress in Mountaineering* was our chief manual for instruction, besides absorbing its stories of climbing at home and in the Alps.

The most influential books post war were W H Murray's *Mountaineering in Scotland* 1947 and its follow-up, *Undis-*

covered Scotland (1951). Both *Mountaineering in Scotland* and Weir's *Highland Days* were written during the war (oddly, both lost fathers in the First World War) though Murray wrote his in the uncongenial situation of a German POW camp. Written on scraps of paper it was destroyed and had to be re-written.

I first came to know Bill Murray from the pair of us and Hamish McInnes being original members of the Scottish Mountain Leadership Training Board, Tom Weir we just kept meeting as one did with regular hillgoers. All the early Munroists for instance knew each other in a way impossible today. A high proportion then were SMC or LSCC. Years on I once wrote a short story (In *The Last Hundred*) set on Schiehallion where a Kinloch Rannoch family met a ghostly figure from the past on the summit. Some time later a letter came from a Sir Torquil Munro in the USA asking if this figure in the story was based on his grandfather, Sir Hugh? I had to admit it was actually imagining Rev A E Robertson, who had been minister at Rannoch. When becoming a director of the then Scottish Rights of Way Society board I found myself facing a Mrs Robertson across the table - the widow of A E R! At that time I also encountered Janet Adam Smith (then Mrs Carleton). It was Janet Adam Smith's *Mountain Holidays**(1946) that first persuaded me to go to the Alps. She made the Alps sound *fun*, and possible for anyone and not just the super-stars of most books.

Hamish McInnes I first met when a friend and I signed up for one of his winter climbing courses, based on Glen Coe youth hostel, then run by the redoubtable, big, Ingrid Feeney, whom one of my school kids described as being 'six feet, in every direction'. She made the Y H popular with the mountain world: Hamish had his courses there, I'd my youngsters, the RAF rescue teams were frequent visitors and there were regulars galore. I recall Johnnie Lees and Gwen Moffat from the Valley team. Johnnie gave the kids wartime escapers' button compasses, a big thrill. Gwen Moffat's *Space Below My Feet* tells the story of her becoming a professional guide, and her *Two Star Red* was one of the first books about mountain rescue. Hamish was to write several. My favourite book of his was *Climb to the Lost World* (1972), describing the desperate ascent of Roraima. Hamish seemed to have a knack of being around for interesting climbs - like the Cuillin Ridge in winter - and had his share of epics. I recall one call out before rescue teams were fully established when an Edinburgh schoolboy had taken a tumble almost on top of Bidean (3773 feet!) and had sustained a head wound. The recovery team was Hamish, the local shepherd, local bobby and our school lads. While there were frequent changes of those carrying the rear of the stretcher, Hamish bore the front, heavy, end all the way down. He, of course, was to design stretchers, introduce metal ice axes, search dogs and much more.

Another great character I met on the hill was Syd Scroggie. We first met on top of Lochnagar in a cloying mist but this didn't stop Syd pointing in all directions to describe the view. It took me a while to realise he was blind. (He also had one artificial leg having been unlucky enough to step on a mine in Italy near the end of WW2.) With a Braehead gang we encountered him stumping along the track from the Linn of Dee to Derry Lodge. Blind. Alone. He pointed out things like deer by the river and a kestrel overhead, to leave the kids astonished. In 1978 he produced a slim volume of poems *Give Me the Hills* several of which I would anthologise in *Speak to the Hills* and *Poems of the Scottish Hills*.

The book he should have written would have been one of jokes for the disabled. He knew many. Wife, accusing husband of philandering demands, 'What would you do if you came home and found me in bed with someone?' The reply: 'Shoot his guide dog'.

Another of that ilk was Ben Humble who was deaf and wrote with enthusiasm of pre-war gangrel days and howffing when the have nots had it all. Ben's great classic was *The Cuillin of Skye* (1952), a real collectors' piece - and one of the most iconic of hill photographs is his picture of Bill Murray standing on the Cioch with a cloud sea below. I nearly ended Ben's life one wild, wet November when driving through Arrochar and came on this figure prancing about in the road, hearing nothing.

Not at all easy, in a literary sense, was taking on various anthologies over the years. *Speak to the Hills* was all twentieth century British and Irish mountain poetry and I reckon it took 2000 letters and/or phone calls to cobble together. (No modern technology in 1985.) Tracing copyright could be a nightmare though on one occasion was forgiven. Various letters to Ed Drummond failed to raise a response till an apologetic card came saying he had been out of circulation; they had caught him halfway up the Empire State Building and he'd done six months inside. Then there was the old dear who only started writing poetry when seventy. She was ninety when I got in touch and she was happy I used two of her poems, but not the third, she considered it 'juvenilia'.

When I had a sabbatical winter off school I headed for the Atlas Mountains, in large part due to the enthusiastic reports of two friends: Tom Weir who had been there twice with Douglas Scott, the second time to make one of his first films, and Gavin Maxwell, best known for the evergreen *Ring of Bright Water**. Maxwell was working on his historical *Lords of the Atlas** so we had often talked about the country and I read some of the book in his seemingly flawless manuscript.

We met later in the Atlas. But it was after the exotic story of the rise and fall of the house of Glaoui was published I had a strange meeting, unexpected wheels within wheels.

I was standing on the Jema el Fna in Marrakech, watching tumblers performing for the crowds, alongside snake-charmers and story-tellers, this evening showground with its beating drums as fascinating as ever. (The tumblers worked up their shows on the Fna in winter and then toured with Bertram Mills Circus in the summer.) I was suddenly accosted by a local; no tout, for his English was educated, the djellaba of expensive material and cut. Where was I from? Ah, Scotland, and he became almost tongue-tied, stammering out, eventually, 'I wonder, I mean . . ., oh, it's ridiculous, but do you, could you by any chance know someone there by the name of Gavin Maxwell?' For the only time in my life I rendered a Moroccan speechless. 'Yes, I was visiting him a couple of weeks ago.'

So, over mint tea then, and visits to his home on subsequent visits, I came to know Mohammed el Khizzoui, one time secretary to T'hami el Glaoui, Pasha of Marrakech, greatest of the 'Lords of the Atlas'. The Glaoui had diplomatically submitted, then died on the restoration of the king (he had largely been responsible for Mohammed V's exile), and his secretary, having kept his head on his shoulders, now lived quietly in the warren of the city medina. He soon came round to why he was initially interested in me. He had been a prime source of information for Maxwell's *Lords of the Atlas* and had loaned various documents, which he would like back. Would I help? It was not to be; on returning to Scotland I was to find Maxwell's home had been burnt down and everything lost. (A rather drastic source of 'copy' even for Maxwell.) I did take Mohammed some copies of the book which was banned at the time in Morocco.

Though Mohammed was naturally disappointed at the loss of the papers his home was still mine to visit. A couple of years later I arrived at his door in the middle of the celebrations for his sister's return from the *haj* and, when I tried to excuse myself, he would not hear of my going away, so typical of the graciousness of Moroccan hospitality.

Came the year I headed from the Fna to plunge into the medina for Mohammed's house - and couldn't find it. I spent *hours* wandering in the maze, no doubt making things worse at every step. I tried several times over the next few months, and the year after, I haunted the Fna and its cafés but the thread was broken. I never saw Mohammed again. This may seem incredible but those who know the medina will understand.

Later, when in touch with Douglas Botting, who was working on Maxwell's biography, I found another side to the story: there had been a falling out between Maxwell and Mohammed, the latter all too easily ripping off a surprisingly innocent traveller. But once wheels start turning they never seem to stop.

The very first post-war Himalayan expeditions (1950, 1951) were made by a dedicated group of Scottish climbers: Bill Murray, Douglas Scott, Tom Weir, George Roger, Tom Mackinnon, expeditions very much in the style of Shipton-Tilman, and which I feel are not always given the credit they deserve. Murray then went on the vital 1951 Everest reconnaissance with Shipton, Hillary *et al*. The mountain was climbed in 1953, and Tom Mackinnon was an important member of the successful first ascent of Kangchengunga, the third highest mountain in the world, in 1955. [Change days, in 2014, some 33 expeditions ascended Kangchengunga, from Italy, Japan, Nepal, Finland, Spain, Russia, India and Bulgaria.]

When a gang of us set ambitions on the traverse of East Top to summit of Nanda Devi we naturally got in touch with Shipton and Tilman. Our ringleaders were Eric Roberts (later avalanched on Annapurna) and Donald Mill (SMC; drowned in Knoydart one Hogmanay). When the Japanese did this route our party split and Eric went off for just Nanda Devi while the rest preferred to bag impressive new 6000m summits in the Sanctuary. Donald, being London-based, visited Shipton several times in hospital where he was terminally ill, I visited Tilman who was shortly to be heading to Antarctic waters, for I already had come to know him through sea rather than mountain doings. Alas, when we returned from India Shipton had died and Tilman was 'missing in action'. I still smile at my first meeting with this remarkable man at his Barmouth home when I was interested in joining him on one of his sailing-mountaineering trips.

I'd arrived a bit early and there was nobody at home so I sat on the doorstep to wait. Soon a figure appeared, dressed in raincoat and hat, dogs at heel, rural Englishman personi-fied: Tilman. Ushered into a cosy room, a match was put to a pre-laid fire, a trolley with a silver teapot was trundled in and we sat toasting crumpets at the blaze. I had to be dreaming. This was not at all the popular image of Tilman. He was certainly not chatty on the other hand; eventually he shot out, 'I've sunk my last two ships'. This was followed by a lengthy silence, 'Nobody will insure me', with an even longer silence and then, 'Do you still want to come?' I still regard him as an exceptional character, the perfect gentleman, and the original 'hard man'.

Shipton and Tilman had first come into my ken through Shipton's early autobiography, *Upon that Mountain* (1943), then Shipton's *Nanda Devi* (1936) and Tilman's *The Ascent of Nanda Devi* (1937), the amazing story of gaining the

Nanda Devi Sanctuary in 1934 and then climbing the mountain in 1936.

Wheels within wheels again. A John Shipton joined me in the Atlas a couple of times and I naturally talked a lot about his father, Eric. Brought up by his mother John was oddly unaware of his father's career and started to read all he could and was soon following, often literally, in his father's footsteps, in the Himalayas and Patagonia.

There was to be one last wheels within wheels concerning Shipton and Tilman. I doubt if I attend more than one lecture every other year at the Alpine Club. On one occasion at the AOB stage of formalities the president asked if anybody had any news of Tilman as concern was growing over the lack of contact. He had gone off months before as guest navigator on a converted tug, aiming for Antarctic islands. A frail old man pulled himself to his feet and quavered, 'I had a postcard from Bill from Rio . . .'. The informality of the 'Bill' and the incongruous picture of the Tilman we imagine *in Rio* made me almost smile but then the old man was Noel Odell who summitted Nanda Devi with Tilman in 1936 and that postcard was the very last contact with Tilman.

Book titles marked * may well still be available - often as reprints - if ordered from book sources/book shops. The two Murray classics were issued as a single volume, as were the two Nanda Devi volumes of Shipton and Tilman, while Tilman's various mountaineering (7) and sailing (8) ventures were also turned into compendiums, as were Shipton's 6 Mountain books. There's a biography on Ben Humble *The Voice of the Hills* by R Humble, and *Gavin Maxwell, a Life*, by D Botting is an interesting read. Seton Gordon's *Highways and Byeways in the West Highlands . . . in the Central Highlands*, reprints, with the original D Y Cameron illustrations can also be found. The seminal 1950 Himalayan expedition was written up by both Murray and Weir: W H Murray: *The Scottish Himalayan Expedition* (1951), and T Weir: *The Ultimate Mountains* (1953).

APPROACHES

THE JUBILEE JAUNT

The thing to do, is think horizons - and go over them.

The trip's name was given retrospectively. Jaunt it was not but we do tend to expect the British trait of modesty to apply to accounts of our dafter escapades. What would follow on from this particular experience would prove to be the greatest reward - the idea of an *event* to encourage others to walk the peculiarly rewarding coast to coast idea.

No crossing is easy. Tay to Clyde sounds easy enough but Ochils, Campsies and Kilpatricks I found rough underfoot. Shortest I'd done was a crossing from Lochinver to Berriedale (Sutherland/Caithness), longest Ardnamurchan to Buchan Ness, which was also the wettest ever, glorious to Acharacle and fifty shades of rain every day thereafter. The Jubilee Jaunt was memorable for the unlikely opposite reason, the *hottest* ever spell of weather I've ever encountered in Scotland.

The planning completed, a couple of parcels posted to places east of the A9, Ray and I drove up to Glenbrittle, dropping off other caches (maps, film, goodies) on the way. The broom was bright, the cuckoos' calling incessant and the

Glenbrittle camp site full this third weekend in May (1977). A diver chattered over. The weather was perfect. For this coast-to-coast, we were additionally going from westmost Munro to eastmost Munro: Sgurr na Banachdich to Mount Keen.

Ray comes from Cleethorpes where a hundred foot contour is called a hill so he was impressed by the Cuillin, particularly as he was a walker rather than a climber. Banachdich is among the easiest of the Cuillin summits however. The lower grass slopes were brittle dry (with lots of hairy caterpillars), cuckoos flitted about and mice runnels were everywhere. We left our 30lb rucksacks at the Bealach na Banachdich and floated up to the summit: 3167 feet. Just Scotland to cross now.

There were still old snow rims and the gully down from the bealach was a hard snow slope. We edged down the trench between snow and crags, Ray none too happy. Lower down the heat was intense and the day's treat was splashing in a translucent blue pool in a stream entering Loch Coruisk. There would be more swimming in the next twelve days than in the previous twelve years. We spent the night in the Coruisk Hut, well-appointed, and the resident climbers had even ferried in a barrel of beer.

The Bad Step was passed on the way to Camusunary then Ray took the track out to walk the Elgol - Torrin road while I made a traverse of Blaven, an easier option in my view. (Walking hot tarmac is not a favourite pastime.) The summit offers one of Scotland's greatest views and I made my worship of Cuillin, Kintail, Knoydart, Sgriol and the Islands. Northwards I could see the Kishorn oil construction yard. I made the road in time to eat, paddle and lounge among the scented hyacinths before Ray arrived. Cows were standing in the sea in postcard content.

We stopped for a brew by the Cill Chriosd graveyard, had dinner at the Broadford Hotel and slept at the youth hostel, bodies glowing from the sun. Shorts and a shirt spread over shoulders had been the day's attire. Next day we walked over lark-reeling moors to cut the corner to the Sleat road and made Isle Ornsay for lunchtime. Beinn Sgritheal, king of the smaller Munros, hunched into the sky across the sound. After that break the oven was turned to its highest setting. I kept a sponge in the small of my back to prevent the sweat running down to create what my sister-in-law called 'nappy rash'. I wrung it out every mile. A wee post office sold us drinks and Ray carried off *three* iced lollies as we tramped on. A pipit chased a cuckoo across the road in front of our noses, a spitfire after a Heinkel you could say. The Ardvasar Hotel was very welcome after fifteen miles. Ray was well enough off not to count expenses (he was paying) and I wasn't complaining though I usually moan at hotel or B&B nights not allowing early, and therefore cool, starts. I lay in a deep bath, with a pot of tea beside me. A full-length mirror revealed a two-tone creature: very pale in the trunk and distinctly red at the extremities.

The ferry *Bute* took us across to Mallaig, the flat Sound duplicating the blue of the sky and upside down Knoydart peaks. We watched the train come in, *Spanish John*, the landing craft, head off with cement and Macdonald, the proprietor, follow in his Cowes-registered cruiser. We brought up the rear in the *Clansman* and had a lazy Inverie day, staying at the estate-workers hostel at the farm. Ray desperately parcelled up surplus belongings to post home and save weight. It is surprising what you can do without when you are carrying its weight. Ray lay in the sun during the afternoon.

At breakfast next morning Ray declared he couldn't go

on, so I went off to climb Beinn Bhuidhe in hope that Ray would perk up during the day. He couldn't understand there being no easy exit from Knoydart and was perhaps too self-indulgent to want to suffer but suffer he did for he lay in the sun again and, when I returned in the afternoon, was suffering real heatstroke. Not nice, being a bit like bad seasickness, only worse, and quite dangerous. Drinks, shade, and rest being the cure Ray was not going anywhere. I had supper, bade Ray farewell and then set off to win back the day: over Mam Meadail to reach Sourlies bothy, darkness falling in the glen but a good moon thereafter, often with the mincing shadows of deer crossing its glow. Bed at midnight, but back on par. Curlews were calling on the sands at the head of Loch Nevis. I'd been at Sourlies a month before when the site was just some broken, overgrown walls. I pulled out rubbish and dug till I broke the spade handle, collected stones and stripped moss off the interior walls, a wee prelude for the MBA work party about to be landed at the head of the loch by the *Spanish John*. The bothy was only a few weeks old.

The rebuilt bothy impressed. During the night there were lots of creaks. Breaking itself in? I would see the bothy quite often over the next few years, once, alas, to scatter the ashes of a friend who had died crossing the Allt Coire na Ciche heading out one Hogmanay. The spate carried him into Loch Nevis. The birch tree group at Sourlies is his memorial. The Allt Coire na Ciche was a mere trickle after days of sun when I hopped across at about 05.30. The made path twists and turns up to 1000 feet, there are lonely lochans and black crags - and suddenly the green sweep of Glen Dessarry. The Mam na Cloich Aird was the best of the fifteen passes the coast-to-coast would demand.

I went over to A' Chuil bothy for breakfast. Tea was

measured by the pint rather than the cup. There was another sweltering two-swims pass over from Glen Dessarry to reach Glen Kingie. Sgurr Mor lived up to its name but had a pleasant breeze on top so, unladen, was a pleasant ascent. The descent was like entering some awful furnace room so I went over to Kinbreack bothy for shade and slept till 17.00. After supper I wandered on down Glen Kingie and then followed forestry tracks till, by Lochan an Staic, I'd had enough and made a bed in the heather with tremendous sunset colours and afterglow. A distant fox call was the only sound in the sweeping silence. The night was cold and clear, perfect for sleeping out.

I woke to hoar frost spraying onto my face - sent down by a foraging coal tit overhead. I'd tea in bed to the burbling of blackcock. The miles of forest by Garrygulach and Greenfield I softened by reading as I walked, something of an acquired skill but much practised, one way of 'gentling the feet by occupying the brain'. From the high pass I went up and down Ben Tee. On top I saw a cloud! Back at the rucker there were three. Was the weather changing?

The descent by the Kilfinnan Falls was a good way to gain the Great Glen, the first of two big milestones on any coast-to-coast. At the Laggan Locks where the Caledonian Canal enters Loch Lochy I scoffed two cokes and a pot of tea. The lock was empty for repairs, the first, I was told, since Telford built the canal. I slept for several hours then wrote up my log before going along to the hostel and a welcome from Mrs Fraser, the warden, who had often welcomed our school parties there a decade earlier. My feet were not so happy, the soles sore, heels tender, the top of toes blistered. By 20.30 I was abed, the sky clouded over. Had the swank of sun had its fling?

Mrs Fraser said she'd heard old people talking of walking

over the hills from Laggan to upper Glen Roy by my route, the Bealach an t-Sidhein to enjoy a dance. The weather being overcast I thought I'd have to aim for Luib-chonnal bothy rather than making another bivouac and set off refreshed by eleven hours in bed. Two of us were to repeat this crossing a few years later on an Ultimate Challenge coast-to-coast when the rain teemed down all day. Our food had been hidden over the bothy burn and crossing would be impossible in the spate so, while still up high, Tony took my gear down direct while I kept to the other bank to retrieve the food and then planned to swim across the big pool at the Eas Ban with it. Almost a mile above Luib-chonnal we found a substantial bridge which was not on the map (and still isn't). Didn't we curse the O.S.

The next day soon saw the sun bullying its way through the clouds so I went up to the Bealach a' Bharnish, west of Creag Meagaidh and traversed Beinn a' Chaorain with its three bumps - which had taken turns as the Munro over the years. The eastern cliffs were still cornice-edged but summer was rushing in, skipping any spring season. Butterwort was flowering and there was azalea on the summit. At Moy I ate into darkness and bedded down on armfuls of purple moor grass to watch the sun set the dome of Beinn a' Chlachair on fire. In the dawn I was given another visual as well as audible blackcock lek.

Today's route took in plenty of empty miles, largely through an uninhabited world, two passes, two Munros and the full reach of the Fara to end at Dalwhinnie on the A9, the second great cost-to-coast distance marker. There had been a frost overnight and clear skies again. Snow patches were frozen hard. Having set off at 04.30 I clattered in to Blackburn of Pattock bothy to startle a family still asleep. I wonder if they knew of the dead deer in the water supply.

The southern end of the Fara, Meall Cruaidh, was the finest viewpoint, even though there is a huge cairn by the summit. The panorama took in Ben Alder, Creag Meagaidh, the Monadh Liaths and the hills of the A9. The A9 traffic noise came up like surf. It was stupefyingly hot after the miles of the Fara. When I found a burn I drank mightily, relaxed by it and woke up an hour later.

The Grampian Hotel was packed by a bus party but Mrs Kettle said she'd 'squeeze me in somewhere'. I wrote in my log: 'the character of any coast-to-coast changes so much once across the A9: great brown fists of hills, still with white nail-rims of snow'. Any hope of easier going vanished as a new heatwave began. (On a later coast-to-coast the A9 near Drumochter was so busy I crawled through a culvert under it for safety.)

Shackled to hotel breakfast times I regretted not being away in the cool hours. Setting off in vest and shorts worried the bus party. 'All that snow up there. It will be freezing.' No such luck. By 08.30 I was dripping. At the end of the day I compared my arms and legs with the previous night's gammon. A redshank bleeped ahead for the deer-busy slopes of Meall Chuaich, there were ring ouzels and dippers and greenshanks too. The Pass of Gaick slotted through the hills; one of the precursor Mounth passes before Wade's Drumochter line. Miles of dusty heather brought on a rare thirst so I gathered heather stalks to make a fire to drum up. I'd left the stove at Dalwhinnie to save some weight. I was too 'weary o' the sun' to do more than paddle. The last paddle took me across a surprisingly deep River Feshie (snow melt I decided - it felt like it) and I went on, barefoot, collecting wood to reach Ruigh Aiteachain bothy. The heather/juniper/pine mix was so efficient it heated the metal plate set above the fireplace and I cooked a huge meal and sat afterwards, body glowing, at the door while a stag in velvet grazed just thirty yards off. When I'd thrown some paraffin on the fire to start cooking several stags outside the window had reared up at the sudden flames.

There was a hard frost and my rucksack made a less than adequate substitute for the sleeping bag which had also been left at Dalwhinnie. The bothy mice appeared to wear big boots, judging by the noise they made. I rose at 04.00 in self-defence, had a long breakfast (bacon and eggs and two pints of tea) and set off at 05.30 through the jaws of upper Glen Feshie to the vast expanse of the heathery Feshie-Eidart Geldie world, a through-route on a prodigious scale. Feeling fit I headed up from the Falls of Eidart to take in the equally spacious upstairs world of Monadh Mor and Beinn Bhrotain, descending over Carn Cloich-mhuilinn which would before long lose its Munro status, being a mere pimple on the shanks of Bhrotain. (Munro was keeping it for his 'last Munro' in order to have a good jolly on top.)

I collected bogwood and at the Chest of Dee had an invigorating swim while the billy boiled, a slot in the rock making a perfect flue for the fire. I dried in minutes and gave my hot soles a good rest before continuing. Out of reading, I'd picked up a biography of Richard Dimbleby at the bothy to relieve the hard road miles but was thoroughly unsettled to be reading his description of Belsen and other Nazi horrors - while about me lay the glorious world of upper Deeside. Six miles on, past the Linn of Dee, I stopped at Mar Lodge and ordered a pot of tea for three and had a coke while waiting for it to come. The waitress obviously wondered why nobody else appeared so I explained I just had three peoples' thirst. My bastinadoed feet took me in to Braemar and at the shop I ate a big tin of pears and drank a pint of milk before going up to the hostel. There I brewed, ate, brewed and still never needed a pee before bedding. And Ray thought he'd had it hot! The day's 25 miles was the longest of the crossing. I now felt more crispy bacon than gammon.

Reading and walking took me up Glen Callater to the singing heights again and heights blessedly free of clawing heather. With everything so dry all the ground was hard and, even with just a day sack, my feet were still bruising. It's difficult to limp on both feet at once. Lying under a peat hag 50 deer grazed onto me and were too hot to care. There were lots of golden plovers crying and a dunlin a few yards off put on a great distraction show; huge eggs for such a wee bird. By Mayar and Dreish I was 'gey forfochen'. After such hours of sun hammering there was no improvement in the lower forest level; just a muggier heat as if the trees were panting. Dan Smith made me welcome at the hostel and I fetched eggs and milk from the farm. 'Even hotter' I wrote, 'feeling a bit off form. A touch of the sun?'

However next day's log began, 'And bounce back on form which was as well, with a twenty mile day - and even hotter'. The day would be the hottest I've ever known on the Scottish hills. At 17.00 the dipping sun angled in under the shirt tied round my waist and raised blisters on the back of my knees. The Sahara never did that to me.

The Capel Mounth took me up to the heights again for some of the biggest peat bogs in Scotland and some of the most difficult country to navigate through. Fun of course. The heights teemed with deer. The Shielin of Mark bothy was a discovery and how many in years ahead would be glad of its shelter on coast-to-coast crossings. I took an hour to swim, rest and eat before leaving the Water of Mark for the final featureless tramp to Mount Keen. It was on this stretch I had that weird experience of setting off a fox which set off a hare which set off a grouse which set off deer. And in another case I startled two hares who exploded off to round the peat hag in opposite directions and then ran full tilt into each other with a crash that sent them flying.

Mount Keen, 3080ft, received a parched 'Hallelujah!' Sgurr na Banachdich seemed way back on another, kinder, creation, before the world turned into a fireball. Years of Moroccan sun had no doubt acclimatised me but I made sure of not becoming dehydrated. I'd had heatstroke once - and made sure never again. I thought of Ray. Twenty yards off on the summit I'd hidden a couple of cans of beer for him. Two years on Ray *was* there with me on a normal warm day, completing his Banachdich - Keen trip, done bit by bit. 'A beer? Yes, please.' The look on his face when I turned over a few stones and produced them!

Mount Keen has one of the earliest recorded ascents of a British Mountain: John Taylor, in 1618, wrote ' ... when I came to the top of it, my teeth began to dance in my head with cold, like virginal's jacks; and withall, a most familiar mist embraced me round ... so that it did moysten throw all my clothes.' Queen Victoria also made the summit.

There were still miles to go to the promised haven: Naked Hill, Hill of Saughs, Badalair, the brown landscape turning to green by the lost village of Arsallary, the lower world a bedlam of pewits, curlews, golden plovers, sandpipers and grouse - to finally reach Tarfside for the night.

Before the walk I'd telephoned Tarfside post office to ask if they knew of a B&B thereabouts and I was put in touch with Mrs Guthrie at the Parsonage. What a warm welcome and little did Gladys Guthrie or Hamish Brown know what would come of it. A decade later her lawn would have thirty tents pitched on it as Challengers bent their routes to take in the renowned Parsonage hospitality. There was a thundery, glowering dusk with a peculiar wind. A cuckoo serenaded me to sleep. (Challengers each May feel almost persecuted by these birds. I was once asked, in all seriousness, if the same bird had been following the walker all the way across Scotland.)

It was tempting just to bomb down the road to Edzell and on to the sea but tarred roads make unfriendly feet and I was walking a mountain way after all. The Retreat, two miles down from Tarfside, is an outstanding folk museum but was shut, so having missed that, I crossed a swaying footbridge and wandered up onto the Hill of Wirren: a sort of ambulatory coda to my hot hills symphony. The hill is only 2274 feet but being on the edge of the big hills had an extensive view: from Clachnaben (to the north east) running west to Mount Battock, Mount Keen, Lochnagar and all the Grampian jumble. To the south I could see the Lomonds of Fife, my home hills and Arthur's Seat where in two days a Jubilee bonfire would blaze. And I could see the sea.

So domed in shape is the hill that for the first time on the crossing I used my compass to ensure hitting the way off I wanted. I came down into a rich agricultural landscape which smelt of honey and was loud with bird song. Edzell was noisy too as a clay-pigeon shoot seemed to be part of its celebrations.

The next morning I walked the 11 miles into Montrose, striding before a cloud-piling wind down to a near-empty beach. The Scurdie Ness lighthouse seemed a symbol of finality. I let the waves wash over my tortured toes, then wended back past kids flying kites to the station - and caught a train home to Fife. There could hardly be a less dramatic ending.

The next night we sat before the TV as the Jubilee bonfires spread out over the country. Taking our cue from the box we looked over the Forth to Edinburgh. The rain rattled on the glass, the roar of the sea came from below the house. Arthur's Seat could vaguely be seen; there was a pathetic flicker of fire on top and then nothing. It was that explosive weather change that underlined my trip was over, what had after all been a right royal Jubilee Jaunt.

There would be wheels within wheels concerning Ray following this innocent-enough walking coast to coast, wheels that ran on, free-wheeling, as if in Greek drama, to tragedy. Ray I had first met when he came on a winter mountaineering course I was running in the NW Highlands and then on subsequent outings. He was well off and liked his comforts hence the 'roof each night' policy of this crossing where I'd no doubt have camped most nights.

When the Ultimate (later TGO) Challenge was set up in 1980 Ray became an enthusiastic and regular participant (he made ten crossings) and became well known to an ever-growing number of challengers. He was also keen to complete walking John o' Groats to Land's End, section by section, as could be arranged, so when I had done my Groats End Walk in 1979 (May to October) he joined me in the far NW, Kintail, Lakeland and Cornwall. He said he'd bring another walking friend along and she, initially, had a single room while Ray and I shared but for the Lakes accommodation Ray and Mary shared and I had the single. Ah-ha! In the next decade Ray and Mary were frequently in Challenge company and everyone assumed they were either married or, in modern parlance, partners. (I'd met Ray's wife!) This was going to give me some problems when writing my *Groats End Walk* book. In the end I kept to the anonymity of using just Christian names. However, as Challenge years rolled on, friends began to send Christmas cards to Mr and Mrs S with 'love to Ray and Mary' and similar greetings. Naturally Mrs S opened these and soon realised what was going on and in the end began divorce proceedings. She found helpful evidence spelt out chapter and verse in a book called *Hamish's Groats End Walk*.

Most friends knew nothing of this saga and Ray and Mary continued prominent in Challenge circles. After his ten crossings Ray largely 'retired' from the event but kept up friendships and attended reunions. Mary even helped at the Montrose finish control. Some of us were concerned that Mary was proving a bit unbalanced, and Ray could not have been all that easy to live with, being very set in his ways. (When Lifebuoy soap was to change its traditional character Ray bought *cases* of the old style in order to have a lifetime supply.) Sad irony. Lifetime was to end shockingly one night for Mary flipped completely and took a hammer to him as he slept.

There were happier wheels turning from the Challenge. The event had been dreamed-up in Morocco and something like forty challengers subsequently trekked in the Atlas with me. One was rather special and was concerned with sea as much as mountains. At the end of the 1980 Challenge I spent a couple of days at the Park Hotel finish in Montrose and had plenty to say about the Atlas to a pair who had also made the crossing and who proved to be the London office staff for Operation Drake. A few days after returning home I was called with the suggestion that while their ship was being re-rigged in Gibraltar that autumn I took the score of trainees into the Atlas and attempt Jbel Toubkal. Could I? Would I?

The beautiful sailing ship *The Eye of the Wind* on which Operation Drake was based on its round-the-world adventures for young adults had come through the Red Sea and the Mediterranean but, before facing November gales in the North Atlantic, needed to be re-rigged - a substantial task. The rigger, Wully Buchanan, and I were flown out by the RAF and while I had the trainees off in the Atlas the ship had every 'rope' renewed. I recall the rigger and I standing to watch *The Eye of the Wind* head off with every sail set for joyous swank. She was such a glorious sight that the tears ran down our cheeks, we orphans, left behind.

The wheels turned again. After Operation Drake completed its voyage the ship was returned to the New Zealand family and friends who were the owners. They spent many months refitting her before heading off for their Pacific home waters. On the Gibraltar-England Operation Drake run they had heard such enthusiastic reports on the Morocco trip from trainees and crew that I was asked if I would join them to sail from England to Morocco in return for me taking them into the Atlas. That was in October 1981 and in July I had also joined the *Eye* on a shake-down trip to sail from Oban up and down the Caledonian Canal and south to Bristol, the highlight for them a night ascent to watch dawn from the top of Ben Nevis.

NATURE WATCH FROM A TENT ON WHEELS

One touch of nature makes the whole world kin
Shakespeare: *Troilus and Cresida*

Ringed plover, avocet, stilt, spoonbill, flamingo - and they were noted before struggling out of my sleeping bag - on waking at Walidia on the Moroccan coast, thanks to being in my camping van, my tent on wheels.

Years ago I attended a Hogmanay meet of the Scottish Mountaineering Club. Some of the members were ensconced in a hotel and some in the club's nearby hut while I, a poor young tyro, pitched my inadequate tent off a convenient lay-by, a spartan experience in the snows of Hogmanay. On the second night a vehicle purred in alongside my tent. The owner was part of the meet and, after supper, I joined him for a dram and black bun inside what he called his Dormobile, which I immediately saw as a glorified tent on wheels. What a sensible idea. Writing this now, 2001, I am celebrating my third camper van's 500th bed-night (the previous two ran up 911 and 871) so it is a good time for reflection.

'Dormobile' was a bit like 'Hoover', a trade name becoming generic for all such products. More accurately, for travel documentation, it was described as a 'camping car'. Since then they have mounted through 'motor caravan' to 'mobile home' with many today costing as much as a house. They are as well-equipped as many houses with TV, microwave, shower and central heating - all the ties and worries which a tent in the wilds is free of, even when the tent can be given wheels. To me simplicity has always been the beautiful.

When I inherited my first 'camper' from my father it was a ready-made V.W. Dormobile but one of the most basic designs possible. I often want to carry a canoe or cycle and most conversions are so cluttered with luxurious furnishings this can't be done.

As noted, one of the joys of a camper is waking in the wilds and looking out at browsing deer, a buzzard on a fence post, weasels working along a wall, or simply the majesty of the scenery. A campsite to me is merely a change of the urban; a view of the motor home next door does not compare with gazing over Loch Assynt at dawn. Sometimes nature can be almost too friendly. I've often woken to the van being gently rocked and this can be red deer, sheep, goats or cows. Highlanders seem most in need of skarting their winter woollies on the camper. When one got its sweeping starboard horn stuck under the bumper the rocking was not so gentle!

On one occasion by Loch Rannoch the loudest sound on waking was the dainty whispering of a gold crest high in a conifer. I made up for that soon after: looking for a wood ants' nest a capercailzie exploded at my feet. Several times I've surfaced from sleep because of a wagtail repeatedly trying to attack its reflection in a wing mirror.

There is simply nothing to beat having such a base in the wilds. Last year I spent the night by a loch (which will remain nameless) where ospreys nest and was sitting at the open door as usual with that blessed first cup of tea when there was a great splash and, just beyond the lochside overhanging trees, an osprey rose with a fish in its talons.

More than once I have woken up to find myself surrounded by water. At Keswick I paddled about to ascertain the depths then sat at the entrance, feet still in the water, to finish breakfast. Adding insult to injury a duck then paddled up and asked for a bit of my toast.

Sitting at the sliding door with feet on the ground was a common enough practice. If it brought speculative sheep or deer looking for handouts it also brought odder encounters.

Once a tickle over my sandals proved to be a slow-worm. On the sands of a Shetland bay wee ringed plovers that normally wouldn't let a human within twenty yards raced and stopped, raced and stopped, all round the van and under the arch of my legs. They only disappeared with a whoosh when a sparrowhawk came round the corner and, seeing me, climbed upwards at an angle and speed that would have torn wings off any man-made flying machine. There was a redshank I once rather went off. The bird perched on a fence post outside the van in the ultra peaceful flow country in Caithness and went *bleep, bleep, bleep* at 03.30. By 04.00 it had not wound down. At 04.45 I slammed a door to make it fly away. Five minutes later the redshank was on the fence post again. *Bleep, bleep, bleep*. At 05.00, ragged with lack of sleep, I burst from the van and threw a basin of water at the clockwork bird. It fled. At 05.10 - well, you can guess. At 05.15 I fled.

These joys are as likely abroad and all my campers have travelled Europe, from Arctic Norway to the Atlas Mountains. (I take the liberty of including the Atlas under the grouping as AA information declared Morocco had 'some of the best and quietest roads in Europe'.)

When my first camper died of old age I bought a similar V.W. van and simply shifted all the furnishings over, with a few modifications. When Number Two needed replacing I went on to a Transit and again bought a van and did my own DIY conversion. This is a task I'd wish on my best enemies.

The only major job I had done for me converting Number Three was the installation of windows and two skylights, one above the cooker to let steam escape. The skylights came with gauze mosquito netting but on the first still warm evening away I watched in horror as the midges wiggled their way through this to reach their victim. Now skylights and all windows have midge-proof netting which is Velcro attached when needed.

Here's how bloody marvellous a camper can be. There was a Meet of our local mountaineering club to Glen Etive and after foregathering in the Kingshouse three or four cars set off for the chosen spot. If we could find it. The weather was on the unfriendly side of nasty: sodden snow being blasted up the glen in a gale. I left my lights on to help the tent pitching. Tents which frequently soared like filling spinnakers, were fought to the ground, pegs banged into recalcitrant ground, the owners sweating in suffocating waterproofs that glittered in the wet. Not a happy scene. As for me, I'd just stepped through and put the kettle on. And then checked to see just how many cups and glasses I could muster. There was a bottle of *Jura* on board. That night - and many nights since - I lie rocked to sleep by the wind, snug and smug at not being in a tent. Am I persuading you?

Being able to walk through from the front was a vital factor in choosing the Transit but it came with a front passenger seat for two people so this had to be replaced by a single seat to make the passage. I was quoted a horrendous maker's price so went to the nearest scrap-yard and found a perfect seat match for £5. I mention these trials and tribulations, savings and satisfactions to indicate there is really no need to take out a second mortgage for a mobile home, if it is a camper van.

Most of my hill days are made from the camper now with the advantage of often being based at the start of an outing whereas those in tents or hotels or B&Bs may have to travel and certainly won't have had breakfast at six o'clock. Early on the hill is the most rewarding option generally least taken.

The camper is a vital part of my work too, for I can carry maps and books, stay on the spot, catch weather for photographs and write up my notes in comfort. With successive publications on the Fife Coast, Skye and Kintail, and the Edinburgh to Glasgow canals, I've gained a better feel for those places by being almost resident. (Each van has had its own record book along with a map of Scotland with a dot for each overnight stop.) Another great advantage of a camper is being able to use it instead of tackling a late night drive home. This can be from an evening at the Pitlochry Theatre, a business meeting at Ft. William, giving a slide show in Aberdeen or just a long hill day.

Simply driving along in remoter corners of Scotland has brought special moments. Like the time in Mull where, as we pulled onto the main road, a sea eagle flapped across our bows, very much living up to its description of a flying barn door. My passenger winced but she remarked that at least it wasn't a pheasant with the bird's propensity to crack windscreens. In Morven something different happened. I was driving slowly along when a roe buck suddenly stood on the road in front of me. I stopped. The buck looked left and right and then dived straight underneath the front of the van. There was a great twanging of cables and bumps before it shot out to the side and through the hedge. We can only think it was a bit dazzled by the sun, became confused and dived for the nearest shadowy shelter - below the van.

Alas, nature too often doesn't receive the warning and we note a sad number of frogs, rabbits, hedgehogs, foxes, badgers and deer lying as victims of car-kill. During my teaching years I sometimes took the more presentable corpses into school for the science department to dissect. One morning I threw the van keys to a boy and told him to off-load a pheasant. The van happened to be parked outside the Domestic Science block when a teacher demanded to know why the boy was there. 'Please sur, I'm just fetching a pheasant from Mr Broon's van'. He, apparently looked from boy to van to Domestic Science doorway, shrugged, and walked on.

So many of the delights of having a camper come serendipitously, whether from wildlife's presence or from encounters with people. One last snapshot. Crossing the Tizi n' Tichka (2206m), the great pass over the Atlas Mountains to the desert south I pulled off to spend the night by lush meadows then bright with mini hooped-petticoat daffodils (*N. bulbocodium*) and later with metre-high orchids. I wanted early morning photographs. All too soon I was surrounded by shepherd boys begging, 'Monsieur, un dirham, un bonbon, un stylo, un cadeau'. I happened to have a cassette of Berber songs playing and when they heard this their faces beamed - and they lined up, clapping and singing along to the music. 'Encore, monsieur, encore!' Later some older boys arrived and spent an hour going through a big picture book I had of Morocco, avid to learn and full of questions. They'd all come up from a lower village that very day to start grazing the summer heights, a transhumance that made me think of the vanished shieling days in Scotland. They insisted on taking me to see a fine local waterfall and, at dusk, one imp returned with the present of a freshly-baked loaf of bread. Treasured connections like that don't occur in crowded tourist sites.

To avoid morning rush hour congestion, when I visit St Andrews I often spend the night before at a nearby riverside spot. Recently, sitting there, outside, with the first cuppa of the day, my eye caught a tiny movement. In a gap among the leafy greens there was a twinkling, a glitter, of something golden brown. It was just a beech leaf on the end of a spider's silken thread which twirled like a mobile in any gossamer of wind. The thread was invisible and the leaf shape so symmetrical that it became a propeller: one way or the other, it spun on and on at every hint of wind, a Tinkerbell wonder, seemingly poised unsupported in the air, enchantingly beautiful, the prosaic made magical.

I'd a joyous nature treat once in Rutland Square in Edinburgh. I'd been at a concert in the Usher Hall and had to be back for a nine o'clock meeting nearby, next morning. Why drive home for a brief sleep just to return? So I was kind to the environment and stayed where I was. My reward was watching a grey squirrel playing. Autumn leaves were piled up below the trees in the square and the squirrel was regularly rushing up a trunk for a few yards, looking over its shoulder and then throwing itself off to tumble into the leaves - again and again. What fun! In the background was the clacking of high heels heading for offices which distracted the squirrel not at all. A man came to the car beside me and unlocked the door. I was sitting, my door open, with the inevitable mug of tea, a tape quietly playing the Mahler of the night before, when the man turned to me. 'I've been watching you from up there'; he nodded to his flat and I thought some disapproving comments were coming. This was Edinburgh. 'You made me so nostalgic. I used to have a camper van.'

Sometimes when driving home at night I've turned off the road home to drive high up onto a Fife hill to spend the night there just for the joy of doing so. I stand there, blessed, under an extravagance of stars with the secretive sounds of nightlife and the cool touch of night winds on my face. The prickling lights of towns break up the blackness below, navigation lights wink in the estuary and Edinburgh glitters, with certain blanks - the familiar shapes of Arthur's Seat or the Castle. Anytime I wake the stars have swung and then at dawn the sun lights the tall towers of the Cockenzie power station, [alas; they were felled in 2015] while skylarks will be welcoming the new day, the dewy cobwebs are exposed on the yellows of the gorse, and silence proves itself the best of the world's noises.

THE TWA DOGS

Every dog has his day

Proverb

That was the title of a poem by Rabbie Burns in which Caesar and the collie Luath sat to put the world to rights. For many years my life was dominated by two dogs, two Shetland collies. Both became dogs of the mountain, both completed the Munros. The second came with the name Ellenyorn Spiders Web (I kid you not) but was called Storm, a most suitable name for a hill dog. Thinking of the naming of dogs, three of us, hillgoers, were once exercising our dogs on the sands at Montrose and, when ready to go, we called out, respectively, *Misty* (German Shepherd), *Cloud* (Springer Spaniel), *Storm* (Sheltie).

Kitchy had originally been a present from my brothers and me to our father when he was becoming less able. Hip operations were a new idea then and he suffered a twice-over failure. The dog became the protective companion for a man walking with sticks then, when father died, the dog became mine. I was teaching at Braehead (next chapter) at the time, so willy nilly, the dog came along. Of course he had been on the hill on innumerable occasions already. (The present of Kitchy to father was a bit like giving someone a book for Christmas in hope of being able to read it oneself.)

Kitchy must have missed a great deal of wildlife as he had no sense of smell thanks to a strange scabby infection on his nose. Despite going to vets and vet colleges no cure was found then, late in life, whatever it was disappeared - and he could smell. How he relished the new world.

Being thrown into the world of school gangs was quite traumatic. Being so fluffy his tail was forever being stood on and, once, with temper failing, he turned to snap - and his teeth clunked on a table leg. Laughter. He did not like being laughed at. Camped in Glen Cannich on another occasion the dog raced round a tent and went flying over a guy line. The lads laughed, then turned to commiserating as the dog limped away from his tumble. Two minutes later he raced up the track to welcome one of the boys arriving, no sign of any limp. 'Displacement activity' they call it.

Within a year of coming on our school trips he had made a miraculous transition and just lived for being away with the boys or girls. In the school playground he would be mobbed, being 'so beautiful', but would completely ignore those who had not been away on expeditions. They, on the other hand, received a tremendous greeting. Kitchy played a very useful part in the calming, healing and enthusing that being in the wilds could bring to sometimes troubled youngsters. Walking down Glen Torridon someone asked a girls' party what breed the dog was. 'Kitchy's a climber' came the reply. One wee boy became very devoted to Kitchy but the family went off to Australia to live. Nine years on I answered the doorbell to find a long-haired man with an Aussie accent who greeted me by name. Before I could respond Kitchy shot through my legs to give a welcome. One of his!

When the school closed down. I went off for a sabbatical, climbing in the Arctic, Atlas and Andes. Home sometime in the middle of this I went up Helvellyn on ski. Nearing the top we saw a school party on a converging ridge and Kitchy took off at once, wildly excited. One of his gangs again! Seeing him coming there were cries of 'Hello, doggie, nice doggie!' and the dog's tail, no, his whole body, drooped. Wrong accent. They were not his.

Kitchy, was a Malayan word for 'Little one', a wording often applied to me, aged eight, when there in 1941 so part of our family language. Kitchy and I once caught up a lass on the mist-covered slopes above the Devil's Elbow when she began to call 'Kitchy! Kitchy!' into the gloom. When I said Kitchy was right there she said she was calling her Kitchy - and then stopped in amazement. Two Shetland collies were bouncing around us. Why? Because two families who had escaped *Malaya* in WW2 had bought *Shelties* and, being small *named them Kitchy*. And we *met*. You couldn't make it up.

Another memory: two keen lads and I, plus dog, were sitting by the cairn of mighty Liathach, then the easy to recall height of 3456 feet, when we noticed a man toiling up. He chatted away and eventually swung the talk to be able to mention that Liathach was his fiftieth Munro. We all swapped glances and I could see what was going to happen. He'd been a bit condescending to the boys so had little response. 'Do you know about Munros?' Grunts. Nods. 'Done some, sonny?' to Alec. 'Aye.' To Derry next, 'So how many?' Derry mumbled his tally of a hundred and one. 'And you sonny?' Alec admitted his hundred and two. The man looked round, visibly shaken, and then pointed at Kitchy and smirked 'And what about him?' 'Him? He's done them all.' As the man fled one of them added, 'Just as well he didn't ask you, Hamish'. (I'd a unique three rounds of the Munros at the time.)

A party at the Carn Dearg hut at the head of Glen Clova became snowed in; the road had vanished, snow was often fence-high so the valley livestock went visiting, and we had marvellous skiing on the forestry tracks. The fields were full of hares, galloping about with the abandonment of children let out of school and Kitchy just couldn't resist joining in their games. The hares didn't seem to mind and he would chase and be chased with the best. They were all daft on that glowing spring day.

Hares seem to be accident prone. On another occasion Storm and I were sitting in a reef of granite boulders, the only landmark in a sea of heather moor, when a hare came racing towards us, seemingly oblivious of our presence. The dog tensed with excitement as the beast came nearer and nearer and finally ran (still at full tilt) straight into the dog. With mutual looks of astonishment the hare disentangled and shot off only to take another header over my outstretched legs. It then set off again, looking back with some pretty black thoughts - only to run straight into a big boulder.

By sitting still so much can be seen. A noisy family of wrens once worked down a burn where we were sitting and one of the birds popped out of the heather and perched on Kitchy's head. A lizard once ran over Storm's back and the sensation must have been like a tickle to a three-year-old because the dog, for the next half hour, was constantly quivering and giving his coat a shake.

Kitchy had, perforce, been up the In Pin and, would 'compleat' on Sgurr Alasdair a few days later, (his 500th Munro. Storm's last was Beinn Eibhinn on a stunning, all pleasure, winter traverse of those hills from Culra bothy.) Kitchy's In Pin was done during a summer camping meet in Glenbrittle: Summerhill, Braehead and Cheadle Hulme schoolboys and a few friends, 18 and 2 dogs in total, enjoying a Skye grilling. After two climbers had abseiled off the In Pin we took it over for the next 2½ hours. Fifteen folk and one dog went up, by the long or short sides.

The Glenbrittle-facing wall of the In Pin overhangs slightly and we noted two climbers had set off up it. Periodically we had been aware of these climbers for pitons were banged in and there floated up the odd word new to the youngsters' vocabulary. Eventually only one lad, Kitchy, and myself remained on top, then the lad with me abseiled off and scarpered. At that moment a hand groped round the edge so the dog went over to see what this presaged. When the climber pulled up he met the dog face to face. To his credit the climber did not fall off but vanished and there was much 'There is... There isn't,' from down below so he had another look. 'There is so an effin dog up there!' echoed round the corries! I lowered Kitchy, abseiled off, released the dog and we set off. When the climbers landed on the summit there was nobody there. I would love to have heard the conversation.

Kitchy (and later, Storm) became known for leading to summit cairns even in thick mist, but I suspect this was because on summits there was a fair chance of finding food. People ate on top of any summit they had just climbed. On one summit Storm lapped up the contents of a cup before the owner noticed. 'That was Irish Cream,' I was told in grumpy tones. A rather tipsy dog tailed us off Mount Keen. Camping in Glenbrittle, our's one of perhaps ninety tents, we were busy cooking breakfast when Kitchy came on the scene towing a substantial string of sausages. They were not wasted.

When I was three months abroad a friend of my mother's took the ageing Kitchy for a walk. A puppy jumped on him, causing a heart attack and the loss of movement in his hind legs. Strangely, our old Siamese cat climbed into the dog's basket and the two faded away together. They were eventually taken to the vet and friends joining me abroad were told not to tell. Unfortunately the vet's bill for 'putting down one dog and one cat' was addressed to 'Mr Brown' and so was brought out in my mail.

Both Kitchy and his successor Storm were proper Shelties, not the nervous inbred powder puffs so often seen today. I was happy to wait till finding good stock. Storm was worth waiting for, the magic of chance bringing us together. Driving through Roslin on the way home after months abroad I saw two fine Shelties being walked and stopped to find where they came from. Home, I rang the breeder who promised to call back when pups were available. When months had passed I rang again. The bitch had missed. We talked then, almost as an afterthought, I was asked if I would consider a two year old. They considered him too big for a stud dog. Show-ring trained, all his medications etc in order, it sounded too good to be true. So I went along and was shown into a room full of pedigree Shelties. One came and laid his chin on my lap. I had been chosen!

Years on we went walkies from John o' Groats to Land's End, wrote a book about the trip, Storm seen posing on the cover. When his previous owner saw this she turned to a friend, 'You'd never know as a young dog he'd broken a leg would you?' I had noticed he walked with a bit of a twist in one hind leg, which would have doomed show ring chances, which was probably the real reason why he was sold. All the dogs I'd seen had been good, big stock*.

Storm's day on the In Pin couldn't have been more different than Kitchy's. I was wardening the BMC/MCofS hut in Glenbrittle over April 1984 a month which began with rather fine winter conditions during which I helped an old friend complete his Skye Munros. (His *first* had been the In Pin, forty years earlier.) So Storm gained a few more Munros as well (he has built-in crampons). Then the weather went sour, so wild and wet we hardly left the hut. The weather tantrum led to what could be called cabin fever so at the first, faint token improvement we set off up the hillside opposite, simply for some exercise and fresh air. The dog raced round in glee, making what airmen refer to as 'circuits and bumps'. Conditions were miserable but out of cussedness I squelched on up until, eventually, a grey shape loomed ahead. Heavens! The In Pin. Thanks be I'd not be climbing it.

Others were! It was swarming (it felt) with youngsters in camouflage gear who, in turn, were being dragged up whether they liked it or not and then were abseiling down the same way, frequently those ascending and descending having encounters of a confusing nature. There was a great deal of vocalising which quickly identified this as a military training exercise. I stood beside the presumed sergeant i/c (you can tell rank by the language) and when I made some mild comment that it was a 'daft sort of day to be having a circus' was told it was (a) good for them and (b) was what had been ordered for that day. (There was probably an unvoiced (c) suggesting I mind my own blankety blank business.)

The phrase 'What was planned' should always come with a health warning. I wonder how many accidents and fatalities are still caused by that inflexibility, what I came to call 'programmitis' after the tragedy involving the Edinburgh kids on the Cairngorms. In lighter vein however I also recall how one of our school parties to Skye reported in the school newspaper once back in Fife, 'We had a super trip to Skye. We climbed every Munro in the Cairngorms'. We had shifted after three days of Skye monsoon. That's flexibility!

This was not my first encounter with military programmitis in Skye. A friend Dave and I were descending off Marsco after a traverse of the Red Hills on a day of extreme heat, when we came on a gaggle of what were then called 'Young Soldiers'. They were all arrayed in bright orange and were struggling to insert one of their number into a sleeping bag. Asked what was wrong I was informed they had an exposure case on their hands, the lad had been staggering about strangely and was becoming incoherent. Their course obviously had not included heat exhaustion on the syllabus, rare as that might be in Scotland. Asked why they were wearing their waterproof tops and bottoms they said they had been issued with them so presumed they should be worn. Dave and I were in shorts and shirtless.

But to return to the In Pin. Between roars at his performers the sergeant i/c and I chatted. Storm curled up and pretended to be elsewhere and at some damnable moment the conversation came round to the dog. I explained he only had a handful of Skye Munros still to do to finish his round. For the In Pin we'd probably need some help. As soon as I'd spoken I realised I'd made a mistake. 'Oh, we'd be glad to help.'

The rain was still assaulting the hills, the overnight verglas was now being shooched off by the water running behind it, passing boots had covered the holds in slime and mud, and I wondered about the competence of the corporal on top who was to give me a top rope. I think the term is 'calculated risk'. The risk in reality was minimal, it was just not an exercise contemplated with pleasure.

Anyway, the dog jumped into the big Tiso sack and off I went. Halfway up there's an out-of-balance move I've never liked and, with the dog's weight on my back, I was teetering on the verge of coming off when Storm leant over and gave my ear an encouraging lick. His arrival on top was greeted by cheers (or was it jeers?) and when I'd lowered him and he was let out of the rucksack the dog set off on a circuit gallop that probably gave the poor squaddies their only laugh of the day.

To be available when climbers were usually arriving or departing at the hut in the month's final heatwave I'd set off to use the last couple of hours of daylight, bivvy out, enjoy the early hours on high and be present to see folk off. The most memorable overnight trip was out to Rubh' an Dunain, the point at the outer end of Loch Brittle, a place of historic (Viking) interest and a fine viewpoint for the Cuillin. We kipped on top of one of the many knolls, dry, with close-cropped heather, and then went down to the loch, Loch na h-Airde, to brew and eat breakfast. We were just sitting there quietly when an otter and two cubs appeared and landed in front of us, no more than six yards away.

Both Storm and I froze, though I could see the dog's nose quivering as he tried to scent these unknown creatures. They splashed in and out a few times before the adult became aware of our presence. She stood upright to have a good look at us - and then came forwards slowly till she and Storm were nose to nose. Neither showed panic, neither showed aggression. Having sniffed each other, the otter returned to the loch and Storm sprawled back on the ground. I breathed again.

In a few minutes the mother otter was back, this time with a big, lively eel. The youngsters were all over her, begging for this tasty bite but she had other ideas and swung the eel round away from their reach. A sandpiper had been sitting on a rock, bobbing up and down and wondering if she should move when, out of nowhere, she received a whack from the eel which sent her splashing into the loch. Her language as she flew off was unrepeatable. This bit of slapstick broke my discipline and I laughed outright. Exit otters, instantly. Storm looked at me as if to say, 'Now look what you've done'.

Both dogs enjoyed the rough grip of Skye gabbro but after a week would wear through the pads of their feet so were provided with Elastoplast padding when on the hill. Frequently, coming to a step too steep for the dogs, I'd turn to give a heave up only to find the dog gone, only to reappear above the difficulty. Storm, at a bidding, from wherever, would launch out in a leap into my arms, which could look quite dramatic. Both enjoyed going in the rucksack, especially in winter when the snow could ball up underneath them. They liked having their heads out to observe all that was going on but in weather nastiness would just curl up inside. I was well trained.

Storm seldom harmed wildlife: 'look but don't touch' had been made clear from the start. Sheep were taboo of course and Storm was trained to walk to heel when any were encountered. We were once descending off a hill to a glen where the shepherd's virulent attitude to dogs (and their owners) was well known. And there he was striding down the opposite slope obviously heading to meet me. And I'd a field of sheep to cross. As we neared each other his expression showed many changes and when we met, we both just laughed. At my heels was Storm but, nose to tail, behind him were all fifty sheep following in happy single file.

We talked sheep and dogs and people, and he told me about a day in the spring where he had seen a couple with their dogs blatantly cross a field through a flock of his sheep. They had three dogs and these chased the sheep everywhere while the owners looked on quite unconcerned. The ewes were in the field for lambing so goodness knows what the damage was, quite apart from the ewes the dogs had worried. One ewe had to be put down, several just died.

There were a couple of occasions when someone offered to buy Storm; one occurred on Brandon Mountain, that magical mountain in the extreme south-west of Ireland. It has a long crest, cut away on one side into vast corrie with steep, cliff-girt headwalls. Sheep were always going on to those slopes and falling down the cliffs I was told by the shepherd who I met staggering along under a load of stobs (fence posts). He was going to fence-off the cliff edge, an astonishing work for every post and coil of wire had to be carried up on his back from sea level to 3000ft.

While he was talking, Storm - the most placid and friendly of dogs - was receiving a bit too much attention from the shepherd's two collies. In the end he turned on them and, in seconds, routed both. Before I could open my mouth there was an awed, 'Do you see that now? You wouldn't be for selling him?'

Crossing from Larne to Stranraer one autumn Storm was left in the van during the voyage. I found him looking a bit sheepish on rejoining the vehicle and saw an empty tub of margarine on the floor. It had been nearly full at Larne. Thinking of what was inside him I gave him a large handful of dry dog biscuits. After an hour's driving we settled down for the night in a known corner where owls invariably hooted in the woods and coots croaked on a lochan. I woke to a distinctly unpleasant smell, and a very apologetic dog. It's the only occasion I've put a sleeping bag in a washing machine.

Storm in his lifetime compleating the Munros and 'Furths' - an overall 459 Munros and maybe 150 Corbetts before old age sneaked in as it does. Not being with me was unusual since we had become well-known as a pair. More than once I met someone on the hill who would immediately say, 'Are you Hamish Brown?' Could have been ego-boosting but, invariably on saying 'yes', the response was, 'Thought so; recognised the dog'.

On Skye, I was really put in my place. We were climbing along the ridge for Am Baseir, had managed down the wee wall so there was only the rooftop final ridge remaining to traverse. This is very narrow and very exposed: steep on the left, sheer on the right. A twist of snow still lay along the crest and Storm, who seems immune to exposure, decided this snow would be excellent for rolling on. Storm rolling about, feet in the air, inches from a 300ft overhang was not good for *my* nerves - he went on the lead. Of course, as soon as we proceeded, we met someone coming the other way - which made me feel the complete twit, with dog on lead going walkies there. All was well however.

'Hello! You must be Storm!'

This fan of Storm's, after brief conversation, asked if he could take a photo of the dog. 'Sure,' I replied and the great poser posed. The man looked up, then waved me to one side.

'Would you mind getting out of the way please?'

Storm sometimes took rides in my rucksack when I was cycling. On one occasion I was able to leave my cycle by the Cluanie Inn above Glen Shiel and then we set off from the foot of the glen for a day traversing the undulations of the fine Cluanie Ridge with the expectation of miles of freewheeling at the end of the day.

Storm was in the rucker on my back with his grinning head out and perched high over my own, a spectacle that received odd and sometimes amused looks from the motorists coming up the glen. A big tourist bus passed and I was aware, out of the corner of my eye, of a whole passing array of startled faces as they saw the dog, but not me whizz past just outside the window. When I glanced back it was to see the bus halfway up the roadside bank - the driver as well obviously had his eyes on Storm instead of the A87.

Storm learned quickly and could follow a range of orders. He loved to 'Track!' (follow footprints) and would 'Go round' in a direction pointed out by waving - useful when I ended gripped on a corrie between Sgurr a' Mhaim and Druim Shionnach. I was on ski, with skins attached and *harsheisen* (ski blades, acting as crampons) heading up rather aimlessly. The slope grew steep and the surface so hard I had to jab through it with my poles to make steps for the dog. The *harsheisen* buckled. To come off would mean a long slide and probably some loss of my epidermis so I went on only to find myself stuck under the cornice.

Well, nearly stuck, but by poking, I found the wall was made of much softer snow so I should be able to fight up - but Storm wouldn't be able to. Pointing back down our track, I told him 'Go round!' which, rather reluctantly, he did, first inching down, splay-footed, from indentation to indentation until the angle eased and then half sliding, half romping the rest. I waved westwards. 'Go round!' He trotted off and chose an easy route up.

Side-stepping up a vertical wall of snow was a novel experience and not exactly graceful but by battering with the skis and ramming the poles in horizontally I made exhausting progress. The cornice soon fell about my head, half of it going down my neck to melt instantly, the rest burying my skis and trickling down the slope. Eventually I could reach over on to the top surface, stuck the poles in vertically and, pulling them at surface level, managed to do a sort of roll up and over onto the ridge. I just prayed there would be nobody there to witness these novel techniques. Storm gave me a companionable lick on the nose. If only one old dear could see him on the hill.

I'd received a letter forwarded from a newspaper which I thought might have been a spoof from some of my friends (spelt minus the r) but eventually decided it was genuine as the shaky hand indicated somebody elderly. 'Dear Sir, I was appalled to read in *The Sunday Post*, about your Dog Storm who is to climb mountains with you. Don't you think this is cruel. The poor animal could be frightened out of his wits and terrified at the heights he has to climb. Please don't be hard on him, he looks such a beautiful Dog. Yours sincerely, one who cares for Animals.'

Storm showed uncanny judgment about river crossings - far more than just instinct. A notable example was crossing the Luibeg Burn in the Cairngorms. The bridge upstream had gone so, perforce, I'd paddled across the powerful burn. The dog followed me out, from boulder to boulder, till he was left perched on the outermost granite block. I'd paddled across to a rocky spit opposite and Storm teetered on his boulder, eyeing the spit opposite, looking up and down stream, hesitating to plunge into the rush of water. You could almost hear the cogs turning in his brain. He eyed it all up once more then hopped back to the bank, ran upstream and out on to the boulders again, plunged in and made a perfectly angled ferry-glide across to arrive on my spit of rock. Had he plunged in from the initial spot, he would have been swept down past the landing place. I'm convinced he knew this - and made allowances for the current.

Storm eventually began to have small heart attacks, on one walk staggering off the towpath into the Union Canal. When he barely made the low hill of Cockleroy I knew the dream was over. I've never had a dog since, from purely practical reasons, but I often wonder if I could. There was something very special about Storm, a rapport I'd never known before, a pure devotion beyond the ken of humans. Coming off the Galtymore range on a walk we did coast-to-coast across Ireland's mountains I sat on a park bench sorting out a parcel of maps, film and Storm's dehydrated food, when a tinker woman with an obviously blind girl came by. She asked would I mind if the girl touched the dog. The blind child ran her hands over his coat several times, then sighed and smiled at me. 'Sure, and he's a gorgeous fellow'. He was indeed.

Storm was a very pukka, pedigree sable/white Sheltie with a family tree going back to the g.g.g.g. parents, half of whom were champions, as was his sire, Fairona Rockafella. His mother's name was Philhope Precious Gold. For those into that sort of thing, the more important stables, I mean kennels, were Riverhill, Shelert and Flockfields. Storm's official name was Ellenyorn Spidersweb. Imagine yelling that from the back door at night. Some of his ancestry bore pretty weird names too: Ratafia, Swagman, Satin Slipper, Such a Lark, Golden Oriole, Rather Rich, Sweet Sultan, Strikin' Midnight.

This ancestry, apart from giving a slight giggle the two or three times I've actually looked at his certificate means nothing to me. Dog-breeding strikes me as being a manipulation of questionable morality. As far as Shetland collies go, in the last few decades, a breed of superb animals, of splendid temperament, always very fit and happy, have been turned into shrunken miniatures with neurotic temperaments, as far from the original working dog as real Shelties were from their wolf ancestry. Thank God Storm escaped from the prison of show ring and stud yard. But it has taken just his lifetime to see the breed ruined.

GOOD TO BE YOUNG

Through the Sixties I was taking boys and girls from a Fife Junior School into the wilds, pioneering what is now, alas, all too institutionalised Outdoor Education, enriching them with experiences. Young years should be active, observing, bright. In selecting, stories as good as the Cuillin Ridge Traverse, have had to be left out, and this outdoor adventuring was only part of the wider, inspirational story of Braehead School under its head R F Mackenzie. There is a lot more to the mountains than just reaching the top.

We had no serious accidents over those hardier, more resilient years. Mountaineering, other than at extreme levels (the preserve of a few), is as safe as day to day living. Among my most gifted lads in that period one was killed while walking along a pavement, hit by a car, a farmer's son was fatally injured by a tractor accident, one drowned on a family holiday and a newly-married 23 year old former pupil died of a heart attack. Jumping into a car is far more dangerous than heading up a Munro. Life is dangerous. Western people today live in a world of mystic expectations that all should be well all of the time. We have a robust ageing population because people grew up in tougher times with real challenges. The strange dichotomy is that today we see as never before people - gifted, driven people - often young people - heading to the hills; there are more skiers, canoeists, sailors, naturalists, artists, musicians - and all the rest - finding satisfactions in chosen activities. We need, and seek, challenges or life atrophies. That all this happens despite the constant denial of facilities or encouragement is a wonderful testament to the human spirit. Education is too often a deadening hand where it should be a liberating experience, making for dull conformity instead of encouraging curiosity, advocating material security with few chances of discovering these other worlds of wonder. 'Everyone needs beauty as well as bread, places to play and pray in, where nature may heal and give strength to body and soul alike' (John Muir).

AT SCHOOL IN THE BLACK WOOD

'Sur, the stars move!'

Back in the Sixties our school had a bothy (just a wooden hut) in the Black Wood of Rannoch, one room crowded with bunk beds and the other both living room and kitchen. Most of the fittings came from the ship-breaking yard at Inverkeithing. For the kids from the coastal coal-towns of Fife it must have been a revelationary change of habitat, but they took to it like stuffing to a duck.

The Black Wood is *big* and our part of the forest was a genuine remnant of the old wood of Caledon that once filled the glens as far north as Loch Maree, mature trees towering from a tangle of moss, berry, water and rock. On the first evening we would have an energetic paper chase - one way of ensuring they went to sleep - but mainly to introduce them unselfconsciously to the wild wood. When a capercailzie rose like an exploding turkey at their feet it certainly felt wild. But even going astray did not need to cause panic. Anyone becoming 'mislaid' simply had to follow water down to reach the lochside road, and so home. This elementary navigational knowledge gave them the freedom of the Black Wood. Our part of the wood was demarcated on the east by the big Dall Burn, beyond which lay the parkland landscape of Rannoch School while, west, the wood rolled on for more miles than would ever be explored. A minor road ran along the lochside, with an old ice house and some huts belonging to the Navy between road and water.

This landscape gave a great variety of bird life and many youngsters became enthusiastic bird watchers. I've a memory of returning to the bothy and wondering at the odd sight of faces crowding a window - until a treecreeper worked round the Scots pine a yard away from the bothy. They sometimes thought there was a bit of magic in my ability to conjure up birds. On a walk I'd tell them they'd see wren, dipper, oystercatcher and goldcrest and, on each forecast, the bird duly appeared. I knew the habitats of course but there was the evening when one of them rushed in to say he'd seen a cormorant flying along Loch Rannoch. As Loch Rannoch is about as far from the sea as you could be this seemed unlikely but it was true and proved not unusual. And why not? The sea cuts well inland from Loch Etive towards Rannoch Moor, with its lochs draining to Lochs Rannoch and Tummel and so to the Tay and the sea at Perth, a much easier commuters' route than round the north of Scotland. I think birding had a special appeal. Nature has no secret agenda, no plotting and posturing. What you see is what you get.

The capercailzie has become rare since those days. For a couple of seasons the wood had a cock bird that attacked humans, which made life a bit exciting. On another occasion some boys were having a dip at the mouth of the burn when there was a crashing of glass from the Navy huts just above. We rushed up at once but found nobody, nor was there a missile among the shattered glass on the ground outside. We then noticed the window opposite had been smashed as well and the glass from it lay inside. Something had gone right through the building. Capercailzie. In case the boys were blamed they went and reported the matter to the local police in Kinloch Rannoch.

Some of the keen ornithologists were invited to do a radio programme about birds and the discussion drifted onto birds' names. One lad explained the nonsense of the name *Wheatear*. This was a misleading Victorian euphemism for the accurate Anglo Saxon *white arse*, and it's what the French say. Auntie cut that bit of the broadcast.

The varied bird life was simply a reflection of the range of habitats. Scots pine never dominates but shares space with birch, rowan, oak, holly, alder and so on. The mix of ferns, mosses, blaeberry (bilberry to sassenachs) made for a diverse ground cover - and plenty of bugs, beetles, butterflies and moths with the most exciting element the wood ants with their domed nests among the hummocks. The road took its toll of wildlife, birds mostly but roe deer occasionally and once some girls found a dead weasel.

If it was necessary to tire them out on the first night, to ensure some sleep, there was no problem thereafter. With the soft Highland air and so much to see and do sleep was instant. On the drive up from Fife they were as chatty as chimps, guzzling crisps and pop and, by the hill road over Schiehallion, mostly bringing everything up again; on the journey home they were usually fast asleep before passing Schiehallion. If not in Gillead, there was certainly balm in the Black Wood of Rannoch.

Schiehallion was the area's dominant peak. The *fairy hill of the Caledonians*, 3547ft/1083m, famed and photographed for its Fuji Yama gracefulness. This symmetry led to the eighteenth century scientist and Astronomer Royal, Maskeleyne using Schiehallion to try and work out the mass and weight of the world and, in so doing, invented contours.

For some hundred youngsters Schiehallion was their first Munro and on its winter slopes skills were learnt that would be applied on Mont Blanc. (They learned to prussic up a rope hanging from the bothy's nearest pine tree.) On this additional habitat of 'hills and heather and peat' above the wooded lower reaches the youngsters saw snipe drumming and golden eagles soaring.

The day Braehead School closed for good (1971) we set off for the Alps as usual and their steps would range from the Arctic to the Atlas - big doings from small beginnings in the Black Wood of Rannoch.

The wood was one of the first ancient remnants to be regarded as a rare treasure and the Forestry Commission (to whom we paid £1 a year in rent for the bothy) have done impressive work to keep the wood growing younger year by year. An old Scots pine forest is one of nature's great spectacles but overgrazing and misuse has lost so much of it that seeing a forest regenerate is heart-warming.

They knew their Scotland. Sometimes, in May we had joint trips with schools like Eton or Marlborough. (I went along as interpreter) and, on a trek across Rannoch Moor, it was to the boys the visitors turned, not me, when they wanted to ask the Where? What? and Why? of puzzles that lay about them. A Braehead group were camped by the railway on Rannoch Moor (searching for the elusive Rannoch rush) when a student friend joined us for the weekend. He had to produce a newspaper before we believed the news he brought: President Kennedy's assassination. We must have been among the last people in the world to have heard.

Very few children read much and none were read to by parents so bedtime stories soon became a tradition. *Rikki-Tikki-Tavi, The Monkey's Paw*, Leàm O' Flaherty animal/bird stories, Saki, bits of *Always a Little Further*, all of *The Prisoner of Zenda* and the, then new, *Narnia* chronicles. We also kept a logbook and every day was written up by someone and they also reported back for the weekly school newspaper. Reading and writing can be fun.

The area was full of historic sites and traditions which they delved into. We found cup marked stones and explored old graveyards (one stone showed a whole family of twelve wiped out by consumption - TB. The song *The Road to the Isles* with its refrain, 'Sure by Tummel and Loch Rannoch and Lochaber I will go ...' led to a major project, described later. On one trip we crossed the hills to Glen Lyon by an old drove road and had a two hour walk to reach Garth youth hostel. They sang the whole way, without repetition, everything from pop to grand opera.

All parties at the bothy learned to camp and look after themselves. Cooking was done on paraffin primus stoves which required considerable discipline. The person who carried paraffin never carried food. Paraffin-flavoured tea was not appreciated. There was an odd spin-off from their having to learn to cook: the school produced more chefs and caterers than any other in Fife, one even working in Buckingham Palace.

The bothy had a gas cooker, gas lighting and running water besides an old Carron range with a *swee* - an arm for suspending a kettle over the fire. There was one desperately misused boy who came up on several occasions to enjoy 'respite from pressure' in headmaster R F Mackenzie's phrase. One day we headed off for the Rannoch hills, leaving him behind to enjoy a peaceful day. When we returned the kettle was simmering on the *swee*, a soup had been made, a pot of potatoes peeled and a pile of firewood laid in.

Kinloch Rannoch was four miles away but they would think nothing of walking there and back just to buy sweets. We ate well always: a proper soup, meat and plenty of vegetables, tempting sweets (trifles, bread and butter pudding, spiced rice and raisin pudding). There was always a curry night, always a pancakes night, sometimes we baked biscuits. Cooking could be fun. We allowed six shillings (60p) per person per day.

There were sometimes boys or girls in the parties who couldn't even afford that cost and the pupils would hold discos nights to raise funds to send the less fortunate to Rannoch. There were the odd horrors of course but how effective was the challenge of Rannoch, and the whole sweep of Mackenzie's vision in Buckhaven, was seen in there being no pupils on probation when the school closed. At slide shows today I am constantly accosted afterwards by former pupils who say how grateful they are for the security and challenge of their school days.

If those years gave me grey hairs there was often a certain humour to ambush me. Groups on arrival were warned that over one night they would be sent out, alone, with their sleeping bags, so they'd better find suitable shelter beforehand. On one visit there was a stack of concrete culvert pipes and when I wandered out to check some of the usual places they used I found several boys lying inside the pipes, like grubs inside a honeycomb. They came in for breakfast after those nights walking ten foot tall.

Another place often discovered, and used, was the ice house, unless it was occupied by a wandering tramp, Hairy

Dan. (This ice house was an arched brick structure sunk almost underground, used a century ago for storing food into summer, after being filled with ice during the winter - a sort of pre-electricity freezer.) If the weather was dry the wise, or lazy, simply lay in the open and how many kids today have had a chance like that? Now you have to fill in a risk assessment form to walk on the beach. Theirs was the good fortune then to have tasted the benison of the Black Wood. I'll end by translating a few of their breakfast time comments.

'A squirrel ran over my sleeping bag.'

'I thought there was some monster in the woods but it was just Shug snoring.'

'A wren family played tig all round me.'

'Sur, the stars move!'

WALKING THE SONG

Happiness is a simple fraction - expectation divided by realisation.

Iain R. Thomson: *The Endless Tide*

Who hasn't sung out the chorus of 'The Road to the Isles', feet tapping to the tune, 'Sure by Tummel and Loch Rannoch and Lochaber I will go / Over heather tracks wi' heaven in their wiles ...' To a school group many years ago the song became rather special.

The words had been the loose heading, theme rather, for a school project, and 'walking the song' was the reward for good work done in the classroom. One early discovery was the origin of the fine tramping song. The tune, composed in 1896, was called *The Burning Sands of Egypt* but the words we know, *The Road to the Isles*, were written in 1915 to fit the tune - and winning a prize for a good marching song for the troops in WWI.

The pupils were a mixed ability group though the term had yet to be invented, drawn from several classes, some keen Munro baggers, some not at all athletic, volunteers however, supposedly non-academic. The germ of the project idea came while driving to our Black Wood bothy, arriving there by Loch Tummel and Loch Rannoch ... The song perfectly fitted the line drovers might have taken from Skye to the tryst at Crief: the pathway to (or from) the west. So my gang came together regularly to study what was basically Highland history in the seventeenth and eighteenth centuries. What was astonishing was how quickly curiosity led to enthusiastic research and topic after topic would race in like waves on the shore, be investigated, and lead on to something else. I decided it would be more romantic to walk to Skye rather than the reverse. We could start from Killin.

My logbook noted, 'Off in the school bus. We had a picnic by Loch Earn and were dropped off at Kenknock Farm in Glen Lochy. The sun was blazing down and the toil up the 1000 ft climb over the Lairig nan Lunn was murder, like going up to an alpine hut only with heavier packs. Cheers when we saw Loch Lyon. Went over the dam and along the north shore, a well-defined wee path. Many sheep shelters brought up the topic of the Clearances again. A few sad ruins. Set up tents at the swing into Gleann Meran. Two folk were fishing from a boat out on the loch. Heasgarnich, scraggy on this side, tipped with snow, but Chreachain dominated. Blissful relaxing in evening cool'.

The heatwave was set to go on so next day we rose very early to put in the miles while the oven was still at a low number. What a way to gain the Moor of Rannoch - the Robbers Pass, Gleann Meran, a *cateran* trail as well as a drovers' siphon. We followed the burn down to Gorton Station and a welcome from an old friend, Charles Murray the stationmaster of this long-gone halt. There was an hour for tea and talk. He regaled the gang with tales of winter on the Moor - going out to thaw out points and coming in to *stand* his frozen coast behind the door. We took the chance of sending two lads off by train to Rannoch Station with all the rucksacks so we 'floated' over the Moor unladen.

Parts of the line here do really float; the peat was so deep that a bottoming was made by layers of birch faggots and the line laid on top. You can still feel the slight undulations when travelling by train. We visited old shielings and were watched by weary deer. A grouse nest contained nine eggs. Some pools called for a break before following the Duibhe Bheag's new forestry road. (The trees are now being felled - and taken out by train from a temporary halt.) The C18 Soldiers' Trenches were visited. These appear to have been an attempt at drainage but were mainly to keep bored garrison troops busy.

Rannoch Moor was baking under the sun, a change from its normal status of 'wet desert', the heather dusty, the peat cracking (so giving easy walking), the burns stale and dying, the odd parcel of hinds perched on knolls for non-existent breezes, the butterworts looking like stranded starfish, the whole shimmering and producing mirages that had tired minds doubting their eyes.

Camp was at a wee lochan by the Garbh Ghaoir, the tents already up and tea waiting. The afternoon went eating and lazing and swimming and, once cooler, Rannoch Station was visited. Some of the gang had already been there and could regale the rest with stories of the railway: the crazy journey over the Moor by surveyors, the runaway ghost train, and explain the weird face carved in stone at the down-end of the platforms. (This was made by the navvies as a 'thank you' to James Renton, one of the directors who had dipped into his own pocket when the project had hit financial buffers.)

Crossing Rannoch Moor is quite a daunting prospect but the early start paid off. W H Murray had said he left six hours for the journey, unladen. The lads, laden, did it in five and camped by the Kingshouse. We had visited Tigh na Cruaiche, halfway along Loch Laidon. 'Imagine living there.' Folk couldn't, as the ruin testified. At Black Corries the party had a good crack with the keeper. The Kingshouse was quite a milestone: a historic staging post and known from our classroom studies. We almost finished off the hotel's stock of MacCall's lemonade. Tents were pitched with the doors framing the Buachaille Etive Mor which several of them had climbed.

Also well-known from studies was the Devil's Staircase next day over to Kinlochleven. Extraordinary to think that carriages once made that challenging crossing. Two boys again took the rucksacks by bus round to Kinlochleven.

On the way up the Devil's Staircase two young men with hefty packs came charging after us, got within 50 yards and collapsed. Our slow steady pace still had us dripping but everyone was amused at this example of the Tortoise and the Hare. Halfway down there were pools not to be denied. Kinlochleven was another important staging point both historically and for us. Refreshed and much liquid taken on board we set off on an even more alpine-like ascent for the Lairig Mor.

The Lairig Mor is well known by those walking what became the West Highland Way and, though nearing the end of that route it still presents a challenge, both physically and mentally: feet pound hard track and the route snaking away ahead seemingly without end. In some ways the youngsters had an advantage coping with the effort. They could let their minds float away, no sin in this classroom. As I drew alongside one lad to check all was OK, the bent head lifted and he turned with the *non sequitur* to say, 'My dad breeds budgies'. Over the next mile I forgot hot feet and learnt quite a bit about budgies.

The Lairig Mor is not exactly lush in vegetation and the barren slopes of the Mamores were reflecting the heat onto us. Sunbathing in a dish aerial must be like that I suppose. We were very careful to keep covered up from the sun and at the end of the trip anyone taking off a shirt presented a two-tone appearance: torso white, arms and face nearing mahogany. Collectively, the effect was a soccer team in an unusual strip. Camp that night was in Glen Nevis and some, after a gargantuan meal, still had energy enough to walk in to the Fort for chip suppers.

Trekking in such heat was cruel besides being potentially dangerous so we telescoped several days by catching the train to Mallaig and sailing in to Inverie in Knoydart on the *Suaira*. No respite from the sun however. We collapsed for an hour in a wood heady with the scent of crushed hyacinths and swam in the sea. Two couldn't wait though and pushed on to the Dubh Lochan where they had camped once before. Being well trained they naturally had a brew on when the rest caught up. One advantage of the fierce sun was the absence of midges. Someone recalled an explanation in a book. 'They don't like strong sun or strong wind and don't appear above ten thousand feet'.

Ruckers were left at the Mam Barrisdale and, as 'We've done half the height, Hamish' everyone was keen to traverse out to Ladhar Bheinn and back, quite a demanding crest, the views of Cuillin, Eigg and Rum (Rhum then), seen through shimmering haze. The alpine flora was looking sad, not many wet places for butterwort, globe flowers or saxifrage. Many lark's nests were found, one with a cuckoo's egg in it.

A green track twisted down off the pass to the flat, long depopulated, Glen Barrisdale. We walked out to the point - Fraoch Eilean - vainly looking for a burn. In one of the wettest parts of Scotland water was scarce. When we did find one, we tried to drink it dry. One lad said his ears were 'frizzled'. The braes between Runival and Skiary were a real test of stamina. Skiary had many ruins and cairns and was lived in till the early C20.

In places the rocks fell straight into the sea so the path was built up, craftsmanship which had stood the wear of years. A farmer at Kinloch Hourn showed us a good spot to camp and, in the morning, we found a big can of milk by the door.

The Bealach Aoidhdailean through to Glenelg was another massive day which was taken without problems by the 'berry-brown boys'. First out a tent in the morning yelled in excitement so everyone tumbled out, then stood about relishing *the rain*. It proved a brief novelty but nicely freshened the jungly climb up past the big house for as wild and lonely a pass as could be imagined. However there were still ruins pointing to lived-days and stances where the Skye cattle would graze on their long trek to markets. To me that was the most fascinating day we had. Such complete emptiness is a rare treat. I remember us sitting by one burn with cups of tea, deer grazing below, an eagle slowly mounting the thermals and feeling we belonged as if born to a timeless world. Sadly, when 'they' decided to run pylons from Skye the line marched this way 'because there was nothing there'. You will not find that day as we knew it ever again. No glen to the west is now uncontaminated.

We slept that night at the mouth of Gleann Beag after exploring the brochs of Dun Troddan and Dun Telve, after washing every stitch of clothing and drinking, drinking ... Skye lay across the Sound of Sleat, a full moon hung above the woody slopes and the clouds were gently washed in the afterglow. The river sang a soft lullaby.

We had two days in hand - and used them. Seemingly inured to the heat they were keen to add another Munro to Ladhar Bheinn. The accepted suggestion was The Saddle - 'looked great when we did the Cluanie Ridge'.

We managed to arrange a lift over Mam Ratagan in a laundry van (imagine that today!) and set off up the familiar track in early coolness but, on the Forcan Ridge, the sun was smiting us as strongly as ever. 'Smitten by the sun and addicted' I happily misquoted. In an article I wrote for a magazine at the time I mentioned how we 'collapsed at the cairn and drank our bars of chocolate'. The editor missed the point and changed the words to 'ate our bars of chocolate'. An even bigger thrill followed: a 'scaffy hunt' along the coast from camp.

This proved thoroughly enjoyable as pools were studied and the tangle searched. We'd brought the biggest dixi and a stove so we could have a brew but by picnic time it was full of the contenders in the 'smallest crab competition' and anything else of interest: butterfish, prawns, winkles, a hermit crab, seaweed types, an ugly Granny fish and much else, including one real puzzle. I'd guddled among west coast pools most of my life and had never met the like. The fish creature looked like a large tadpole with a vivid greeny polka dot on its back.

Our wanderings had taken us along to the islands at the 'Camusfearna' of Gavin Maxwell's *Ring of Bright Water* with their views out to the blue islands and not so far Cuillin. We diplomatically stopped as we knew Maxwell received too many unwanted intruders. But he was something of a marine biologist wasn't he? He'd have reference books. We all wanted to know what we'd found. We also wanted to use the dixi for brewing tea!

So I sent a couple of the boys with the dixi and with firm instructions about being polite when asking what it was. They didn't come back so, feeling like Noah, I sent two more. When they didn't return we all went over and found everyone on the floor with books spread as they searched for the fish's identity. It proved to be a Cornish sucker fish, found mainly in the Scilly Isles. Maxwell then suggested he send it to the Natural History Museum and the fish was duly pickled and dispatched.

Later I would hear Maxwell's account of the encounter. He'd been writing when there was a knock on the door. Opening it he found two wee boys who thrust a can at him with an immediate, 'Can you tell us whit that is mister? No, not they wans. We ken them. That yin!' And he didn't know. 'We'd better look it up' he stammered. Doing so, the other two arrived and were soon drawn in to the search. 'It felt a bit unreal. These self-possessed naturalists appearing two by two out of nowhere.'

The boys saw the furry infant otters Mossy and Monday who came out from below the floor to be fed and, after tea and cake for the party, headed for home. We sang our way up the track and home by the wendy road above the Sound of Sleat with the sun setting the Cuillin pinnacles on fire across in Skye - and, finally, last day, we went over the sea to Skye and, even having had such enervating sunshine for our road, there was still the braggart in our steps.

The last picture then: the Kylerhea ferry over the kyle with several of the party sounding like couriers as the visiting tourists in their cars heard how drovers swam their beasts across these narrows and pointed out the inn where Dr Johnson and

Boswell stayed. They explained about the military road to Bernera Barracks and the Clearances. I could only smile. But they knew their history, a history which they had married to geography (and memory) over the hot, long days. We stomped off down the clanging ramp with voices ringing out 'It's the far Cuillin that is pulling me away ...'

CANOE CAPERS

Back in the Sixties I was sold a canoe for £5. I'm still using it. I used it for over 50 years. The canoe became mine because the teacher selling it was 'skint', and the school had moved on so was building canoes in the new fibreglass material. My wood and canvas canoe was an antique when I bought it.

The school was on the shingly shore of the Firth of Forth so that is where pupils learnt to canoe. Only good swimmers were allowed to canoe - or sail - which was one way of encouraging pupils to learn to swim. My canoe was unsinkable even without the addition of buoyancy but I had polystyrene in the bow and a net of ping pong balls in the stern. Damage usually just meant a canvas patch stuck on with black Bostik and some more paint. To buy a modest seaworthy canoe today you'd need to add some zeros to the price I paid.

Not all the changes are completely necessary. Canoe-ists are presented with the same 'must haves' and fashion demands of every sport and pastime. We had great fun with those ancient canoes. They took us to inland lochs and sea lochs and we ran most of Scotland's big rivers with them. I once laughed during a portage when I found a nephew's state of the art modern canoe was actually heavier than my old *Carrick*.

Paddles were always the weakest part of canoeing equipment and eventually I always carried a spare, and used one-piece paddles. An escapade on the Forth taught the need for this care. For some reason of wind and tide I ran into a weird sea off Longannat power station, waves popping up everywhere in random spouts, each capable of tipping me over. As I struggled for control my paddles broke at the join. All I could do was overlap the broken ends and tie them round and round with cord - the guy lines of the tent I had on board - in a rough and ready splint.

I'd never canoed the River Forth with school parties: too dull for lads who learnt the game off the Buckhaven shore but on my tramp from John o' Groats to Land's End which also took in linking the most northerly Munro (Ben Hope) with the most southerly (Ben Lomond) it struck me as a good way to reach home at Kinghorn without breaking the 'self-propelled' rule. So the *Carrick* was left at Loch Ard ready for when I came off Ben Lomond.

Once down onto Flanders Moss and the carselands the canoeing *was* dull, with high banks giving no views and the endless links requiring a great deal of distance paddled for little real distance gained. (The dog just curled up and went to sleep.) Things livened up when tidal waters were reached. The canoe was left overnight on the outskirts of Stirling and when I returned at an unearthly hour to catch the ebb I found vandals had kicked several holes in the canoe. Fortunately, no struts were damaged so the new waterproof tape was soon slapped on - and we continued.

Time and tide dictated another night stop and I managed to use a jetty to get ashore clean (the upper Forth is all gooey mud at low tide) and settled against a high fence, tent draped over paddles for a shelter as the weather was fine. I was in the middle of supper when a posse of security guards with an

Alsatian dog arrived. There were notices everywhere apparently, but none facing the sea, saying 'Keep Out! No fires!' The site was an explosives depot! Luckily the sergeant proved a former pupil, and he vouched that my story of walking Britain end-to-end and being with a canoe on the Forth was quite likely. Looking at the acres of mud I was left to wait for the 0400 high tide. There was some NATO exercise at the time and off Rosyth a dozen warships were anchored. Canoeing through them in the pre-dawn light made me a bit nervous but I was not even challenged!

Come to think of it the Tay Estuary gave me a fright too. A Braehead gang had a great time exploring the great reed beds and had come over to Newburgh and were ghosting along below the sheer walls of a factory. I was in front as usual, half dopey with the heat, when suddenly a pipe jutting out of the wall shot forth a great gush of steaming hot water and had it been a couple of seconds later I'd have been scalded.

At Perth the boys had been set to do a survey of the harbour area to see what variety of industry existed and what use was made of the sea access. They found one example of what could be termed green quarrying. The Tay was being dredged and the material brought ashore was graded and sold in various sizes of sand and gravel - a perpetual source. Some of the grains of sand could have started on Schiehallion one of the boys suggested.

Having the school bothy in the Black Wood of Rannoch canoes were taken up and used on Loch Rannoch. One winter some keen lads took canoes they'd made and despite the cold had fun exploring the loch. Launching was no problem at the mouth of the Dall Burn but, having crossed the loch and wanting a leg stretch, we found the north shore rimmed with ice. A recent film of Arctic icebreakers had showed how their bows rose on the ice and broke it down so I decided this would work equally well with the canoe's angled bow. So I charged the ice. The canoe failed to mount the ice which simply drove two great gashes into the canvas! Some spare clothing was jammed into the holes before the canoe filled and these, first wetting then freezing, made excellent patches. The boys in their fibreglass canoes had no problem. Over various trips the school canoed the whole way from Loch Rannoch to the sea.

Some lads and I once had a great skating day over Rannoch Moor, the only time I've worn a climbing rope, crevasse rescue gear and lifejacket simultaneously, and this suggested a fun canoe outing - right across Rannoch Moor- which proved a bit of a logistical exercise as well. We did the crossing the next summer: several boys, three teachers and the 'heidie' who was always game to try anything once. Once probably proved enough for canoeing. The boys knew the schools' canoes, the head just took one from store - and it leaked. He had to stop periodically and empty out the water. One teacher, with a 'shoogly' arm from polio had canoed across the North Sea; in a kilt of course.

A car was left at Bridge of Orchy station and everyone then went up onto the Moor in a Land Rover, with the canoe trailer in tow. At the other end of the crossing the canoes were to be taken up to Rannoch Station, thence by train back to Bridge of Orchy where camp would be pitched while the bus and trailer were retrieved. Everything worked well though the Rannoch station master was nonplussed about payment. 'Never had canoes before'. In the end he decided to charge by weight. The *lightest* canoe was proffered every time and a sum done.

Half way along Loch Laidon a great whaleback of rock lay just below the surface and, as leader, I found it by grounding gently. I stepped out, pulled the canoe over, and climbed in again. Later the headmaster reported how it appeared to the rest some distance behind. I apparently stepped out of the canoe for a short stroll on the water before continuing. One lad, seeing this, gasped 'Christ!' to which a mate quipped 'Naw, naw; no Christ. Jist Hamish'.

The islands on Loch Ba and Loch Laidon were noticeably tree covered compared to the rest of the desolate Moor, a classic example indicating how the Highland landscape has been deforested and demeaned by overgrazing through the centuries.

The only near-disaster occurred while descending the River Tweed when a boy, despite warnings, got caught in the branches of a fallen tree. He was unceremoniously yanked out by his hair.

We finished the Tweed descent at Kelso as there wasn't much of technical interest thereafter. We were half-drifting lazily along towards Rennie's Tweed bridge when we realised there were about thirty swans on the river ahead. Something alarmed them and they turned up-river to get airborne. This takes swans a lot of effort, and distance, and we were closing quickly. They were going to crash right into us. It was like being attacked by a fleet of Concordes! Only at the last moment did they gain lift enough to skim mere inches above our heads, the turbulence of their passing gusting over us and water splashing onto our heads.

Looking out to Inchkeith as my home did then we frequently canoed out to the island - and once continued on to the Lothian shore - so came to know it in most conditions. Caught by sea mist we once reached the island by following the whirring flights of homing puffins. On a day of intense sun dog and I became so drowsy we fell asleep and it was only a porpoise surfacing close by that woke us. Instead of being off Pettycur we were facing St Serf's tower at Dysart.

On successive visits to Inchkeith I towed back beachcombed companionways off boats which made a useful stile over the garden fence. Good wood from the shore would eventually floor the loft. Over the years I noted plastic bottles with origins in both the USA and Russia.

I think the happiest solo trip I ever had was on the west coast. I launched on the River Callop which runs into the north end of Loch Shiel near the Glenfinnan Monument and camped by a lonely stand of pines set in natural woodland echoing to the calling of a cuckoo. Near the south of the loch I landed on Eilean Fhianain (St Finnan's Isle) to see an early Christian church. An old hand bell of the period is still there, a precious relic. The island was also the traditional burial place for Clanranald. Islands became favoured burial places as they removed the risk of having newly-interred bodies dug up by wolves.

The short river gave an exciting run down to the sea near Castle Tioram then I went through the tidal sound of Eilean Shona to the open sea. I had a leg stretch on Samalaman Island - to the surprise of an otter - and ended by camping on the Ardnish peninsula. Next day I caught the train from Lochailort to Glenfinnan, collected my car, collected the canoe, and headed home.

A canoe was sometimes useful as a way of reaching a desired hill or interesting place without having to walk or drive a long way round. On the occasion I climbed Ladhar Bheinn across Loch Hourn from Arnisdale, I passed under the stern of what I took to be a cruise ship; until, above me, I saw the name *Britannia*. (The Queen was on the way to open the Kylesku Bridge.) Ben Alder cottage was the happy base for a weekend of hills - reached by canoes down Loch Ericht. Our long lochs offer great scope for that sort of ploy. A school party raided the

Loch Lochy Munros (Meall na Teanga and Sron a' Choire Ghairbh) by canoeing across the loch. We also used Loch Lochy youth hostel for canoe-exploring the Great Glen's lochs, rivers and Caledonian Canal.

Loch Oich drains by a river to Loch Ness which is more exciting for canoes than the canal. Doing this we swept round a bend where green lawns ran down to the river from a mansion. A lady standing on the bank called out in an imperious cut-glass accent, 'What do you think you're doing?' I'd passed so was in no position to reply but our tail-ender did. He said, 'Canoeing' - and disappeared.

A nephew, a school friend and I once canoed the whole Great Glen, south west to north east, the direction of the prevailing wind, but strong winds made Loch Ness very hard work, almost paddling one-armed to keep off the lee shore. Alltsigh youth hostel was our base and each night we found a safe place for the canoes, hid paddles and lifejackets and thumbed or bussed back to Alltsigh. We ran the River Ness to the sea. There is something special about reaching a major town where river becomes sea. (Aberdeen, Perth, Inverness) for, by contrast, canoeing is so quiet and rural and a great way to observe wildlife. For instance we'd found a then rare osprey nest on that trip.

From Loch Lochy we portaged along the *Mile Dorcha* (the Dark Mile) to Loch Arkaig to raid Corbett Beinn Bhan and stop overnight at Invermallie bothy. Haunting footsteps in the night turned out to be grazing garrons.

Beinn Loinne was reached across Loch Cluanie with launching made difficult by a great expanse of bare shore thanks to an unusually dry summer. Loch Loyne whose dammed increase flooded the old Road to the Isles from Tomdoun can give an odd spectacle in dry summers with a bridge apparently sitting in solitary state out in the middle of the loch. Loch

Mullardoch, so big the locals call it 'the Atlantic', was to catch me out on another dry summer. A canoe along its length to reach the western hills seemed a good idea. The bare shore was a black, peaty goo which made launching both tricky and messy, so it was a relief to be paddling off into the golden path of sunset waters, the dog's whole attention focused on the calling of a loon. Loch Mullardoch is the dammed combination of two lochs (Loch Lungard and Loch Mullardoch) and an hour later we had the shock of seeing they had reverted to being two lochs again with a merry river draining one to the other. This was ironic for as a youth I'd headed north to pass between the lochs (as shown on my 1/6 prewar One Inch folded map) only to be faced with the huge new Loch Mullardoch and the devil of a diversion.

The setback this time proved a gain for we camped there and then, one of those serenely quiet and lonely spots away from the world. I lit a bogwood fire and brewed a last cuppa on the flames. On the shingle I kicked what looked like a float for a fishing net but it clunked as stone, not wood, so I picked it up and saw a delicately decorated whorl from a prehistoric spindle. The canoe had to be lined both up and down the rocky link between the lochs but we had our hill day and a second, equally happy, night at the camp spot.

Loch Maree, the largest loch in the north, not only gave access to the hills on its northern shore but allowed an exploration of some of the islands. One Loch Maree island, Eilean Subhainn, has a loch in it and in that lochan is an island ... Isle Maree is another with early Christian associations, St Maelrubha, a saint and missionary second only to St Columba, having his base there. Older superstitions saw sacrifices of a bull right up till the seventeenth century and for centuries the insane were brought to the island for horrendous 'treatment'. I've written more on this already. Loch Maree is endlessly fascinating.

Lochs and rivers were once more important as lines of communication than the land. We canoe, or boat, or sail for fun. How different for prehistoric man discovering this great landscape. Some of the oldest habitations in Scotland were on Western islands. Canoes could have taken these early adventurers to St Kilda even, forty miles beyond the Long Island. Not a paddle I'm prepared to make, at least not in a fifty year old canoe which cost £5.

HIGH ON MONT BLANC

Bliss it was in that dawn to be alive,
But to be young was very heaven.

Wordsworth

Recently I came on a 27-09-1969 cutting from the *Glasgow Herald* in which I described a traverse of Mont Blanc which was rather special at the time (and still is) so I dug out that season's logbook and have written up the trip, not originally intended for publication but it could just interest others - oldies - who were active in those primitive times. Why was it special?

Well, we were a somewhat unusual party, seven of us, Ian and David (Nabby), both 15; Ronnie, 16; Andrew, 17; and 21 year old student Bob (later an honorary SMC member) who celebrated that landmark with champagne on the train from Victoria. There was also fellow teacher, Ann, a keen LSCC member. Right through the Sixties I was employed full-time taking boys and girls from Braehead School into the wilds, this from the mining coastline of Fife - the first such appointment in a state school and I became much involved in what developed. A mountaineering tradition soon sprang up in the school and their 'escape from the classroom' (title of a headmaster's book) would have a strong influence in their lives. They would not have been on Mont Blanc otherwise.

Ian, with an irrepressible laugh, had an odd ability of catching wild birds with his bare hands. At Zermatt we'd see him dive into a bush and come out with a black redstart. (After admiring it the bird was free to fly away.) He was the middle of three brothers, each coming with enthusiasm already strong. Alan, the youngest left school with over 100 Munros sclimmed - and was one of a party who set off for the Alps the day the school closed for good. Rob and Ian set up a butcher's business. Dependable Nabby would become a nurse. In 1972 after leaving school, he joined Bob and me and others for a fine season climbing in Norway. Ronnie had done less in the hills but, as a neat, self-possessed lad, was very much at home in the Alps. All were efficient campers and capable cooks, used to long unsupported trekking trips through the Scottish Highlands. They were there because they wanted to be, with their personal dreams of climbing bigger hills. We were a 'Meet' of 14, which included my brother and his wife, a former pupil with his wife, others who were not climbing at all or who only had two weeks of July holiday. Alec (wee Eck), a baker's apprentice, was one of these but he did manage the 'Munros' of the Diablerets and Mont Vélan. (After one ascent he casually mentioned he only had one lung.) Sadly our Alpine summers came late in the school's history so predecessors who had climbed summer and winter, and done things like the Cuillin Ridge, missed out. A skilled ex-pupil, Joe, had joined us in the Dauphiné in 1964 for an epic on the Meige (p. 186). Another, Sandy, joined us in 1968 and 1970, Jim in 1970 taking part in a fine traverse of Lyskamm, Castor and Pollux. The school closed in 1971 which ended the Alps connection. I was always impressed by the youngsters' stamina. I don't think they ever thought they were not up to any challenge but, on the other hand, they were remarkably disciplined and unfazed by failure. I mention all this simply to indicate their at-oneness with the mountains. More, as a professional instructor, I knew they were safer and better than the generality of people on the hill. And they were good company (most of the time!). At the swimming pool in Sion, someone listening to their thick Fife accents, asked me where they came from, and what language were they speaking?

There was a school tradition that when anyone passed 50 Munros they were given a copy of the Tables, a wee book, *Focus on Mountain* written by Tom Weir, with a foreword by John Hunt (and autographed by them) and I took the recipients out for a celebratory meal. Latterly these seemed to be saved for the Alps and on this occasion I had to fork out on raclette suppers in Martigny's *Hôtel du Rhône* for Ian, Nabby and Alex. Martigny and Zermatt were our favourite camp site bases.

On the 3rd August 1969 we took the wheels-screaming rack railway from Martigny up the Trient Valley into France then set off in the middle of the day from Chamonix: a bus to Les Houches and the cable car up to Bellevue (1790m) where we had something to eat before joining the tramway from St Gervaise on to the Nid d'Aigle (2386m). (Some of them had camped at Loch an Nid in Scotland and were able to translate: *the eagle's nest.*) The Nid was as far as mechanical propulsion would help. One lad suggested such uplift was cheating, but hadn't offered to walk. The weather had been deteriorating and we set off in mist and rain wondering if it would be a case of Duke of Yorking: up to a hut and down again - and all that money lost on the uplift. They had largely financed themselves by much 'tatty howking'. There wouldn't be a second chance.

The rain came down hard at times as we slogged through boulders, mud and snow to a ruined hut on the edge of the Glacier de la Gria, a depressing world of many shades of grey, above and around. Glaciers are not the pristine white expanses of popular imagination but we had met this gruey world often enough not to be downhearted. We found some shelter in the ruin then crossed the glacier to tackle the endless-feeling zigzags of a 'slobbery rubbish *arête*' to the Tête Rousse Glacier. There was some thunder growling in the murk. Despite heavy rucksacks with supplies for possibly four days (bags of Reddy, a trade name of a new invention called *muesli,* and Ann's rucker full of Chamonix *baguettes*) we reached the Tête Rousse Refuge (3167m) in 'under book time', something it was a matter of pride always to do. Only once installed did conversation come round to the strange buzzing everyone had noticed on the *arête*! It snowed. The hut was cosy enough and at the bowls of coffee stage after supper the hut rang to songs from Germans, Swiss, Italians and Scots (strangely, no French).

The hoped-for weather window seemed to have gone astray so it was seven o'clock before I looked outside to find the sky clear and welcome frost. We hurried to head off, at least to recce, for I was concerned about the big central couloir on the face which had to be crossed and down which people tended to knock stones. I'd seen this previously and just a week before there had been a fatality. We scurried across on two ropes. The main danger would be in the afternoon when those who had been to the summit began to descend from the Goûter refuge, tired physically and mentally, the time when accidents so easily ambush. We had to have everything right.

We solved any other stonefall problems by then taking an

original (well, non-guide) line, ascending a rib leading directly up to the refuge on its perch above the face. Nothing could come down on to its crest. The rocks were frozen (*verglas*) but the snow firm and it would 'go' with care. We treated it seriously enough and roped up, moving together or belaying as required. The higher the better it proved, with more snow and good scrambling and what felt rather odd, the last belay being to the railings of the Goûter refuge balcony (3817m).

We were early so lazed and ate and drank and watched the mobs streaming up the route we'd carefully avoided. Many were not climbers who had employed guides for their one ambitious ascent of a lifetime, to reach the highest summit imaginable. (The syndrome these days ranges from Ben Nevis to Everest.) Many arrived weary and already suffering from the altitude and sat around looking miserable and unsmiling for most of the day. Our lads must have been a sore trial, so obviously full of beans, (and eating voraciously). They actually laughed at times! I noted one older guide scowling at them now and then but he and his client and our gang were first out the hut next morning. Bed spaces were not allocated till late in the day and who says 90 into 60 won't go? We were crowded in with Italians but they later vanished so we had room enough but it was still a stuffy, claustrophobic, noisy, typical hut night.

This route up Mont Blanc was first taken in 1861 by Leslie Stephen, F F Tuckett and their guides Melchoir Anderegg, J J Bennen and Peter Perrin. The first ascent of the mountain was in 1786 and came up the snows of the NE flank, our proposed way down, partly for the historic association and partly to avoid the crowds of the *voie normal*.

The first ascent of Mont Blanc is seen as the firing gun for what became alpinism, aiming for new peaks and passes and thereafter filling in ever more improbable details. The

Geneva scientist H B de Saussure offered a reward of 20 gold thalers for the first ascent and, after several attempts, the local crystal-hunter Jacques Balmat and Dr Michel-Gabriel Paccard duly reached the summit on 8 August 1786. A year later Saussure made the ascent, as did the first British climber, Col M Beaufoy.

Early starts always pay off. Clouds had built up in the afternoon but this was a good weather sign and we were up at 2.30 and stepped out at 3.25, into a world of gripping cold, with a half moon and a glitter of stars overhead, a glitter replicated in the lights of towns far below. Lights away on the plains were like the Milky Way. On a flat area above the hut we strapped on our crampons and organised our ropes. I had Andrew and Nabby while Ann and Bob were a foursome with Ian and Ronnie. The old guide and his client were off first, we were next and others soon followed. There was some leapfrogging and we were the third party to summit. And I'd wager we were the first back in Chamonix.

There's a long pull up to the Dôme due Goûter at 4304 metres, not technical but in some ways the crux of the day. Not much chat, 'Steady as she goes', companionable moon shadows on the velvety snow. We dipped to the Col du Dôme beyond with the darkness easing away. We could pick out climbers on the elegant, pristine, fin of snow of the Aiguille Bionnassay ridge.

The Refuge Vallot (4362m) was a chilly metal box and we only stopped to leave some food and drink there. We'd be back, starting the descent line from the bivvy hut. I can't recall much detail and wrote little in my log. The whole ascent now (the Bosses Ridge) seemed to be constantly repeating itself, rising rooftops, then a dip but always more rise than dip, a potentially disheartening symmetry requiring a certain dour concentration. We stuck cheerfully-enough to the task:

no complaints, crampons placed carefully, ropes handled fluently, a known discipline. Scenically it was superb and at one stage the crest was so narrow that we teetered along with one foot in France and the other in Italy. Eyes now and then flickered ahead to gauge the time and distance remaining. With our tortoise steadiness we had overtaken more often than we'd been passed. Twice the old guide and his client who had set off at the same time paused and we passed them, then we'd have a P-stop or drink and they passed, the client grimly determined with the reward nearing. We climbed into dawn, the world exploding mountains on mountains out to horizons and dropping to the shadowlands far below.

The summit was almost an anticlimax, an area spacious enough for casual movement, which was maybe as well for our exultant spirits, though celebrated quietly enough. Looking at photographs taken then there are controlled grins, satisfactions that will never disappear whatever life will bring. Mountains, any climbing, demands a discipline and reliance on all involved and it was moving to see it in these youngsters. One of my most moving moments came when, after shaking hands with the guide and his client, the guide nodded at our gang and smiled, 'Ver' nice'.

The pre-dawn chill slowly eased and the colours of the sky behind the arrayed Alps changed from icy opal to the warmer rosy tints then, with explosive brilliance, the sun broke free of the jagged earth and entered the perfect sky. Westwards, the pyramid shadow of Mt Blanc stretched sixty miles into the distance, an awesome spectacle. The whole world was ours.

Everyone felt they could have gone faster but we had reached the summit in three hours, an hour less than book time. 'Slow and easy goes far in a day' I often quoted. There was a wind which blew a nasty surface spindrift and Ian's feet were freezing so they were warmed by being shoved up under Ann's duvet. It doesn't take much of a wind at 4807 metres to produce a windchill factor. The view was interesting, picking out other known areas, seeing the familiar Paradiso-Dauphiné to the south while, east, the Valais backed up, peak on peak, and the long Oberland scored a white horizon. Whymper complained that the view was unsatisfactory, 'there is nothing to look up to; all is below; there is no one point for the eye to rest on' - just like on top of the Matterhorn where there's none of everywhere else's focus on that monolith. My eyes looked to Mont Maudit and Mont Blanc du Tacul for a friend John King and I had gone that way to the Midi téléférique on a 1964 traverse. On that occasion we had been alone on the summit when suddenly there was another person there. He was real enough: a scientist on some project that entailed him staying 24 hours a day for a week on the summit. He had just popped out from his snow-cave lodging.

Whymper did not mention the view *down* and that, almost alarmingly, was where we were bound; a far cry tae Chamonix. A brief reminder to the boys that descents were more chancy than ascents and needed equal care and concentration and we set off, rapidly dropping back down to the Vallot, passing others coming up, with their guides, often looking 'green and gasping' (Ian), suffering but persevering. Good on them! Great would be their reward and, as soon as they began the descent, they would find strange renewal. Theirs would be the smiling faces in the refuge that night.

We had something of a binge at the Vallot, made sure crampons were tight and set off, curving down to the big snow basin of the Grand Plateau, then bearing over, down as fast as possible, to the Grandes Montées with leering seracs off to our left. The Petit Plateau was hardly noticed but the

Petites Montées gave Andrew, Nabby and me some good bumslides - a popular technique. (One of the best ever was sliding more than a 1000 feet off a Loch Quoich Munro, with one dire result. I've a photo of the two lads holding up their trousers with the seats worn completely out of them.) We regrouped at a rubbly area then hurried on again to safer ground where we could relax; just 'mere crevasses' following.

The first crevasse was the best/worst of the day. At another Ann managed to jam herself in it. Crevasse rescue techniques had been practiced at home, often at the school's Rannoch bothy where ropes to prusik up were hung from the Scots pines. At long last the Grands Mulets (3057m) was reached but the hut surrounds were so unappealing we just passed by for the Bossons glacier and had a drinks and nibbles pause at La Jonction.

Progress was rather chaotic thereafter and our wild glissades and scurring along rather horrified a party we passed. There was one crevasse with a ladder over it which made me think of images of the early Victorians with all their paraphernalia and strings of porters - all who came over the decades by this toilsome route. Rocks were banging away onto the Bossons Glacier, there were water channels and ice towers, all very fine, but rather going on a bit I felt. At last we found a spot to cower and take off crampons, then sped along below the cable cars of the Midi téléférique, passed the site of an old lift and reached the Pélerins Glacier by 'a nice dander'. The glacier was all granite blocks and deep but clear crevasses and we teased through it, the last modest demand.

Once across there was a great removing of sweaty garments and most changed into shorts. Quite a contrast with the icy cold of the summit. At 11.30 we were relishing cokes and/or beers at the Plan de l'Aiguille (2910m), halfway station of the Midi téléférique and more than happy to use it for the last Munro-footage of descent to Chamonix. The valley was blistering hot, the contrast setting faces ablaze. *Coupe maisons* were consumed, then steaks and chips and five 1½ litre bottles of lemonade. We sat in a noisy content amid a piquant shambles of rucksacks, discarded clothes, mitts, crampons, ropes and ice axes. We received odd looks from some passers-by but they could never understand just what we hugged to ourselves. We then went for the slow train back to Martigny.

FURTH OF BRITAIN

MATTERHORN EXPERIENCES

The bright face of danger

R. L. Stevenson

My first season in the Alps, 1962, had been enjoyed in Arolla, camping among the pines and, with long weeks of student freedom, we'd climbed just about every local peak. We also had the village idiot drive his cows back and forth for the fun of seeing what they could do to tents and gear. I'm just surprised my insurance claim wasn't challenged, 'Did a cow really eat parts of your primus stove, sir?' ('Yes, two legs and the sooty screw-in burner.')

That first fine careful rapture of course gave endless views to the not so distant Matterhorn. Irresistible. Sadly all my mates went home, there were no Brits at the Zermatt campsite and none at the Hörnli Hut, except 'peasants' gawking on the Belvedere tables. The season was ending.

Then an aspirant guide, keen to fill up his *fürerbuch*, suggested we went together, at a nominal fee. We set off at 04.00. And were back at 08.30. 'Why?' we were asked. Told, an old guide in moustache and felt hat who could have stepped out of Whymper, declared 'That is no way to treat the Matterhorn! Drinks! Drinks!' I think Edi Graven, my guide, was happy. And my logbook called the hill's lower part a 'coal bing'. The postcards look fabulous.

I'd done my homework and had surprised Edi by naming off all the features of the route. That's the way the world starts, up the Alps with a Whymper. Historical interest initially took us to La Berard next season then the lure of Zermatt called us back. Rock *and* snow in abundance for Breithorn, Alphubel, Monta Rosa and the Dent Blanche. Ah, the resilience of youth, for a traverse of the Matterhorn was second on our 'wants' list and gave a memorable seventeen hour day, the first traverse of the season on 23 July. A lot of snow everywhere. 'Might stick it all together' suggested Egg (John Burslem).[1]

It is a mountain of wonderful shape. Wherever we had climbed in the Valais or even away in the Dauphiné we looked across miles of snow and rock to this stark tooth snarling up above Zermatt and biting into the clouds. When up it before we had not even carried an axe and had scorned the fixed ropes; this time, with full paraphernalia, it gave us the most desperate hours of our young lives.

We were up about three o'clock to a morning that showed the hazy lights of Zermatt far below and the black citadel itself faded in mistiness above. Running along Monte Rosa the lightning flickered silently. When the first parties eventually set off we quickly joined in the mad queue so as to be in the van. We could just do without torches though above us we could see the torch beams of the first parties wandering about in the dark. Any suspicions about the weather were swept away in the rush. If the guides were content, who were we to worry? The pace was slow with the guides dragging clients along on tight ropes. Rhythm was impossible and we took every chance of passing parties. The various parties then shook down and a regular pace became possible. By couloirs and chimneys and rotten gullies the route wound up the edge of the east face. It was still somewhat plastered with snow and even then stones were loosening to slither off for the seracs below. Beyond the Michabel the sun touched the clouds a lurid red. There were three of us on the one rope: the Haggis, the Egg and the Camel (Malcolm Copley), and we rejoiced in the simple animal activity. Below us pressed an English Naval officer who, having seen the peak from an aircraft, decided its ascent was a 'must'. He travelled out on a scooter, was passing forty, had little mountaineering experience; but whatever we felt, we could only admire the élan of his venture.

We climbed on the heels of the party ahead. At one stage we had a race for a hold with the result that the man ahead quietly, unsuspectingly, sandwiched my hand under his boot. At the Mosley slabs there was an explosive chaos; the ranks broke to swarm up, guides crossed ropes and hauled and shouted in the wild scramble. It was a disgusting exhibition which caught us like the tide as we had to wait ten minutes for the Camel's anorak which had cleverly untied itself and started a private descent.

It cleared the route ahead anyway and we enjoyed not being in a crowd. Far down a couloir on the North Face we could see two figures. They had set off the day before and were still low down. We were to wonder later how they progressed; did they win up or on to the Hörnli or were they among the seven who died on that and the next two days on the vile mountain? After our forced wait at the Solvay Refuge we carried on along the crest of the ridge, a pleasant change, though demanding some care with snow and ice on the rocks. We came to the long snow slopes that can be seen from the valley. We flicked the rope round the great iron pegs as we passed and were soon on the fixed ropes of the shoulder. There was no hesitation in using them this year. The Camel was beginning to feel the height and effort but the steep section passed and the final slopes were at an easier angle.

We were on the summit at 07.45. And I was greeted by name! There was Edi, my partner the year before, with a client. We shook hands and had a brief chat. He told us nobody had gone down the Italian Ridge as yet this season. Yes, it will 'go'. One party ascended yesterday. There will be tracks. No problem.[2] We took photos on top and gazed at a fine panorama of nearer peaks: the groups of the Michabel and the hills to Monte Rosa, the Weisshorn, Rothorn, Gabelhorn and the Dent Blanche - a ring of fine memories and bright prospects.

The Camel roped up with the Navy chap to descend the Hörnli. Egg and I put on crampons to go along to the Italian summit, a wafer of snow above dizzy depths, but then had to take them off again to start the descent. The rock was pink and steep. We came to the first rope and the Echelle Jordan - and the first verglas, wicked, transparent films which were invisible until the questing boot slithered a warning. Though the slope was steep and exposed, it was easy enough to move together or lead through. The final tower must have been impressive to the early explorers. It gave delightful climbing. We could see the Crête Tyndal below, a rooftop of snow reaching out in a long ridge, with a fine thread of footprints along the twisty crest. Miles below lay the deep purpled valleys of Italy. It was good to be alive in such a world and we laughed at the swinging choughs.

We left the last of the ropes for the Crête. The snow was firm enough as we began the unwinding of the route, no great difficulty but never dull; rather like the Cuillin ridge with snow added. The Nose of Zmutt was etched against the sky and voices came from the ridge there. The season's first improving spell of weather was certainly bringing out climbers on all the routes. Suddenly it was snowing.

It came down in little fluffy ball-bearings and ran swishing over the rocks until it became a voluminous flow of white movement. We had had this before and it simply made it like Scotland anyway. (We compared it with a day that Easter when Egg and I had left the CIC Hut at 2pm, just 'to look at' Tower Ridge and had gone on to force the route in a fine fight that lasted six hours and gave us half an hour's daylight on top in an impenetrable fog, and no map.) So we swung on down, regretting only the vanished track and softening snow. The rock was friable too and needed careful handling. We had a bite to eat. When not moving together or leading through Egg was usually in front seeking out the route, I behind giving what protection was possible before following on.

We went down some soaking slabs, the first of many, and our vibrams did not slip, though our nerves certainly suffered. We cut steps down and across an icy couloir, the ice a mere veneer and no belay possible. As we rounded a prow of snow, we noticed a smell of singeing; my scalp began to creep and my hat quivered on my head. There was a hissing-hum that was not just the running snow. With a yell I threw my axe into the snow and the rucksack beside it. We scampered up to the shelter of some rocks and cringed down. There was a flash that shook us like the blast of an explosion and the mountain echoed with fierce thunder.

We were marooned in the growling clouds for over an hour. It snowed continually, warm and wet. Three times we approached our axes only to stir up a buzzing, as of bees about our heads. We cowered, very small indeed while clouds boiled about, avalanches crashed and the snow swished over everything in streams. Egg found a crumpled fag but, having no dry matches, shot out his hand at a flash only to cry 'Damn! Missed again!'

There was another flash whose blast smote us and then a gradual passing of the storm along the Valais. We came out stiff and stretching to collect our gear. Voices drifted out of the clouds and as they broke we saw the small figures on the Zmutt. They were about the size we felt. The hard work began.

We paused on top of the Pic Tyndal for a psychological meal for we seemed to stand above a sheer drop with no footprints to indicate the continuation. We checked the time there, and elsewhere, but it had little meaning then and is forgotten now. The mind simply boggled at the whole and just grimly worked at the next rope's length. It was a crawl: one run out after another, moving one at a time, but with security for neither, a long memory of patient suffering, endless hidden danger, ceaseless labour, hours of it.

Incidents are remembered like solitary waves on a shore. Some fine gendarmes actually gave some enjoyment and almost fun as far as the Corde Tyndall. There we found a pair coming *up*!! First an Italian guide. He was equally astonished to see us. He and we together then hauled up his client, like drawing a cork. Comic: the guide yelling 'Presto! Presto!' and the wail from below, 'Momento! Momento!' They vanished into the murk, axes buzzing *furioso*. Down the Corde and a wee wall gave the last of what could be called enjoyable going.

Down to the Linceul was dreadful, everything covered in ice, water under it and topped by new snow. (Egg: 'Just like Glen Coe'.) The rock was unstable too and Egg would edge down (once a skite) and I'd follow, one bit the most nerve-wracking moves ever: there just could not be a slip. We traversed on up to a rib to the start of the Mauvais Pas. No rope in place and few expected fixed ropes were thereafter. The Mauvais Pas was fun, and easy but round the corner a shock: slabs which normally would have been more or less walked down were covered in ice and slobbery snow. I hacked and laboured till I felt done then went up to Egg to suggest we abseiled as he'd said he had a good belay, which, on testing, proved a loose rock. Demoralised I set him to work hacking across, then led through and up to the next ledge. We led through endlessly down by the Grande Tour. Being steeper we were given the pleasure of just wet rock to climb. There was a shout on spotting a rope, a wee snow slope, a shoulder, loose *éboulies* and there was the *refuge*.

Egg found matches and we found and scoffed stale, blue-mouldy bread as we were ravenous. We re-garbed and squelched off to the fray again. Loose snow led to slabs where the ropes were missing. How we loathed slabs by then! We spent friction-creeping hours on water-running slabs, everything dripping. The vertical rope was there but not knotted. A finger cramped on it. We were tired enough not to bag a piton we could have won.

Down to the Col du Lion was easier but still dangerous in the moving world of wet. (On the other hand we couldn't have taken a freeze-up in our soaked state.) At the Col du Lion the wind eddied and we looked down snow-ripped couloirs. Memories of Whymper's fall! We climbed to the foot of the rocks of the Tête du Lion and traversed left on a mix of unstable rocks and snow which avalanched at the slightest provocation. The snow was littered with fallen rubbish and one rumble overhead left us staring up into the murk. Nothing came. Corners and couloirs continued. As there was no protection we moved together. Egg had a gleam in his eye and went at things viciously, almost not caring and must have hated my dour canniness. Some snow slid off our trench of track, grew and grew, picked up rocks and plunged out of sight with a roar. The large snowfield eventually came, we dug heels deep and descended. The slope held. The cannonade paused. Slowly, like waking from a dream, we began to believe we were through.

We revived, we talked madly, sped from snow slope to rocks to snowslopes, unroped, rushed down the rocky *promentoire*, hurried down a large gully and just bum slid the snow slope below in case of rockfall. The Abruzzi Refuge appeared on our level and we passed it to reach the wonder of grass and unimagined meadows of soldenellas.

Breuil still seemed a long way off but we descended fast, pausing once to tidy up a bit for we looked a sight. And here, I must interject a memory not in the log. In Zermatt a few days earlier we had gone to the English church where some holidaying bishop conducted the service. We'd sat right at the back seeing everyone was in respectable clothes but, came the moment, the request was made for the two men on the back row aisle seats to uplift the collection. So, row by row, a man in a white suit and Egg, in worn rugger shirt and the seat out of his jodhpurs, advanced row by row to stand before his lordship. A prayer was said, the pair turned, and to this day I can remember how the bishop's eyebrows shot up. We had also visited the museum which was a mistake as every object on display had some connection with a tragedy on the Matterhorn.

The valley down to Breuil (now Cervinia) had waterfalls that sprayed us, and our feet tramped the most flowery meadows imaginable. Down the street we bought plums, sinking teeth into the gorgeous sweetness then, for us, an extravagant spaghetti meal and steaks, fruit and coffee before finding a *pension* and arguing down the price of beds under the rafters. We were also celebrating Egg's twentieth birthday.

Our day had proved a seventeen hour one, done in the third week of July. Later we heard most of those descending the Hörnli had been marooned in the Solvay. The Camel and navy lad took five hours descending. Two people were killed and we wondered how the pair we met going up fared. There was a rope on the North Face we'd noticed. Two days later we met Hamish McInnes who was there to film Bonington and Clough on that face. Two weeks later (August 5) the Matterhorn 'season' ended. I decided that was quite enough of the Matterhorn for me.

---

[1] John had earned that nickname while at school (St Bees) by trying to incubate some wild birds' eggs in his bed, with the inevitable result. He also swallowed a worm out of curiosity then, feeling it might be rather uncomfy, swallowed half a cup of earth as well. His outwardly casual appearance hid great dedication and, as a doctor, he spent his life working on the wild borders of Nepal, Bhutan and Tibet.

[2] A few years later I thought I might try and contact Edi again and use his offer of a good climb together for free. When I got in touch he was not available all that season: he was under contract for the Hörnli - up and down that sorry route day after day with untried clients. My heart sank.

A STUBAI SKI DAY

I slept with my head to the window so watched the sky slowly change from the starry velvet of alpine skies to the silky, cloudless clarity of daybreak. A chuckle of choughs on the rocks. The Dresdner hut was palatial, more hotel than howff. The Stubaier Wildspitz called.

We went up the Daunjoch gully to skin across the Daunko-gelferner, eating distance in that satisfying rhythm of sliding skis, left ski, right ski, left ski, right ski, till one marched forward almost mechanically, the mind floating away, content, relaxed. From the Unbemachte (col) skis came off and we roped: Charles, Gordon, Jenni with me. We creep over the bergschrund and climb steeply, with the club's guide Lorenz thumping good socket steps. This led to the surpringly narrow NW ridge, the other side dropping sheer to a glacier wrinkled as streaky bacon. The ridge's rock presented ample juggies and the snow was firm, again giving the satisfaction of steady movement. And so we arrived on top of the Wildspitz, 3340m. There was a cross on top of course. In summer there would have been scores of gawpers or worshippers.

We had the statutory naming of peaks, then took in some calories (from chocolate, raisins and dried bananas in my case) and my liquid choice of cold tea. We passed the two other ropes on the way down and suffered their pouring snow onto us as we unroped and put on our skis again.

We went round to the Unbemahte, more brêche than col, and zigzagged up from it, binding creaking, a gentle swish of skins, to then climb a snowy ridge for the Ostl. Daun-kogel, 3332m. Only one other rope followed. Back on ski we traverse east to drop down a steep bulge, the ski edges rasping on the icier surface, and gain the Shanfelferner which we follow 'home': ski perfection, on our own chosen line, swinging back and forth, lingering, savouring the artistry we marked on the pristine canvas of snow. This is how an eagle soaring must feel. A bit of *wedelin* to finish, then leaning on our sticks, breathing hard, legs with a comfortable complaining, looking back to wonder at the dazzling world we had so impertinently marked. The tracks would soon go. In a couple of months they would be slopes overwhelmed with alpine flowers, our impertinent intrusion immaterial.

Supper was sausage and sauerkraut, Kaisersmarren or omelettes with ham and spinach. The wine was the best yet. Savouring too that contentment from the day's symphonic experience of alpine wonders (Strauss did it rather well). This was our penultimate Stubai day, the next gave us the coda, the splendidly named Schussgrubenkogel.

HILLS WITH HOLES IN THEM

That Alpine witchery still onward lures ...

F. R. Havergal

1. TAFONATO, CORSICA

In May 1972 Alistair and I flew from Marseilles to Corsica to meet Barclay Fraser who was there with his family on holiday, camping in the wilds while based on his Dormobile. The year before Barclay had joined me in Morocco and we'd toured there in my Dormobile before exploring across Spain on the way home. He had also been to Corsica before and persuaded me and Alistair to come out during our world-wandering sabbatical. He was one of the kindest, pleasantest persons I've ever known, a mentor to whom I owed much.

In this 1972 visit we did some site/sight-seeing in Corsica but were regularly taken up to valley heads to set off and explore the mountains. I liked Corsica (apart from the barbed-wire *maquis*) and had fond memories of cyclamen growing in stately beech woods, finding eyrie-like *bergeries* (bothies supreme but steadily being abandoned, as had our *shielings* in earlier times) while above this level crowded inspiring jagged peaks of rock and snow. We always went to Corsica in spring when the natural world was fresh and new (scented cistus, lavender and lilies), the screes still covered in snow (rather than *éboulées*; *trés pénible*), and the weather kind before the summer smiting of Mediterranean sun. And of course, Corsica is an island, always a bonus, one that doesn't half remind everyone it was the birthplace of Emperor Napoleon.

On this occasion we were dropped off to wend up to the *bergerie* at the Grotte des Anges, where we pitched our tent *inside* a shack as the afternoon saw a strange wind blow. Paglia Orba's blunt cone had whorls of cloud going round it like a playground roundabout and in the night we felt the hut shake as if ready to be pulled into the maelstrom. Strangely, no torrential rain followed. So we traversed Monte Cinto, 2706m, the island's highest peak, though less dominating than Paglia Orba, 'the Matterhorn of Corsica'.

My log noted finding a ten foot line of pine processionary caterpillars and we traced their spun thread line to their nest in a tree, football-sized and made of what looked like cobwebs. I was thrilled as I'd read about them when a boy in a book, *The Life of a Caterpillar*, by the French naturalist Jean Fabre. (The hairs made our itching powder, a mercifully brief craze at school. Birds know to leave them alone and the notorious Borgias made use of them as a useful poison.)

We were off at 05.30 with a woodpecker knocking on the door of morning and on top of 'Pally old Orba' (2525m) by 09.40, the summit a towering prow with a great deal of air around and below it. We went via the *Voie Sud Ouest*, no harder than its given PD for all the snow banking the '*tunnels amusants*'. There was one *à cheval* bit, one nice chimney and snow from the Combe des Chèvres. We then hurried, down as up, and round to snack above the Col des Maures (2125m), waiting for figures we'd seen to appear in the 'hole in the elephant's bottom'. How small the figures were when they appeared in the *trou*, the hole in the summit of Capo Tafonato. I wrote in my log, 'Where can such an exposed fin of peak be ascended so easily while being so spectacularly exposed? We went up from the Col des Maures over rock, scree and snow to reach a large snow flank below a big pink overhang, splashed as if with paint, by yellow lichens. We left our sacks there and went on with just cameras and some nibbles - and a rope. Up a first ledge, inch round a perched block, the exposure multiplying at once, and continuously present thereafter. At the Pierres Blanches there was a wee *source* and then scrambling led to a ledge crossing to the *trou*, a horizontal, Napoleon's hat-shaped hole right through the peak. A blockage there to go over and ledges down to the *vire*, the crux of our ascent. Phenomenal exposure for the peak is simply a vertical wafer of rock with this window just below the summit. We walk through the hole; on one side a view to snowy mountains and the sea, on the other the eye following the valley now far below.

'Ledges and easy chimneys (odd bits of snow) reached the north end, then through a small *brèche* behind a rock thumb, more snow, then a final chimney to a wall which we skirt and so reach the summit (2343m). The best of the view was to the great shadow wall of Paglia Orba, with Cinto behind. There was a visitors' book to sign, showing about 40 ascents from the previous year. We must have climbed a dozen peaks over our stay but none matched Tafonato.' (I described Corsica's peaks more fully in *The Great Walking Adventure* Oxford Illustrated Press, 1986.)

2. Prisojnijk's Okno, Julian Alps

One of my favourite books has always been *Alpine Pilgrimage* (1934) by Julius Kugy who lived in Trieste and became a pioneer of climbing in the Julian Alps in the decades before WW1. His description of bivouacs inspired me to follow suit on many occasions in many ranges. I often quote his words: 'The cold rouses me, and I hear the gentle murmur of the Bistrica in the depths of the Vrata glen. But instead of breaking the stillness of the night, it seems to deepen it. I look upward, heavy with sleep; black rocks overhanging, and the ghostly sheen of the fretted snow-wall; high over the cleft, the stars pass in slow succession. The figure of my companion crouches in the fantastic gleam of our bivouac fire. Sparks fly up from the fresh pine branches; a smell of resin, and a clear crackling of logs; the light flickers; then once more the sinking shadows, the distant song of water, and an infinite silence about us. So the mountain night passes in the beauty of a dream. If you have thus dwelt in the secret heart of the mountains, beholding the full glory of their revelation, as they unfold their signs and wonders from the going down of the sun to its uprising, nothing can efface the memory of such nights.' Amen to that.

July 1976 saw a dozen of us from an Austrian Alpine Club group enjoying the Julian Alps, a bit late for the outstanding flora but giving plenty of scope for varying abilities and ambitions. The jagged, naked limestone peaks rose brutally out of verdant valleys in a shocking contrast but there were many large huts on high so, once up, it was possible to climb peaks without having to descend to valley level each time. We naturally climbed Triglav, 2864m, the highest, fine summit. Rows of spikes and wires mark many routes, something I deprecated, but there were other areas where nothing of man was allowed to intrude. All very organised of course in Tito's Yugoslavia, [now Slovenia]. We must have climbed half a dozen of the best mountains, all of great character. One summit, Prisojnik had appealed to me as it had a hole (*okno*) in it, a hole as vertical as Corsica's had been horizontal.

After one high expedition we descended to the Trenta Valley. This took us through pine forests, then beech, with here and there rifts with trees heaped in the valley from winter avalanches, our descent ending in waterfall-fed meadows with attractive shingled barns and the bright houses of Zlatorog (622m) where we stayed in a hut and relished washing clothes and selves. The church had a fine interior, the ceiling richly painted with angels. The museum had a display of old climbing gear, some from Kugy, some from his guides Andreas and Jože Komac, Oitzinger *et al*. They were commemorated on a plaque set in a rock near the Alpinetum Juliana (Botanic Garden), set up by a Kugy climbing companion, Albert Bois de Chesne. From a map I realised the notable statue of Kugy lay up-valley so set off to see it - and had an unexpected 1000 feet sweat. But there he sat, head turned to gaze up to Jalovec and the mountains where he had seen the birth of climbing in the Julian Alps. We dined well in the *refuge*, with a good array of mountain pictures on its walls, and one of a frowning Tito.

Next day a bus wended up thirty bends to the Vrčič Pass (1611m) and we booked in to the Tičarjev Dom, another gingerbread house of a 'hut', dominated by the 2643m hulk of Jalovec. We simply dumped our belongings in a dormitory and set off, at 11.00 with 2547m Prisojnik our goal. I was one of the first back, at 19.30!

We skirted up under rock walls on scree to an arête, with ever-expanding views, till suddenly, we came to the *okno*, 'a vertical hole through the mountain, bigger than Tafonato's horizontal slot. Onto bare rock thereafter and a rib above brought in the exposure element for the rest of the day. Twist round left and up to a corner where pegs on a ledge led onto the airy crest which was then followed. Care needed on some slabs and steps and old wires looked dicey. Hardly 'walking' and a harder right flanker saw the party dwindle. We joined an easier route for the final pull up. Prisojnik. Great spot. Triglav was still very snowy. Now for the hole.

Much of what followed was 'hairy': frighteningly exposed, poorly protected, 'a way not taken' very often. Regrouped (those continuing) we descended slabs and a chimney pitch to land on loose rubbish. Agag-treading. Not a friendly *okno*. The rest was complex and strenuous yet needed full concentration - old pegs and wires, endless pegs and wires, ropes and overhangs, protection often missing... It was a superbly set exercise but took many of the party well outside their comfort zone. After two-three hours the treeline was reached. Long traverses. Always 'interesting': a pair of chamois bombed us, there were sweeps of snow to teeter across, and always wires, down, down, sprayed by a cooling waterfall, final screes and the road - at 1180m - so that gave a cruel 500m uphill trudge to finish. My thrill had been seeing two wallcreepers on the cliffs, rare birds of grey and red, which looked like butterflies. All up that road the *okno* slash loomed high overhead, 'like a wound' - as if we needed any reminding of a unique day.

3. MONTAGNE SAINTE-VICTOIRE, PROVENCE, FRANCE

Montagne Sainte-Victoire appears in many of the paintings of Cezanne and for that reason alone was a lure. But it also had a hole in it: I could have a triptych of 'Hills with Holes in Them'. An attempt in February 1976 was snowed off, so I hoped a May 1978 visit would be more successful. I'd enjoyed three months in the Atlas, sailed Tangier to Sète with friends hoping thereafter to join my campervan in Marseilles and Ajaccio. I'd most of the party's camping and climbing gear on board and also several pairs of skis homeward bound from the Atlas.

I wondered how I'd get on at Sète, laden as the poor van was. The *Agadir* had set off late afternoon for a colourful sunset behind the Rock of Gibraltar. I went to bed early: every seat on board seemed to be facing a TV set with a bullfight showing. The next day we travelled steadily along the Med to arrive at Sète early the following day. My van was stuck in behind several *camions* so had a long wait even to move. My passport was looked at with a magnifying glass. Curious, I asked the official why. They were having a special exercise that day. Too much *kif* smuggling. I told him of my Tangier precautions. Seeing he was wearing a *douane* badge with crossed skis I queried that and indicated the pile of skis I had on board. He was a member of a crack mountain border ski team. As I had been last off the *Agadir* he was happy to talk and when eventually I drove on towards the next official, hand already raised, I glimpsed the man behind give a signal and the hand up turned into a sweeping gesture for me to drive on out. All round the sun-smitten search area every other campervan was being taken to pieces, everything out. They would be there for hours.

I drove by Arles into the hills towards Mont St Victoire, did a bit of a recce before parking, and set off for the hill, still 70°F at 20.00, a real sweat. The weather looked a bit threatening as I followed waymarks up and along over scrub, scree and slabs, dominated by big rock spurs. 'Lucky local climbers' I thought. Features noted from below came in order then scree led up towards the huge longed-for hole. Avoiding the screes I simply climbed up and through the hole to the other side of the mountain, popping out at dusk and arriving at the big summit cross at 21.30. 'At last' I wrote in my log. 'Triptych complete.'

An old monastery down a bit was now a tourist hut but judging by the noise there wouldn't be much peace in it so I just bivvied, settling in with a big moon. At 01.30 I woke to find it was raining so scuttled back to the big hole, which was very dark and the rock slippery. A stub of candle helped and I found a flat area and went to bed again and only surfaced at 0900 with voices above: a family who decided the hole was not a descent route. Clouds were blowing *down* through the hole and it was raining hard. The rock was like ice and I went up and out in stocking soles, then headed along to the Pas du Berger and the zigzags down, with one nasty slab and a final chimney. In an 'alp' below I spotted the 'Refuge Cezanne'. I sat out another shower in a cave, before heading for my van, hot drinks and dry clothes. Perversely, I'd quite enjoyed my third hill with a hole through it.

I decided to sleep at coastal La Coitat only to become lost in Marseilles (not for the first time) then heavy rain had me draw in for a coffee break. Going on, the wipers wouldn't wipe. *Encore du café*. Then the dashboard became all lit up and the engine refused to start. More coffee while swotting up my AA phrase book for the next day - the day before the ferry to Corsica was booked, with two people meeting me in Marseilles and one at Ajaccio. It rained harder and harder but I managed a running start to turn left and stop at a phone box. After dark there was a full scale thunderstorm. My feelings can be imagined. On bedding at 22.00 the lightning was flashing all round, the van guttering spouting like gargoyles. So much for the guide book's 'Mt St Victoire is particularly nice in May or June'.

Local cats welcomed people arriving for work. At 0800 I started on the phoning, through to Touring Secours first. Where was I? Heaven knows so I hijacked a local to take over the call. I'm sent to stand by the road: 'a man with a beard and small book' - an optimistic perusal of the Corsican climbing guide. An exhausting day followed. What became clear was that the VW was going to be *hors de combat* for at least a week till parts could arrive. 'By heavens, I've had to talk French today. And follow directions from garage to garage before ending in the family run VW one. Can't risk Corsica with electrics haywire. Come back for it in a few days? Now, I've somehow to transport everybody's climbing gear to the boat *à pied* by myself and hopefully meet the others arriving by train. I go in to the port and find there was no car vacancy to Corsica for three weeks. So I phoned Mr Pino at VW who must be sick of me and he said he was happy to garage the van till the middle of June. The Pinos were a delightful family and *très sympathetique*. We had companionably finished off a bottle of pleasant Moroccan wine (*Vieux Pâpes*) which I'd only just opened and I offloaded eggs and milk from the van. I had a night in the Hotel Terminus des Ports, also *très sympathetique*. I cut down to the barest essentials but still had to shift a huge Tiso rucksack (c.80lbs), a hefty kitbag and one tent. On my last visit to the Pinos they were already pulling out the engine. I found a crowded eating place by the port; busy usually meant good value, and it was. I needed it. And even the rain had stopped. *That* is another worry: Corsica is great bivvy country - when it's dry. Write this up while everything is fresh in mind. It could have happened on a remote mountain *piste* in the Atlas.'

Don and Martin duly turned up and were loaded up like camels, the *Napoleon* bore us to Ajaccio where Ernst was, helpfully he thought, waiting at the *vehicle* exit! 'Loads of fun and games but at least now a shared game.' My last act before we were departing the camp site by taxi was a dash to the loo. When the handle was pulled the system seemed to explode and I received a jet in my face while another jet shot over the partition to be greeted by female screams. I somehow half-fixed it, all I could do if we were to catch our train for Corte - and fled. Heaven help whoever flushed the loo next. How deliciously relaxing climbing mountains was after all that. I never took my camper abroad again.

THE MATTER OF THE MEIJE

If we ask why then we need to ask why we ask why.

In 2014 Peter Macdonald wrote an article in *Loose Scree* entitled 'Remembering Philip Tranter' which brought out another of life's weird co-incidences. I knew Philip and my climbing log of July 1964 had mentioned seeing his and Blyth Wright's names in a hut book on the Meije. What I learned fifty years on was how we both arrived in La Berarde a week apart, both our gangs camping, and then both burning down tents before heading off for epics on the Meije.

Philip was a super-powered person, interested in everything to do with mountains. He was the first person to make a second round of the Munros, the first to do the 'Tranter Round', one of the ringleaders of the Corriemulzie club; alas, he died in an accident while driving through France on the way back from a good climbing trip in the Hindu Kush. One non-hill memory I have was of the pair of us as guests at some dinner and being rather bored as a Methuselah droned on with his speech. Philip gave me a nudge and whispered the name of a splendid Scottish hill in my ear and we then let our minds drift contentedly as we recalled our various days on its slopes. After a few minutes I whispered another hill name in Philip's ear, and so it went on. (The idea is not copyright.)

Philip, Blyth and a Neill, climbed the Meije in a somewhat

disorderly fashion, arguing and going astray and their slow ascent being punished by an afternoon storm below the glacier, complex route finding and abseils, an avalanche of new snow, and the hut only reached at 9.15 - for a near foodless night. We can all remember such days. Ours was a good steady climb till on the final section. Here's the story of our doings which I recorded not long after in the long-gone *Blackwoods* magazine.

La Meije was the last of the great peaks to live on unclimbed into the last quarter of the nineteenth century. In 1870 the Pic Central was ascended, but it was another seven years before Père Gaspard and his son led the French soldier Boileau de Castelnau up the Grand Pic - 13,081 feet (3987m). It is a mountain of fierce beauty, betraying an uncompromising aloofness and immensity that had impressed the early travellers to the Dauphiné.

The first ascensionists had a hard time of it. Old Gaspard made his will before setting out. Their descent was made in the face of a blizzard and, slowly being covered in an icy crust, they endured a bivouac under the inadequate; protection of an overhanging rock.

There are no easy routes up the Meije, and the traverse is still regarded as 'one of the great classic expeditions in the Alps'. A larger party of us had enjoyed weeks of good climbing in the quiet French Savoy then, while some returned home, four of us headed for La Berarde. The Meije would be a fine conclusion to the season.

Who wouldn't thrill at the road up to La Berarde? My log declared it 'the most exciting I've met in the Alps'. Robert and Dick, were students, I was a teacher and Joe was a former pupil of mine and a gifted climber. We arrived at dusk and started the usual tents up and food on routine. A snooty loud-voiced individual asked us to shush as his baby was trying to sleep. Instead, we soon had the whole campsite awake.

My log recorded: 'Tents up and food on. A few minutes later Dick let go a Gaz cylinder when changing over. It whooshed all over the place. As we had two candles and another couple of stoves alight, the inevitable happened. Boom! Thirty seconds later, with a ring of gibbering French spectators, we were seeing what we could retrieve from Robert's *Mountain* tent. The people next door helpfully threw a bucket of water on the flames - without removing the bacon and butter cooling in the bucket. My *POM* tent was damaged at the entrance facing Robert's. His was completely burnt out. Our posh neighbour then started to tell us what to do. We told him what he could do! Turned in eventually, all squashed in my tent . . .'

There was another Tranter connection here. I'd more than once seen Tranter's ploy of joining up tents for communal efficiency on his 'feich trips' exploring Scotland and I'd copied Tranter's 'Nally' set up with our school parties. Two school Pal-O-Mine tents (*POMs*) were pitched facing each other and linked by an additional flysheet to form a sheltered porch/cooking area - and we had done something similar at La Berarde.

The next morning was spent in tidying up after the night's fiery fiasco. We salvaged what we could. Luckily we were wearing our climbing clothes, and boots, axes, crampons and ropes had been under my flysheet. I sewed up my damaged tent.

After a snack and coffee on a terrace, the four of us shouldered rucksacks and set off up the path beside the Torrent d'Étançons, several miles of easy walking with a profusion of Alpine flowers. We reached the Refuge Châtelleret in about an hour and a half.

On my previous visit we had been there likewise at the end of a grimy, impecunious climbing holiday, and with the hills cloudy and the valley broiling, the necessity for a bath had overcome even the frightfulness of immersing in glacier water. We had stripped to dip in a cloudy pool only to be subjected to a piercing wolf-whistle! Panic! But it was only a marmot.

Marmot sentries were again whistling away as, after a good meal, we continued. Other people were going up too, but knowing the paths through the bouldery moraines, we outdistanced them.

Looking up the Étançons Valley the Meije presents a high wall with a ragged crest ('Like broken glass on top of a dyke,' Joe described it) which splits up the skyline into the various 'Pics'. To the left, tacked on below, like a square handker-chief is the Glacier Carré, which sloped down to a huge cliff which had to be bypassed on the left, by the long projecting buttress of the Promontoire. Below this was a hut, the Chat-elleret, as far as 'tourists' managed. My previous knowledge helped as we wanted to reach the higher Promontoire *refuge* before all 16 beds were taken. There was the usual squalor however and 24 of us crowded in. (This crowded aspect of the Alps, and the general taming of nature, would see me seeking quieter ranges in years to come. My idea of hell is to be imprisoned on an overcrowded bed-shelf in a high hut with no ventilation and regaled all night with an interna-tional orchestra of farts and snores.)

Robert was not going further but was happy to botanise. Dick, Joe and I, rose at three and set off at about three-forty. Three older men were in front as we set off along the *arête* of the Promontoire. Sound rock and bright moonlight made it a delight. Some loathe the early Alpine start, but I find something magical in it, a sort of unutterable basic silence, and a closeness to the material of the world that is almost spiritual.

The climbing was interesting, and after a while we traversed across the flank of the ridge into the Grand Couloir which we then climbed. We had passed the older three and in turn had been passed by five young Frenchmen. The French lads were inclined to knock down stones which funneled on to us. We muttered imprecations at them.

We came out onto a broad terrace called the Pyramide Duhamel, about two hours from the hut. The peaks, Les Bans, the Ecrins, Grande Ruine, the Rateau, all previously climbed, rose out of the mist to catch the rosy first light. We gazed awhile, till others began arriving, then followed the French youths, twisting this way and that up the great face - never very difficult, but good climbing. They went astray not infrequently and we later ignored their route-finding. Above us there was a slovenly crossing of ropes, a constant babble, and every now and then a yell of 'Pierre!'

We arrived at the foot of the Glacier Carré, where our pause to don crampons allowed the older three and another rope of two to go past. As the snow was crisp and firm it seemed strange that they were not wearing crampons. We had to plod slowly in their wake as they cut steps, alongside the Doigt, and the Pic next to it, and along to the Brêche du Glacier Carré. There we left crampons and ice-axes; there was no point in carrying surplus baggage. Only the rocks of the final Grand Pic spired above us, quality rock-climbing pure and simple.

The Brêche is an impressive breach in the wall. Below it lies the Glacier Carré: a steep rectangle of snow ending in a drop of nearly two thousand feet to the Étançon glacier at its base. We had come up the left edge of this rectangle and then along its top edge, hugging the bounding rocks. On the other side of the Brêche the wall falls even more impressively down to La Grave.

There were eight of us clustered in the Brêche, and we watched the five French lads on the 'Cheval Rouge' above us. We had misgivings about following them up rock which looked loose in places, but when the others set off we deemed it safe enough to follow suit.

About two hundred and fifty feet up the crag, there was a yell of 'Pierre!' and a selection of rocks whizzed past with angry whirrings. As we were about to shout our anger, there was another great yell, and looking up I could see a huge pile of boulders bounding down - like a satanic dumper truck spilling a load into a quarry.

Joe was out to the right, on the open face with no protection. Dick flattened into the slot of a chimney. I ducked down under a step. There was only time to crouch where we were. Beyond Joe the other five were tensed, but out of the firing line.

A huge block exploded just above Joe. The rest poured over and about us, various bits bouncing off my rucksack. Helmets were unknown in those days. I only had tiny finger-holds and could have taken no shock, nor could I have held Joe had he been swept off.

I looked down after the falling rocks. Two figures, roped together, were just traversing round into the Brêche. They stood frozen in the line of steps. The careering blocks were exploding into the snow slope, bursting in bubbles like boiling porridge. A chunk the size of a football hit the front figure in the face. He fell over his axe. The second stood, shocked, far enough back to remain unscathed. Moments later the one who was hit slid off down the tilted slope. The second was then dragged off where he stood and the pair went sliding and rolling helplessly down the longest part of the Glacier Carré. They shot off the slope and vanished.

It took forty minutes to get the French to start their woeful descent. The three older Frenchmen did not have crampons. They went between the other two, and crept down as a long rope of five. We crawled behind, staying above them.

We collected our gear, and the two ice-axes from which a bloody track ran down the snowfield. 'At least the first man knew nothing,' Joe murmured. The temperature had risen, the bitter morning cold had swiftly turned to a mist, then sleety rain or snow. Never did a hill seem more ill-set against us.

A rope of three, from a different route, joined us, one a girl who abseiled into our gaze with great *élan*. Now, we were eleven, with the five still descending. Nobody had brought abseil lines. Ours was in the Châtelleret, for a guide had said it was not normally carried. So climbing ropes had to be used. All the party were competent enough but the older men were naturally slower.

The rocks were streaming. I remember seeing vivid blue cushions of Alpine forget-me-nots. The broken bodies were lying about three hundred feet above the foot of the wall - a difficult recovery.

We reached the big terrace at last: no view. Only later did we read the guide-book warning: '*En cas de mauvais temps, les difficultés augmentent rapidement*'.

After a while the others followed us down the Grand Couloir - too soon, for we received a whirring volley of small shot. We took to the side wall and traversed onto the crest of the Promontoire. An 'Aiguille' (Le Gendarme Jaune) was stark against the glacier, but I did not feel like taking photographs.

At the hut Robert had soup ready, then led us down - in

sleet and snow - to the Châtelleret where we had a big meal and gave first-hand accounts to be radioed to the rescuers. The weather cleared as we left the Châtelleret and the Meije stood frostily clear, a thin line still visible down the Glacier Carré. We reached camp at 7pm, and hid, leaving the loquacious French to deal with the newsmongers and gaping tourists, while helicopters flew up and down the valley.

Robert slept under the fly-sheet that night to let us sleep with a modicum of comfort. I'd one exit in the night and was struck by the tranquility of the world asleep, the roughness of reality gone away like dew, the peeping dawn hushed, opaque as a late Turner landscape. Another reality. The next day we bought *Le Dauphiné*. There it was, spread over pages, lots of pictures, interviews, speculation, the lot: '*Drames de la Montagne. Au Glacier Carré dans le Massif de l'Oisans: Deux alpinistes pris sous une avalanche de pierres, dévissent et font une chute de plusieurs centaines de metres.*' French Press language is even more over the top than ours. '*La montagne a de nouveau frappe sans pitié ceux qui l'aiment. Ce matin, deux alpinistes ont inscrit leurs noms sur la liste déjà si longue ... Le premier alpinist ne put éviter les projectiles, et fut frappe en plein visage ...les deux hommes tomber dans le vide ...*' We put the paper aside.

A large helicopter landed near the church, and two long bundles were carried in. We were told the dead pair were brothers. We slept while it rained again, and woke to see the machine - a grotesque insect against the silvery wetness - fly off to Grenoble.

After an 11 hour sleep we washed and dried everything, making an even bigger shambles on the site (you can always pick out the Brits!). I sat in a café to write up my log. We pigged ourselves on a curry enlivened by bananas, currants and peach jam.

We left La Berarde at six-thirty the next morning, creeping out of the sleepy hamlet and down that frightful road along the cliffs. On the back seat, on some bends, you swing right out over the void - much more frightening than climbing!

The others were homeward bound. I went on to Chamonix to wait for a friend with whom I would climb. One night I went in to see Rébuffat's 'Entre Terre et Ciel'. Out to the reality: the town lit up and Mt Blanc high and lifted up above the dark valley, creamy, rosy, as delicate as a wedding cake. 'Beauty can dominate fear. To go upwards is essential,' I wrote in my log, quoting Rébuffat, and fell asleep among the noisy cicadas.

OPENING THE ATLAS

There is no foreign land. It is the traveller only that is foreign.

R L Stevenson

Having been to the Atlas for the winter of 1965-66 and then 1966-67 I more or less fell into the habit of going there regularly: 53 visits to date, usually for three months at a time, sometimes double that, a dozen years of my life in total. The Atlas satisfied at all levels: a great climate to reward all aspects of mountaineering (still in its mysterious exploratory 'Silver Age'), the families and friends made among the welcoming Berber peoples and their companionship on our trekking, the fascinating cultures, history, cuisine and wildlife that became engrossing. And all relatively inexpensive! Morocco became a second home, returning to much that was known, as comfortable as slipping on an old jacket to go out into the garden. Most visits were with friends or others enthused and many returned again and again. I could fill a book alone on the Atlas, well, have done two, *The Mountains Look on Marrakech*, Whittles, 2007, describing the 1000 mile, 96 day end-to-end trek of the Atlas, an excuse to write about every aspect of the mountains and the people and *The*

195

High Atlas (Treks and Climbs on Morocco's biggest and best mountains), Cicerone, 2012, which is as much narrative as guide - and I challenge anyone to look at the pictures and not want to go there. Those pictures are perhaps more 'me' than all the words I've written.

HIGHLANDS AND HIGH ATLAS

When the great Scottish explorer Joseph Thomson tried to cross the High Atlas Mountains in Morocco to the fabled city of Taroudant in 1888 he was stopped by the danger of warring clans on the pass. In Scotland a couple of centuries earlier a Lowlander's journey across the Mounth could well have faced the same problem. Both countries have maps with the names of clans written in large or small print across them. The big difference is that our Scottish clan geographical areas have virtually gone; in Morocco so far there is only a dilution. I am seeing Scotland as it was.

Oldies like myself who were stravaiging north and west half a century and more ago can remember the Highlands before electricity came, can recall the smell of paraffin, trimming wicks or pumping up pressure lamps. When I first started my annual months in the Atlas in 1965 these were replacing acetylene lamps and it is only in the last decade electricity has been making its way into remote mountain villages. Cooking under a Tilley lamp today in the Atlas takes me back to gutting mackerel as a boy by lamplight in a wee scullery under the stairs at Carrick Castle. But it is the Atlas villages themselves, and the Berber lifestyle, that has the greatest similarities.

Crofting hamlets in Highlands or Hebrides tend to have their houses strung out in companionable proximity, their fields attached, communal grazing above; in the Atlas the houses will be more clustered on a spur or barren area with the fields terraced below and the communal grazing above, a very similar pattern and the more I see it the more I notice the similarities.

The casual visitor often comments that women seem to do all the work for they are seen in the fields tending cows or gathering fodder, spreading the laundry to dry or attending to a large brood of infants. Joseph Thomson might have superficially noted the same in Scotland and my comment might parallel his closer study: who do you think built the terraces and houses? Division of labour on these lines is not unique to Atlas and Highlands either; all too often the menfolk had another priority in clan lands: fighting.

As in the Highlands many Atlas valleys will be dominated by a *kasbah* (a castle) where, in times of trouble, there would be temporary shelter. Such might also be the home of a *caïd* (chief) though this was often a later addition. Berber villages were usually determinedly independent and 'ruled' by the elders, a St Kilda parliament if you like. Life in the Atlas hadn't changed in centuries when Joseph Thomson made his observations. Fighting was certainly still common as clan raided clan or made common cause against central government in Fes or Marrakech. A sultan's word meant no more to a Berber chief than did a Stewart's edict to a Lord of the Isles. The historical similarities are striking.

In Scotland, with the disintegration of the clan system and an enforced peace, there was the chance to successfully cultivate more land. The potato made this easier too. The outcome was a population explosion and eventually the surplus was having to move out, to the cities where the Industrial Revolution required workers, or overseas where Britain was painting large areas of the map of the world pink. (The

Clearances were a brutal, unforgivable, extension of the situation, not a cause, the failure of the potato crops a tragic exacerbation.) In my lifetime I have seen this evolution in the Atlas: the equivalent of the blackhouse has gone, replaced by the white and now, not infrequently, the equivalent of a bungalow - but so much more stylishly traditional.

When I cycled about the Highlands as a boy I was never stuck for a bed. If a youth hostel wasn't available I'd just knock on a door and speir and soon be taken in by someone. I was never charged for this hospitality. Wandering in the remote Atlas I've more recently had exactly the same sort of hospitality, something those who only know the tourist traps may find hard to believe. This is my most evocative comparison and one as mysterious: that a people so warlike and independent can also be so friendly and hospitable. They may lack material goods but personal relations, hospitality, friendliness, cultural traditions and family solidarity still survive. For how long? Roads and electricity have seen every village sprout a rash of dish aerials, opening life to the greedy contaminations of the west. Visiting Rousay (Orkney) a few years ago I was told not a single original old family remained. Scots had, and still have, some choice of moving to other lands, young Moroccans don't, a dangerous dissimilarity.

One home I stay in every year is owned by a man named Mohammed but as every other man is a Mohammed he is known as Mohammed Beri, 'Mohammed the sheep', because he once introduced a new breed to the valley. He is also one of the first mountain guides, runs a B&B and acts as travel agent, besides being a crofter, a good replication of the varied jobs needed to maintain a croft today in North Uist say. I've stayed with Donald the Post and Erchie the Bus.

Lingering with us but still important in the Atlas, is the crofting world's system of communal efforts. I can recall, in 1970, when a storm cut the Atlas road to Mohammed's village, someone from each home was required to take tools and go and restore the *piste*. Mohammed was busy so he sent me! But for his most recent house extension he has had contractors in from Marrakech.

Expounding on these similarities on Mohammed's roof terrace someone looked at a flock of sheep and goats drifting across the slopes above cultivation level and pointed out there was a mighty difference between that stony desert and our wet Highlands. But was there? The Atlas landscape, like our own, was once forest, and like our own, was destroyed by man's activities. Overgrazing and mismanagement ever since has made one no less desert than the other: one is simply dry desert, one wet desert. Joseph Thomson noted geological similarities too: in Morocco all laid bare, in Scotland covered in a poverty of grass or heather or bog.

One old tradition which has completely gone from Scotland but is very much alive in the Atlas is taking flocks up to the summer grazing grounds, the *shielings* (Scotland) or *azibs* (Atlas). Looking south from Marrakech with its old mud walls and palm groves it is almost shocking to see a horizon to horizon mountain range bright with snow. Three times higher than the Scottish Highlands the practicalities were the same: after snow melt and spring growth and seed-setting the flocks wended up to higher ground to live in pretty basic shelters till the frosts of autumn and the dying grass would send them down again. A Seton Gordon description of shieling life a century ago sounds like an Atlas description of today.

Though the mountains look so impoverished, where there is water, two crops a year are taken. Winter barley will be harvested in May, and maize sown, which is then harvested in October. As with all farming there are periods of intense activity and times of quiet, all the more hectic in the Atlas because of its greater variety of crops than is ever possible in our soggy, windy world. They have such honest weather in the Atlas.

Because it is basically crofting with small fields on steep valley flanks work is still done by the sweat of men's brow - and women's too. Any hamlet will have a group of round, flat areas with a post in the centre: the threshing floor. When ready the grain is trampled on by a line of mules going round and round. It is then winnowed by hand. On the plains, as in our Lowlands, the whole process is completely mechanised but this has not had the same detrimental effect. Crofting thrives in the Atlas.

Ploughing is primitive but effective for the situation, a simple wooden hand plough with the *sock* and *coulter* metal parts we see so often on gravestones in Scotland. Mills are frequently still water-powered, made from local materials of stone and wood and designed exactly like the Viking-style mills once used in Orkney or Shetland. Many homes will have a loom. I've a butter churn at home which is made of recycled tin that was meant for sardine cans. Recycling is nothing new in either setting. The similarities are endless but perhaps truer of the Highlands fifty or a hundred years ago. The Atlas however had kept its isolation and independence longer.

A decade after Joseph Thomson another Scot trying to reach Taroudant was Robert Cunninghame Graham. Failing at the same pass for the same reason he tried to sneak over by a remoter route only to be arrested by one of the 'Lords of the Atlas', the great chiefs who had come to dominate, rather as the Campbells had in the Highlands earlier. Gavin Maxwell's *Lords of the Atlas* tells their equally bloody story which only ended with Morocco's independence in 1956. Very recent history.

When Joseph Thomson travelled there, or at this time of Hooker, Ball and Maw a decade earlier, the Atlas was completely *terra incognito*. Thomson was the first to correctly speculate on what was the highest Atlas summit but it was not climbed till a dozen years after the South Pole was reached. The Berbers, like the Highlanders, had every reason to be both suspicious and antagonistic. Morocco was the closest country to Europe but the last in Africa to be grabbed by a continental power. Neither Highlands nor Atlas wanted outside interference or exploitation.

Both would succumb, the Atlas much more recently. Seeing the greater prosperity of the towns they agitated for a greater share of comforts, hence the move to have electricity in the mountain villages (Morocco is rich in hydro power) and road access of some sort, whether dirt track or tarmac, which allows the export of produce so much more easily. I can recall some years ago on a rugged pass, the path longer and harder than the Tourist Path on Ben Nevis, meeting a string of 90 laden mules. They were carrying sacks of potatoes, the equivalent of, from Corrour say, along to Ben Nevis, up and down it (the equivalent of the pass), to their nearest town (Ft William) there to find lorries to take the spuds to market in the Lowlands. The villages they came from are now linked by road. And didn't the Wade and Caulfeild roads not subdue the Highlands more effectively than armies?

Scotland's connections with Morocco were strong. Through much of the nineteenth century Britain's representative in the country was Sir John Drummond Hay while another confidante of the Sultan and his military man was the exotic Caïd Sir Harry Maclean, from a Morven family (the museum in Tobermory has some of his artifacts). And, in 1901, with isolation crumbling, Isabella Bird (with homes in Tobermory and Edinburgh) rode over the mountains to the great castle of the most notorious Lord of the Atlas. Morocco could so easily have become British but in the great carve up of the world at the start of the twentieth century the deal was France had Morocco, Britain got Egypt.

The world-dominating Romans pushed into Morocco (their Mauritania) but, when they came up against the Atlas Highlanders, went no further. In Britain they pushed north only to find a like unconquerable people and, with a certain despair, built a couple of walls. Some similarities go far back! Both sets of Highlanders have always remained aloof, separated from Lowlands by language and traditions, shielded by geography and with the armour of history. I find myself at home in both cultures.

DOING TIME AT TACHDDIRT

- and there's always the interior of Morocco

Saki

Tachddirt was interesting as a climbing base because it offered both summer rock climbing and winter climbing at the same time depending on which side of the valley one decided to exploit. Angour's big rock face looked south and the Moroccan sun soon stripped off the snow while, Aksoual, a huge sprawl of mountain presented a north aspect of Himalayan snow. When our 1965 expedition gear was held up by a dock strike - in the UK - Rog and I headed south from Tangier for a recce and went up to Oukaïmeden, the small ski resort, hired skis and from the top of Jbel Oukaïmeden saw over to Aksoual and were mightily impressed - as had been Tom Weir and Douglas Scott a decade earlier. When built, pre WW2, the lift on Oukaïmeden was the highest in the world (and makes a few initial days skiing a good way of acclimatising). Rog and I skied over the Tizi n'ou Addi (*tizi* is pass or col) to Tachddirt and liked what we saw. There was a *Club Alpine Francais* (CAF) *refuge* built in 1929, more bothy than alpine hut, but beside the highest permanently occupied village in the Atlas (2314m), and sandwiched between the great peaks of Angour and Aksoual, it would become a favourite base.

When we eventually winkled our gear out of Tangier we did a deal with one Brian, who hailed from Papitoetoe in New Zealand, that he would take us and the clobber to the Atlas in his Land Rover in return for our adding him to our three months of Atlas explorations. Brian had been world-wandering for years. He was an aircraft engineer and whenever finances ran low would go to the nearest airport and invariably find work. He wisely kept off the climbing, unlike Leo, the last member of our group. Leo was a good skier, Rog and I beginners, but he was game to try 'proper climbing'. This January, the south face of Angour was still very snowy and Aksoual looked like some melting *meringue glacé* confection. We had come on a particularly snowy winter.

Tachddirt was also our first stepping into the local culture. We had hired a mule to carry our gear over the pass from the road-end base at Imlil and this was led by a delightful wee muleteer, Bourgemâa. On arrival we had some food and invited Bourgemâa to join us at the table - which got dirty looks from a French group on the terrace above. Not done it seemed. Rog was small too and he and Bourgemâa set to later on for some wrestling, Cumberland-style. The French were scandalised. When we eventually returned to Imlil[1] we were invited up to Bourgemâa's home for supper and a real friendship with the family began. Near the end of the season someone in the village had been fined a goat, which was slaughtered and divided among the households. And a small portion was allocated to us. We were part of the community. We very soon allowed families we lived with, or trekking helpers, to provide our meals: home produce, fresh and tasty, uncontaminated by any processing. Bourgemâa and I once raced each other from Imlil to the Lepiney Hut, a five hour tramp which we did in 3½ hours. Bourgemâa and mule won but he sat in the hut wracked with coughing for the rest of the day. Sadly, he was tubercular and had to go and live in Casablanca for his health. His 'business' was continued by small brother Mohammed who would be our chief helper over the next forty Moroccan years. After the second year we always lived with the family, rather than at the Imlil refuge. His Targa Imoula became my second home.

Really the only facilities of the Tachddirt hut were iron bunks, a tap with concrete basins, and a separate loo block, hole in the floor style (but a hole in the wall made it 'a loo with a view'). The setting was what mattered and with its terraces edged with almond blossom and the constant sun we had 'a kingy fester spot' as Rog put it. An early log entry reads: 'The village at sunset was busy with herds coming in. The houses are all huddled on top of each other, built of mud or stone, flat-roofed and with few windows - in the better ones these are painted white round an iron grill. The beasts are herded in at night (warm farm smells). Fires are of scrub, which is carried home in huge bundles that bow the women double. Women are unveiled and favour orange colours in their garb. The men wear *djellabas* and tattered *selhams*. The children are very poorly clad. No lights go on at night and there is no sign of life until the sun hits the village at 09.30. Blue smoke leaks out then and the animals wend off to scrape food from the barren slopes'.

My log also mentions our getting to grips with Angour, a mixed rock and snow ascent which, to me, was more interesting than just rock climbing. 'Hard to know where to begin this day, the biggest any of us have ever had. Must have been 3000 feet of climbing, mostly III but, at times V, always interesting [euphemism for scary!], very exposed but with the sharpest clarity to Aksoual.

'We started at a snow gully as the sun hit us, a tricky, thrutchy 100 foot up to a spike, one essential foothold an icicle. The frozen fall above was tried then Rog went round, right, to gain a nice rock rib instead. After those test pieces we had some easy snow plodding then sloped up to a gully on rock. After a bite we move together for about 400 feet, up to the foot of a huge rock face split by cracks. Complex moves led to a chimney (VS) which began with a cave pitch. Rog stood on my head there and made a good lead on. Slings helped Leo and we had to haul up our sacks. The route became quite sustained with few alternatives. Scramble onto a knob, then descend slightly and up on snowy ledge with a belay in a cave with the exit round and up a wee frozen waterfall. More rock and snow led to a wafer of snow to gain the top of the big crag. Up another rock rib we stop for some food: spicy sardines, lemon-water, an orange, Kendal Mint Cake.'

The climb was very mixed but rockier higher up, and the rock very friable. Often the big buttresses were flakes/prows jutting out, each having to be climbed (endless chimney pitches), or bypassed on snow gullies. Belays were often somewhat token. Rog led most of the route, often ahead, while I looked after Leo who was, after all, on his first real day's climbing. We joined the plateau of this strange mountain at what appeared the highest point of this big face of cliffs and gullies, and trudged through snow the 400 yards to the 3614m summit.

Angour is a great plateau *berg* with cliffs round three sides, gently sloping on top, with a stream draining its heart and slowly changing from small mountain stream to cliff-girt gorge waters. The *voie normal* heads up from the Tizi n' Tachddirt to break through crags and follow round between the stream course and off-side cliffs: a very atmospheric approach - our way off, reaching Tachddirt at 16.45. Brian had tea ready.

Aksoual, in contrast, proffered miles of mountain facing towards Tachddirt, a very jagged crest, mostly over 3700m and the highest point 3910m. I'd read about Tom Weir and Douglas Scott climbing the face and could pick out their line. Right of it a more continuous ridge ran all the way to the highest point, the longest, most dominant feature. Rog and I set our hearts on this. Let me quote the Weir/Scott day on the mountain, to compare with ours. They also had come over from Oukaïmeden.

'At 5am the fire was lit, eggs boiled in the tea water, a quick breakfast scoffed, and with food in the rucksack, rope and ice axes at the ready, we were away down into the depths of a gorge to ford the river by jumping from boulder to boulder, then climbing over a hill shoulder lying between us and our mountain. In daylight this took only one hour. In darkness, as we were to discover fourteen hours later, it was a very different and heart-breaking story. Everything was frozen hard, the steep snow just above the gorge forcing us to cut steps even at modest angles, then by a gully we reached iced rocks and scrambled steeply out of shadow into sunshine on a silver saddle surrounded by red rock towers projecting against a blue sky. It was good to be alive and faced by a real exploratory problem on virgin ground.

'Our reconnaissance of yesterday was paying dividends. We recognised the rock rib which we knew would lead us to a bulging overhang, by-passable by going left on snow. What we had not bargained for, however, was the snow getting soft so quickly, forcing us to stay on the rocks, playing a game of hide-and-seek between the overhang and the snow, enjoying thrilling situations that continued for 3000 feet, and led us to another of our landmarks, a rock arête which we hoped to climb for 1500 feet to its top. It proved easier than it looked so we were able to move together, and at 2.30pm we stepped on to the summit, the climb having taken eight hours with only three halts for food, delightful halts on sunny ledges.'

I've several times checked the figures but the gorge crossings at Tachddirt is 2291m and Aksoual's summit 3910m, the difference 1619m, 5311 feet. Knock off a thousand feet for the easy slopes up to the start it still left a lot to tackle in a day. With the great depth of snow and underestimating the scale Rog and I flogged about half way up before realising it was not going to 'go' that day, even having set off at 05.30. You cannot hurry progress in heavy snow. The next year I was determined to 'bag this plum'.

The following year nine of us hired an old Bedford minibus for £60 and drove out to Morocco[2]. Rog, keener on rock, went off for Anghromer, 3892m (below the Tizi n' Tachddirt) which we'd traversed on the first season, and seen good rock possibilities, (we'd a fantastic return on ski from that outing), so Clive, a Lakes guide, joined me for Aksoual. To deal with the scale we set off the day before and climbed up to bivouac left of the ridge proper, saving several hours.

We had a miserable night, a big boulder being no shelter from a sneaky cold wind and we spent the time fighting for warmth. I'd my head in a snow hole and my cagoul over my rucker into which I'd wiggled as far as possible. I noticed Colin moving elsewhere. Rising is easier in such circumstances, but before we returned to the hut we'd be on the go for 23 hours. Just as well we didn't know.

We spent the first two hours just going up a fine arête to reach the crest of the main ridge. And we enjoyed the climbing, easy enough snow with lots of rocky steps (and chimneys to surmount them). After 700 feet we left a cairn, crossed a gap, another chimney to a rake across a tower, another 600 feet, then more dodging and chimneys, another 600 feet. Memories are vague. Too much to assimilate and no note-taking Rog. I'd a long break on top of one pinnacle as Clive had to retrieve his dropped ice axe. (Later on the trip he bashed his head with the said axe and was patched up by Gavin Maxwell of all people - of whom, see the end of 'Walking the Song', Ch 5.) There were successive towers, each giving good climbs though I noted it was 15.00 when confronting the fourth tower, 'tired, late, with heavy sacks, we skirted it on steep snowfields, then the crest up to the summit crags. Cut round behind them into the sun, unrope, and plod on, then more step-cutting on hard snow and a final scramble to the 3910m (12,714 ft) summit, 17.00'.

We took lots of photographs and hoped to reach the Tizi Likemt (3555m) in the light remaining. This pass is about 3400m, a great summer slog and famous ski descent in winter. We could sit and bum slide all the way down. We should have read Weir more carefully. The sun set, all too soon, in a swank of colour. 'We brewed and continued by torchlight. A 3769m peaklet was a pech, Colin feeling exhausted. Every variety and size of gendarme gave good scrambling under the starlight. I found a species of saxifrage I didn't know. Colin noted a Painted Lady[3], and there were dainty Alpine accentors about. A sheltered sandy spot called for our bivvy. We slept for two hours, until the stars misted and a wind again made life intolerable. We brewed, relished instant apple flakes, and set off, Colin refreshed, I feeling weary and my torch reduced to a dying flicker. We coped with some big gendarmes and at last had the Tizi Likemt looking nearer. Snow slopes shooting off to the left at a reasonable angle tempted us. Just going downhill would be bliss.

Out came our axes. We descended funnel after funnel, gully after gully, on every type of snow, just praying there would be no vertical drops. We finally exited onto big snow slopes. My turn to be whacked and I had a 45 minutes snooze while Colin brewed and then we spanked on down. The snow became harder down the Tizi Likemt corrie and then, luckily, we hit the known water channel and its path which we followed along to its start at the gorge mouth. We soon set the dogs of the village howling and reached the refuge at 04.15. Of course the guardian had locked up, perforce, we bivvy again on the terrace.

While at Oukaïmeden, Tom and Douglas had noted a gully along from Aksoual's summit towards the Tizi Likemt which they planned to use on their descent, once they found it. Here's their variant from the summit. '. . . something ominous was happening to the weather. Our immediate concern was our couloir of descent, and how to get across the rock towers between us and it, for they were more formidable-looking at close range than they had appeared from far below. Wasting no time, we dropped to the foot of the first one, saw there was no direct way up but threading the face like a barrel hoop was a snow tilted ledge, dangerously soft and exposed to a big drop, a tense traverse that took us to the base of the second tower, where the mist was curling. This one had an obvious line of weakness, and in forty feet of difficult rock climbing we were on easy ground leading us to an airy summit crest, with an abrupt drop to the final tower. This one we took direct by its steep arête, Scott vanquishing its overhanging edge as if he were starting the day and not on the exposed top of a remote mountain after long hours of hard climbing.

'Now to get off this last one and find the couloir! In mist and snow it is hard to judge distance. We knew we should not proceed too far, so at a likely place started down, slowly at first, then when no rocks interrupted, we decided it would be safe to sit on our backsides and let gravity slide us down. It was exhilarating, we were moving fast and in good control, until suddenly we had to throw ourselves back on our ice axes and brake on the edge of a drop. Nothing for it now but to uncoil the rope, and climb down a series of awkward pitches of rock and ice.

'Once down this we were in the true gully and realizing that until now we had been in a side branch. Daylight was going fast and we fairly shot down the next 1000 feet. Darkness was winning the race, however, not only the darkness of night but the darkness of storm. It was time to get out the torch ... a flash ... a crackle of thunder, followed by stinging hailstones the size of small peas ...

'Torch in hand and blinded by frequent stabs of forked lightning, we stumbled down the gully, keeping to the centre as far as possible in order to avoid holes, like miniature crevasses penetrating to the stream running far below. The peaks were clear now, as we could see when each flash of lightning outlined them in quivering purple. There was a nightmarish quality about the remainder of the descent in a wet world of ravines and waterfalls, loose stones and side-gullies ... It has been remarked that electric storms can have an invigorating effect on tired men ...' And, when they reached the hut they found the guardian had locked their food cupboards, (but not the door) so it was supper-less to bed.

'We certainly slept well that night, and once we got the cupboard opened put the eggs in the pan and ate a hearty breakfast before taking a leisurely walk round Tachddirt to greet the villagers, have a tour around and enjoy the plentiful bird life: shorelarks, black wheatears, lesser kestrels, black redstarts, alpine swifts, rock buntings, choughs, partridges, grey wagtails, dippers and woodpeckers as well as common species.'

After good new routes on Tazharhat or classics like the OSO on Toubkal, and a visit to the Lac d'Ifni Rog and I returned to Tachddirt for one last big climb on Angour. In the intervening weeks the snow had largely vanished. A bit like Aksoual, this would go up the Central Buttress. Remember this was at a time when all one carried were a couple of slings and krabs, a few pitons and nuts which came from one's garage rather than Tiso's. Neither of us had helmets or harnesses - they hadn't been invented. Climbing was serious. One just could not fall. Rog was more into rock climbing than I was but confessed we'd 'rather pushed the boat out'. A very interesting day.

One climb is rather like another. My early delight was having half a dozen lesser kestrels flying around and, all day, the usual choughs who seemed to be making personal remarks. I'll swear they were laughing at my becoming completely wedged when struggling behind a chockstone in one of the endless chimneys. I could neither go up, nor down, my rucksack was jammed, and Roger hauled ineffectively from above.

I was amused by Rog's making a careful route description (Scottish traditions were freer) for it soon went crazy. He described half a dozen pitches between 70 and 150 feet, varied comfortable climbing at a good enough standard, then simply recorded, 'Climb straight up, 960ft' - and meant just that. The featureless rock simply had no belays and no protection. Pitons were useless. One overhang disintegrated on us. In the end we largely moved together, the most delicately footed cats in the country. The exposure had teeth. If either of us made a mistake we'd both be disgustingly dead. I count it the most alarming situation I've ever been in on a mountain. Interminable. We had seven very interesting hours from start to plateau. Rog graded the day IV, V, D/TD. ['Very interesting' in this case was 'brown trousers scary'.]

I never did anything like that again in the Atlas, partly no doubt because I quite fancied living to a ripe old age and partly because climbing itself was changing with the explosive arrival of new technology which, for me, saw climbers loaded down with gear and too much time spent static. I wanted to move. On another Angour route my log noted, 'Long periods freezing while Rog struggled up. Not fun at all'. Technology put me off harder climbing. And in the Atlas there was an element of mountaineering that was proving irresistible: the magic of ongoing exploration. Here was a range like the Alps with next to nothing known or recorded for much of it. We began simply to head off into the unknown on regular treks, taking in peaks and climbs *en passant*, eyeing other lures and going for them, with camping, staying in villages, and all with companionable muleteers' beasts doing the donkey work. Moving was the thing, milestoned by cryingly-beautiful camping spots. This led eventually (1995) to a 96 day, 1000 mile end-to-end Atlas traverse and in the record of that I put a symbol against the best camp spots - and realised I was marking them all. (Tom Longstaff, writing to W H Murray said, 'Mark your red-letter days by camps not summits - no time there.) Three of us finished these baptismal years with a journey that hooked me completely.

We started from the Lepiney Refuge and ascended a 3000ft gully up the face of Tazharhart, a vast plateau but, unlike tilted and drained Angour, it offers a 'desert de pierres, plat, nu, vide, si haut perché qu'on n'aperçoit rien sous le ciel'. We traversed it to drop down into the Agoundis valley to stay in a house, well fed by delightful people but, for the only time ever, were ferociously devoured by bugs all night. The next day we hired a mule as far as it could manage as we went up and down through very wild, uninhabited country to end at a *tizi* at dusk, looking down a long gully to the Lac d'Ifni. We cramponed down 2000 feet by moonlight and found the perfect bivvy spot under a huge boulder.

The *lac* had icebergs floating on it. Beyond is the start of the south-flowing Tifnout river, the infant Souss which then drains all southwards along to the sea at Agadir, and had a dirt track following its course. We hoped for a lift out and, at the first village, came on a lorry with a big log on it (valuable walnut we learned later) but he insisted he was going east, not south, to a place not named on our map. That however might lead helpfully on to the main Tizi n' Tichka road over the Atlas so next day we literally rode the log all day long as it ground its way along below the mountains. The driver took us in for the night and the next day an even bigger lorry continued going east, under what we would call our 'Ridge of Dreams' (Chapter 8). This time, there were two huge trunks with a third on top. Slow travel but largely painless - on legs and feet anyway. We duly reached the main Ouarzazate - Marrakech road. And the rain rained. The scale, the wildness, had been astonishing, the people encountered so friendly and hospitable, this had to be the future. Doing time at Tachddirt was to open doors to many of the richest experiences of a lifetime. Hamadula.

---

[1] Imlil then was *only* the car park, CAF hut and small guardian's hut; hard to believe seeing today's thriving town.

[2] Two incidents with this van are worth recording. Thanks to the bad roads we lost one of the big bulbous headlights when driving across Spain. This didn't really matter as we never drove at night but going down to

Marrakech on one occasion we were pulled up by a policeman at the entrance roundabout who told us we should have two headlights and to have it fixed. A few weeks later we had exactly the same encounter: same place, same policeman. He was a bit narked and told us he could fine us on the spot. Bedford headlights not being likely in the *souks* and we being financially distressed again we did nothing. Finally, well-laden, leaving the Atlas for good on the long haul home we were somewhat nervously nearing the inescapable roundabout when, oh no! there was the same policeman.

A fair cop. What happened then struck me as being so very Moroccan. A stork was carrying a stick for its nest in the city and as we reached the point of no return the policeman turned to follow the bird's flight until we had passed.

Somewhere on the Atlantic coast a day or two later we came on a sandy strand which proved irresistible. Everyone, except me, stripped off to race for the rushing rollers. I'd a foot in a duvet boot to protect a big toe which I'd broken a few days earlier - while bird watching. (I'd spotted a brambling, far south of its range, and was racing terrace to terrace keeping it in sight when I went sliding down a bank and bang onto my toes. There was an audible snap.) So I was told to put the kettle on.

When I looked later on I couldn't see any sign of the revellers till there was some movement among the dunes. When I looked through the binoculars it was to see heads pop up and then disappear or a crawling body slither down a slope. What were they up to? As the bird-watcher of the party I was blamed for their experience: thousands and thousands of swallows were migrating northwards, going hell for feather, and the lads were convinced they were at risk of being hit. Visions of what that might mean ('I didn't want one going right through me,') led to them taking the evasive action I'd seen.

[3] Bristol University arranged for us to mark Painted Ladies, and some Bath Whites, butterflies which crossed the Sahara from West Africa, flew over the Atlas Mountains, and then the Bay of Biscay, to reach the West Country, an astonishing migration. We did so happily enough but we did wonder what the local shepherd boys reported home when they saw us rushing around like madmen with our huge nets. When in full flow tens of thousands of butterflies would be blowing through like autumn leaves. Some we marked turned up in Clifton itself! The marking involved making small dots of coded colours on the thorax.

The Ridge of Dreams

> *...the fatalism necessary to the enjoyment of Morocco.*
> E. Wharton: *In Morocco*

I've a snapshot of three dusty, sweaty, scruffy climbers, in stocking soles, hands dangling mountain boots, standing among sprawling tourists by the swimming pool of the posh *Grand Hotel du Sud* in Ouarzazate. The pool was not to be denied. We'd not washed in over a week. I did warn, 'Jump in. Don't dive, or you'll have your Y-fronts round your ankles - or worse'. The place name looks a bit of a mouthful but *Ou* in a name is a *Wa* sound and a final *e* is not pronounced - so try growling Waar-zaz-at. In 1979 Ouarzazate still had a feel of *Desert Song* about it, the edge of cultivation, *Beau Geste* desert close by and, thankfully, this first posh hotel up on the hill above the *souks*. But, best explain why we were there.

If you cross the Atlas from Marrakech to Ouarzazate over the great pass of the Tizi n' Tichka there is no doubting what a barrier the Atlas Mountains make. Looking up to the western aspect of the range from Ouarzazate they give the impression of a long rampart, a defensive wall, as if safeguarding the citadel Jbel Toubkal, at 4167m the highest summit in North Africa.

From that mountain heart which I'd come to know well my eye had often been drawn from Toubkal eastwards along that undulating crest, 60km without dropping below 3200m. What a traverse it would make! I found no record of other visits - so there were no 'helps'*. With my long longing it became our 'Ridge of Dreams': well worth waiting for but it could so easily have proved a 'Ridge of Nightmares'.

Technically it was not difficult but its remoteness was serious and escape would be difficult and long: either down to the desert south, miles (days) from any easy way back over the range, north into some of the roughest, most vertically-challenged country. Towards the Toubkal end, when I first went to Morocco, the highest crest peak was 4001m, Iferouane, which made it a lure for friends who had done all the Toubkal 4000-ders. It was then lowered to 3996m. In 1922 it was climbed by a French party under the impression it was the highest summit in the Atlas. It wasn't but from it they realised Toubkal was and in 1923, after one attempt stormed off, Toubkal was climbed for the first time by outsiders. The Atlas was - is - not tame country. The Iferouane end of the crest saw some multi-day ski mountaineering trips over the years but there have been almost no other visitors.

Our team came together in 1979: Patrick, whose two weeks off from engineering on the rigs set our parameter, his friend Peter (both competent climbers) and Patrick's older brother Tom who was roped in though not a regular hillgoer - and, ironically, would be the only one to complete the trip unscathed. On March 6 I spent a frantic day at our Imlil base on the logistics and then getting the packing done, everything into man/day loads and arranging four locals to porter up the first brutal ascent. There had been no time to acclimatise for the trio. They were somewhat reeling with the culture shock of Marrakech and the wild beauty of the drive to Imlil - in a crowded bus and more crowded shared taxi.

March 7 saw us leave Imlil before dawn, which greeted us on the Around flood plain of the now popular 'Toubkal Trail', then it was on up to the shrine of Sidi Chamharouch where a twist in the valley leads on up to the Toubkal *refuge* and the highest mountain's ascent routes. At the shrine however we turned off up for the Tizi n' Tagharat, 3456m which had been the climax of a British expedition in 1879, the first real Atlas mountaineering sortie - by Joseph Hooker

(Kew fame), John Ball (first AC president) and George Maw, the last alone reaching the *tizi* (col), encased in blizzard snow. From shrine to *tizi* is about 6000 feet. Our four cheery helpers stopped for mint tea at the shrine and caught us up when we were putting on crampons at the snowline 2000ft up. They borrowed our ice axes, leaving us feeling a bit naked, but as they were romping up in *djellabas* and wellies it seemed a fair distribution of resources. We cramponed up the gully for 3000ft.

On the *tizi* we took one look at the big snow basin beyond and a 500ft rise to another col, where our traverse proper would be launched and promptly bribed the lads to carry on to there. We were weary and ready for brews, and they had carried up our 40lb packs while we carried nothing. Cloud had kept the sun off the ascent gully so it didn't soften as expected and on the way down one of the porters had a long slide. We never did learn the full story.

Patrick was feeling sick with the altitude but we still shouldered the packs and made for the Tizi n' Terhaline, rejoicing to be on our crest. Tom later confessed to being rather overwhelmed by where he was and at his first bivouac experience. Like most this simply involved scraping out a ledge (ice axes have many uses) and lying in the excavation - lined perhaps with prickly scrub under our Karimats. We had our only meal of fresh produce and I'd sneaked up a bottle of *Vieux Pâpes* so there was an incongruous mix of roughing it and living it up. We happily drank Patrick's share of the wine. 'Mogadons' helped the twelve hours of darkness to pass. With the brilliant stars of Africa overhead most bivouacs were a joy.

The pattern was there from the start: rising just before dawn to melt snow or use prepared water for brews, a couple of hours on the go (to warm up), breakfast (super-muesli and brews), then a regular pushing on with brews every few hours till mid-afternoon when we'd dig or build our bivouacs and prepare our one main meal. For four days of this (the easy part) the weather played cat-and-mouse with us but sunsets were always explosively spectacular and nights a chilly extravagance of stars.

Names won't mean much, even if pronounceable, but the Tizi n' Ouourai, at 3200m was the lowest point of the whole trip. Wind and the constant threat of snow led us to an *azib* (goat shelter) but it was full of snow. The scale impressed: two hours just vanished cramponing up to the ridge for another long giant, Adrar-n-Dern, 3853m. We outflanked Iferouane, 3996m to dump our loads and then tick off this highest unladen. Lunch was salami and *biscottes* (toast), which had the unfortunate trade name 'Grim'. Snow showers swept by yet somehow never caught us. This was all easy ground but the long ridges of poor snow were tiring. A black sky hurried us down to the next *tizi* bivvy. Jbel Sirou (Sirwa) the volcanic plug to the south, which joins High with Anti Atlas was plastered white. A big storm grumbled to the north. In the morning our bivvy bags were ice-lined. This was mentally draining for me. The others hadn't experienced lightning or a serious storm on big mountains nor could imagine what any retreat would entail, and we were away out on a limb.

The Tizi n' Tighremt c. 3400m was one of the few summer passes over the range, beyond lay the heart of the Ridge of Dreams, where we'd not drop below 3700m again. We had a conference there over a needed brew. This was our last reasonable escape line to the south. Abort? Though early we decided to bivvy and decide in the morning. The wind blew both ways over the col in turn, it snowed, but sunset somehow burnt off the grey and across the desert we could see the lights of Ouarzazate.

Faith was rewarded, dawn came clear, barometer rising. With regular discipline we traversed peaks and brewed on the cols, a twist in the ridge taking us northwards so on that night we saw the lights of Marrakech. Valley cloud had dispersed and when sunset burned itself out the cold was ferocious (3728m). I was writing my log till too dark to see and at that instant a full moon rose as if a light had been switched on, the mountain world painted ghostly white. 'Absolutely superb, whatever the bivvy brings,' were my last diary words.

My sleeping bag was inadequate and, thoroughly chilled, on rising, my innards just emptied and I faced our most serious day feeling rotten and with no calorie-intake. We were now committing to the three major peaks, switching progress, as it were, from Mamores to Cuillin in a step. We had an abrupt waking as we moved onto exposed but impeccable rock, one roof giving a classic *à cheval* stretch which reminded me of the Bietschhorn. Peter was in his element, searching out the 'good bits', grinning at us. I skipped eating, the thought of salami made me retch, so I wandered on slowly. Traversing the Western Zat peak, 3850m, had me whacked. Was this what cyclists called 'the knock'? We had a long break before climactic Taska n' Zat, 3912m, our highest point since five days before on Iferouane. I could still appreciate the buttress of pink granite that led to the small flat highest 3912 point. Peter had a brew waiting for me, its effect quite noticeable in a spurt of energy.

The 3818m East Zat peak lay ahead of us and we pushed on to try and get beyond it where a descent would be more practical if needed. The barometer was falling. We gained this last big summit in failing daylight but the ground beyond was harder, not easier, so we bivvied where we were, c. 3800m. Peter gave me his warmer bag and we all snuggled together for warmth. Tom dosed me with a cocktail of pills. We all slept well.

I was a bit wobbly to start and as Tom had not climbed much we roped for what was an enjoyable climb down. By the foot I was hungry, even for salami. Obviously better. But Peter wasn't: he had torn a knee ligament. (Doctor Tom hoped it would reduce his speed a bit.) The western sky was a wall of black, the barometer in freefall, but we were through. Descent now would only entail a day's march to reach the Tizi n' Tichka road. We set off down.

After about 1000ft of cramponing we sat on our bottoms and slid the next 3000ft, to Peter's relief. Gorges, crags, sheep trods, complex ground, but *down*. We came on an *azib* beside a stream. Tea without melting snow! We brewed and brewed. We made our main meal to savour the spot then it was on down to the dirt-track, the under-the-Atlas road, playing pied piper to children at a village but the tail falling away as night fell. We had our seventh bivouac, aware that the rolling clouds were down on the ridge, almost certainly snowing hard up there.

Long johns and mitts were bound round Peter's knee and he hobbled the morning away. When he reached Agouim on the Tichka road we'd already demolished several litre bottles of fizzy drink. Peter only had a mouthful before we squeezed into a communal taxi for Ouarzazate. We were hitching in both directions: north for the long Atlas crossing to Marrakech, our base, or to nearer Ouarzazate, south, for immediate relaxation, hence our odd presence in the poshest hotel in town. The next day the 2260m summit of the Tizi n' Tichka to Marrakech was sheeted in ice and the spindrift blowing wildly. Nobody needed to comment. We had escaped a 'Ridge of Nightmares' and can keep our 'Ridge of Dreams'.

*Michael Peyron, doyen of the Atlas, noted an Italian party traversing this
    ridge in the 1930s and a French ski traverse by Cominelli was also
    made in the 1970s.

COASTING WITH CAMELS

*My dream was of big dunes, lying listening to the songs of
surf, eyes bright with sunset and the ocean's shine.*

One lesson learned: don't pitch a tent downwind from a
camel. Camels leak. And every dog in the district will enjoy
overlaying the impregnation. I don't think Vango would
approve.

Definition: a camel is a creature designed by a crazy
committee. An old enough observation but living with the
brutes again recently didn't alter the basic accuracy. What
else, besides a hedge trimmer, could tackle an argan tree,
Arganier spinosum with its warning scientific definition? We
had plenty of argan forest, limestone plateaux, flowery cliff
tops and vast strands for our short trek down the coast with
camels. [The tree is now *A. sideroxylon.*]

Trekking in the Atlas is among the world's best and
has enthralled me for a lifetime. No centrist activity can
match the natural progression of going on, day after day,
up valleys, over passes, taking in peaks and pleasant places
with good companions, in an improved climate and with
surprising comfort. Mules are normally used to carry all the
gear so one walks unencumbered and mules mean muleteers
(good companions too) to look after them - and us. Picture
a standard day.

Up early, sunrise pictures on setting out, cool and refreshed,

221

tents down and the muleteers left to strike the mess tent, load, follow, overtake and be on site for the arrival in early afternoon, mess tent up and brews ready. The early start always pays off, walking in the cool, finishing in the heat, giving the day room to breathe, to relax, to have time 'to sit and stare'. All one carries during the day is some food and water, some defences against the sun or wind and, of course, the camera. On arrival, a space is cleared of stones and thorns and the tents pitched, brews consumed and the day free, to wander, look at birds and flowers, photograph sites and sights, read, write up diaries, apply plasters, enjoy a dram - the thousand and one notes that go to making a harmonious day. Supper and sunset, and another day has sped away. Time stands still at the start of a trek but goes supersonic by the end.

I first met camels in the Central Atlas where the Jbel Sahro Aït Atta tribe have grazing rights in return for an association two hundred years ago when various tribes actually combined to halt the eastern expansion of the Glaoui Lords of the Atlas. These transhumants yo-yo from Jbel Sahro (the Sahara Atlas) to the high pastures of the Great Atlas.

We had set up camp by a small spring when the invasion started: yells and shouts and dust glittering on the crests in the sun as boys drove down a flock of sheep and goats. Behind came a string of camels, slow-stepping, sturdy, laden with goat-hair *kaima* (tent), belongings in carpet-panniers, small children and hens perched on top of loads. One camel even had its baby riding pick-a-back. A couple of dogs ranged alongside. Men, lean and fit, faces wrapped round in colourful scarves; women, in many hued layers, blowing and glittering in the sun; children, carrying children, singing and laughing, hardly broke stride to greet us, 'La bas!', before spilling down a rocky scarp to their decreed transit camp. Later they came with skins (and plastic containers) to fill water at our well. In the morning they had gone and by our cook tent had left a present of buttermilk. Our Ali had baked bread in the evening, over a scrub fire, and a watching imp took an armful back to their quarters.

For a century the coastal strip round Essaouira has had ongoing work to reclaim what was desert and defend the scrub forest from the sands blowing off the beaches. This deservedly popular tourist spot is where most visitors see camels for several come to the esplanade so tourists can perch on top and have their photos taken or even parade along the sands. Most don't, believing the adage that they are 'dangerous at both ends and uncomfortable in the middle', and on top of a camel you feel at least two storeys above the ground. Climbers call the feeling 'exposure'.

I was more interested in watching the camels bringing tree branches from inland down to the dunes in the continuing fight to stabilise the shoreline. They used *hundreds* of the beasts, an impressive sight. Cut out the sea 'background' and you could have filmed *Lawrence of Arabia* here, (they filmed it elsewhere in Morocco), and it was that incongruity of sea and camels that made me think of trekking with camels down this coast. The main road from Essaouira to Agadir keeps well up and inland from the sea which gave the coast a certain mystique and inferred the landscape was too tough for a road. That was a lure; besides, I live on the coast, have always heard the two mighty voices (hills and sea) and been addicted to travelling afoot. Here was much to spark the imagination.

The practicalities of realising the dream proved ludicrously simple for my regular mountain helper, Aït Idir Mohammed from Imlil, had contacts on the coast and could set up the whole exercise. Fellow coast-living Fifers Richard and Edith joined me for the novel venture. We met Mohammed at Essaouira, a night in the Hotel Sahara, which sounded appropriate. Next morning we were bundled into a pickup and went south, half an hour, to Sidi Kaouki, beyond Cap Sim, the point that ends the *four hours* of walking Essaouira's strand. We were to meet our two camels there. Our rucksacks and the boxes of food Mohammed had brought sat in a lonely pile. As far south as we could see the sands were bare. No camels!

'Not to worry', said Mohammed. 'Set off. We'll catch up,' - and he started bawling into his mobile phone while we ambled off along the big sands, accompanied by two good natured dogs, one fluffy and black (part collie), one buff coloured and legs buffed to ridiculous shortness (a dachshund contribution perhaps). They were obviously good friends and played endlessly with each other, chased the tideline plovers and tried to catch elusive 'sandy loupers'. We assumed they'd return at the end of the beach. They didn't. Nor after the second strand. Nor the third when we were ten miles from the start and shortlegs was worn out.

Those strands were magic: imagine St Andrews West Sands, Luskentyre, Sandwood Bay, one after the other, flowery headlands in between. Mohammed and one camel man caught us up. The camels had mistaken the rendezvous but were passing along by an inland route. Essaouira is known and sometimes notorious for its wind, the *alizé*, and we assumed cooler walking, but the afternoon became roasting hot. A local lad caught us up and we wended up to his croft-like establishment where he provided mint tea along with bread hot from the oven which we dipped in honey, olive oil or *amlou*, the last a dip tasting like peanut butter and made from argan oil, almonds and honey. 'An acquired taste' a guidebook noted. We acquired it instantly.

We all slept for a couple of hours then went out to find the camp. The dogs had disappeared.

Looking down from a crest we saw a picturesque shrine, the whitewashed Sidi Mbark and, next to it, the familiar white shape of a PWD style tent. Bars of rock closed the small valley with a stream spraying over in a succession of falls, big dunes beyond, and the tide snuffling on the shore. Camels came and went all the time and nobody passed without popping in for tea, the refreshing mint tea of Morocco. We pitched our personal tents and settled in. All too soon the sea quenched the sun and the stars were hung in the sky. The boss camel man had driven two camels down the coast, pitched the big tent alone and did all the cooking. Each night he made a soup from fresh ingredients (coriander prominent), followed by a *tagine*, a sort of stew of lush fresh vegetables and meat or eggs, the meal rounded off by sweet melons. You can have backpacking; give me mules or camels any time.

Day Two began with the regular 'up at six, off at seven' and gave quite a different world. We climbed up a ravine to a shelf or plateau along the coast, cliff-edged, undulating, a few villages inland, a few barley fields on the harsh limestone and the slopes covered in argan trees. The argan is indigenous to the SW of Morocco, a small tree of vicious thorns yielding a fruit akin to an olive. Inside this fleshy outer is a hard shell and inside it a small kernel, which, crushed, gives the gourmet argan oil. Goats are encouraged to climb the trees and devour the berries, thereby stripping off the fleshy outer parts, and the nuts are then collected, half the task done. It still takes thirteen hours of work to produce half a litre of oil. Much of the production now is from southern cooperatives run by women.

We had a big gully to cross, the coast suddenly vivid green with a bushy euphorbia. Coast walking is no easy alternative to hill walking. The cliffs were bitten into by bays of pristine sand and we picnicked and paddled in one, an eye on the rising tide. Another, shy, dog attached itself to us and over the hours grew friendly, nudging our legs and grinning - and disappearing at the end of the day's tramping. Women were searching rock pools for squid and a trader with a donkey was weighing and buying them on this remote path. A ragged point brought us to another huge strand with the *kouba* (dome) of another *marabout* (shrine), Sidi Ahmed, our destination.

The wind had risen steadily so camping on dunes was inadvisable. The white shape of the big tent was perched among argan trees several hundred feet up above Iftane, a row of fishing huts on the sands. How Llacen pitched it single handed was a puzzle. We had fun with our small tents which did their best to become kites. Blue-painted boats came in with the tide and we went down to find a stall had opened, selling water, fizzy drinks and basic foods. Who says you can't drink a litre and a half of coke straight off? Dehydration isn't a monopoly of deserts. We slept to the roar of surf. Perhaps the day's most delightful memory was of the morning's encounter with migrating swifts: for several hours racing, swooping, endless birds had been making their surprisingly silent way up the coast.

Day Three was punishingly hot. By eight o'clock I could have wrung out the sweat from my shirt as if I'd been washing it. The coastal scenery was on a grander scale and, ahead, loomed Cap Tafalney, which would have to be gone over, not round. We had assumed a fairly inland route at the start of the day but low tide allowed us to walk round a headland on sand, a double strand with miles of untouched, tide-wrinkled sand. We had a 'pieces and paddle' pause before the last secretive bay, the ridiculously steep path up the cape all too visible. The super heat however created a slight breeze for the ascent, over 300 metres in no distance at all.

On top was a wide plateau of argan forest, bright with yellow flax flowers, red poppies and the blue and white of statice. An hour of dappled forest led to an equally harsh descent. Limestone cruelty. There was a bigger fishing village, Tafadna, a dozen blue boats hauled out and a long sweep of pretentious buildings as if the place had been meant for a resort, and failed. The camels, as ever, had beaten us to it: the white tent stood by a river/lagoon. The breeze had become wind and the wind strong enough to raise a dust storm. The afternoon was something of a survival exercise, seeking shade, calm and liquids, life reduced to simplicities. The sealed tents still had a film of dust over everything when the wind vanished at dusk. Night herons flew down to the estuary. A distant mosque sent out the evening call to prayer. Llacen produced another welcome, delicious meal as we sprawled on the matting in the big tent, lit by a candle tied to the metal pole. A tanker came and delivered oil to the pump house of the local well then a JCB roared up and parked alongside the camp which, far from wrecking the romantic element, gave wonder again at the sheer tenacity of life in hard places: tough people in a tough landscape (and seascape) with every possible inch cultivated and every possibility worked.

Our fourth day did take us inland a bit, following a track which was being prepared for the tarmac, passing several villages of harsh, glaring limestone, fields, and olives and argan, a world divided by walls and heaps of field-cleared stone. The Yorkshire dales, with sun. Hotter than ever for the last day, sunburn gone from medium rare to well done. At a village, Iknioun, we were to end our trek in a house. We entered through an arched entrance passage into a white courtyard and colourful guest room - and the welcome mint tea and hot, fresh, delicious bread to dip in *amlou*. After a siesta one of the many sons of the house took us across fields and forest for a walk along the edge of the sea, or at least the edge of the slope tumbling 250 metres to the sea. The females of the house made a *couscous* supper and, before that, Edith had her feet and hands patterned with henna. The hospitality was gracious and friendly. The guest room clock had struck three on arrival, to the tune of Home Sweet Home, and gave a different tune every hour. The clock was removed when we bedded down! We slept well.

We only had limited time so next day piled into a wee Renault van which took us inland to the coast road, to Tamanar, whence a shared taxi took us to Smimou, whence a shared taxi took us to Essaouira. Mohammed then caught a bus to Marrakech. We stayed in the Hotel Sahara, the big treat being showers. Water. The camels had carried big containers of water to our sites from wells, some of it a bit brackish, none of it wasted in washing us. (We used Wet Wipes.) We had one big and one small camel, nicknamed Big Bottom and Little Bottom, that being the general view we had of them, if any. We left first, they arrived first. They seemed to do everything in slow motion (energy saving?) but were immensely strong and surprisingly speedy. Another lesson learned: you can't compete with camels.

The experiment had been a great success. The coastal scenery was splendid throughout and gave a good mix of horizontal strands and 'strenuous verticals'. (On hills one usually chooses the angle of ascent to suit, on the coast a path does the dictating, often fairly brutally.) Another two or three days would have been useful, and logical, ending the trekking where the main road comes down to the coast. Next time maybe.

LADIES ON MELTZEN

Looking south from the battlements and palm groves of Marrakech, away over the deserty plains, the High Atlas fills the view, stretching horizon to horizon, and often presenting an improbable sweep of glittering snow.

On the first morning of every visit to Marrakech I still climb to the rooftops at dawn and look south to the mountains of my life. From eastmost Jbel Rhat to western Erdouz I have climbed them all and, as a friend once joked, I could actually pronounce their names. (Try Biiguinoussene!) Quite a few visits passed before I could sort out that view with any confidence. It baffled early travellers and they often headed for what appeared the highest, a fine cone rising above the generalities, which is Adrar Meltzen, 3595m. (Jbel Toubkal, 4167m, stands further back, further in, by no means prominent.) Adrar Meltzen, Meltzen the Magnificent, went on my 1976 bucket list when our local Braes o' Fife Mountaineering Club were visiting.

One problem was the absence of a map of Meltzen, a regular Atlas feature in those days - first find your mountain, then climb it! The Toubkal massif had been extensively explored in the inter-war period when France had set up its Protectorate and a surprising number of *alpinistes* worked in the country as geologists, surveyors, engineers and foresters, (de Segonzac, Neltner, the Lépiney brothers and others). Climbing gained a boost when the great roads over the Atlas were constructed, the Tizi n' Tichka to Ourzazate and the Tizi n' Test to Taroudant, so commerce as much as the sword pacified the Berber mountain clans. Then came World War Two and then the struggle for independence so it was mid-century before mountain activity resumed. The Atlas Silver Age. Life was still fairly primitive in 1976 when five of us set off for Meltzen armed with my local knowledge and a Michelin road map of Morocco. Anne, Janet, Susan, Bob and I were part of the Braes o' Fife Mountaineering Club meet. We first crossed to Tachddirt (already mentioned), the next valley east of Imlil, for a few days.

The head of the valley, Tizi n' Tachddirt was 3172m and from it there was a clear view of Meltzen down the Ourika valley. This was our approach, rather than heading up the Ourika valley from where it debouched onto the Marrakech plain.

We set off from Tachddirt at 05.00 with a mule carrying our ruckers but the guardian soon passed its handling over to a wee boy. The load promptly fell off. We watched a lammergeier being mobbed by choughs. Endless zigzags led up towards the *tizi* (pass) and we had quite a wait once up as the mule couldn't cope with a breakable snow crust. There was a bitter wind and the lad asked for matches. He then lit one of the dry, thorny, cushion plants and stood over the flames, holding out his *djellaba* to trap the heat. Smoke seeped out at his neckline.

At one time the CAF had a refuge at Timichi, half way down this upper Ourika valley, but it had gone. [Now there's a comfortable *gîte*.] The descent was a regular progression of traverses above gorges and then zigzags down, often to finely-perched villages, each with its terraced fields, the lower ones explosive with almond blossom. The hours slipped away. A hot day. Packs growing heavier.

In the end there was the deepest gorge of all, forcing us to grind uphill again, to what luckily proved the last traverse. Weary, we considered bivouacking but a rest and another brew revived us. A flight of bee-eaters passed overhead and there were rock buntings and black redstarts about. We enjoyed an eyrie-like view down to the patchwork fields running up from Setti Fadma to the shrine itself, where there is an annual festival attended by thousands. Many would camp in the valley bottom on the floodplain, something no mountain Berber would do, yet how many pilgrims were only one or two generations away from their Atlas origins and had already lost the feeling for mountains? A flash flood a few years later carried away and killed over a thousand pilgrims.

We were soon trundling down the zigzags to the valley bottom, to a *piste*, to houses of concrete, with iron patterned doors, civilisation of a sort. Being early April the Setti Fadma hotel (such as it was) was closed but folk at the *maison forestière* directed us across the torrent where the Café Azagza made us welcome. We arrived to a clock chiming with the notes of Big Ben. They could provide rooms. These proved to be in a bare concrete block a quarter of a mile down-valley, set on terraces ablaze with the blossom of apple, plum, cherry and almond. Two rooms had slatted beds, the only furnishing. 'Welcome to the Ourika bothy' someone laughed. Having walked two days in one we quite happily cooked and ate our two days' supplies in one.

The Oued Ourika waters rise on several valley-head passes, the flow heads roughly east before, where we were at Setti Fadma, turning right angles northwards, to flow down a beautiful valley to the plains. Coming up the Ourika for Melzen is the logical approach and was the way early travellers tried: Hooker, Ball and Maw in 1871, Joseph Thomson in 1888, both parties stopped in their tracks by hostile tribes, and Lt Washington, RN, in 1829 had been successful as he was part of the respected Drummond Hay consular visit to the sultan in Marrakech. He managed to climb out of the valley, towards Meltzen only to be sent packing by being fired on from above. He became Admiral Washington and had surveyed and charted the Moroccan coastline in detail - while the mountains still were shown on maps a single, long, fuzzy line with few names or features known. In my early wanderings our parties were often the first 'outsiders' any village had seen yet, far from being shot at, were welcomed with fantastic hospitality and helpfulness - as here - where instead of a bivvy in the rain, we'd been given such shelter as there was. [Setti Fadma is now a thriving pilgrim and tourist *town*.]

We woke to a view of deeply-plastered peaks, Rjoute, above the Ourika valley bend looked like Fuji seen through the blossom. We filled a kitbag of gear which could be left. One soon learnt that the genuine necessities are few. We left the kitbag at the Café Azagza and had a coffee with the youngsters running it. There were three Oxford students breakfasting after their bivvy in the local graveyard.

A bouldery valley swung round to Touchte, the last name on the road map where a *piste* was being constructed. There was a working mill at the top end. We reached a valley bifurcation and took the bigger stream heading in what we felt was the right direction. There was a sort of line on the map that might be path, (it proved to be the symbol for an intermittent river).

Impressive cliffs hemmed us in and we were often scrambling up smooth boiler-plates, a bit like an enclosed Coire a' Ghrunnda. Bob was lagging, weakened by gut trouble and, after a brew stop, decided to go back. To our delight he took the omnipresent tail of kids with him. We continued, crossed the stream to a goat track and soon realised this branch was a no go. A shepherd by voice and mime conveyed the same message.

The route up the other valley rather 'played tig' among tiny fields and the stream-bed itself. We stopped to brew under a numbered walnut (what a local was paid for a tree here would sell as veneer in Paris for a thousand times more), there was a fine fall on the cliffs to the left, dippers whirred upstream and black wheatears hopped among the rocks. Clouds were coming down so we decided to follow the stream as far as possible, bivvy and tackle the peak from wherever we were.

Our gorge narrowed and the path was occasionally built up across bare rock sections, once simply going up a rock islet in the stream. We passed a fine bivvy site under a boulder. (If only we'd known.) Another barrier was passed and zigzags up a steep slope led to *azibs* on a grassy knoll. The air was juniper scented. A *seguia* (small irrigation channel) led to the other *azibs*, the Atlas equivalent of *shieling, bérgérie* or *saeter*. We were still too low so, again, pushed on after a brew, in saturating wet which soon turned to steady snow. The gorge narrowed and widened as if jaws were opening and closing to devour us. We began losing what was left of our goat path and scrambled on through the wavering, feathery flakes with very little visibility. The Michelin road map of Morocco was not very useful! Another rock band loomed but a scree fan to the right had a trace of the path working upwards. Every step up was one less for the morrow but some of the gang were obviously tiring. The extra effort paid off however.

In the lee of cliff at a wee *azib* I left the girls brewing soup and went on to recce a bit and found a big enclosure and more *azibs* so we carried up to there. Most of these *azibs* were built of mud and branches, not very appealing in the now heavy snowfall. We found one with a small fireplace, tin shovel and plenty of litter so we squeezed in and carried on making supper: soup, tinned ham, with beans, onions and spuds (ages to cook at that height), apple flakes and 'brews to bursting'. Between courses we found our bivvy nooks and crannies: Anne and I in niches under the cliff and Susan in a small cave while Janet opted for the cookhouse. About six inches more of snow fell overnight.

Susan's spot was a bit damp but I'd a space blanket between me and the spongy sheep-and-goat-droppings ground. I'd bedded with the expectation of retreat so when I woke at six to blue skies and a blazing world of whiter than white it was like receiving an electric shock. As snowy Rjoute faced us we had to be in a flanking corrie of Meltzen. All we had to do was climb to the ridge and follow it to the summit - anyway that was my encouraging simplification. After tea, porridge, pieces and tea we set off at 07.30.

I was to plough a furrow all the way to the top but luckily was of the age and in a peak of fitness to even relish the demands. The worst was gaining the ridge but, with the feel of scree and scag below the snow, our conditions could have been an improvement. We must have flogged up a thousand feet. We took a good breather on gaining a slight dip on the ridge (Susan was lagging) and simply gazed at the view. The north flank was even snowier and would have been off-limits. Our ridge ran down to the Tizi n' Ghelis and the weird plateau of Yagour, a vast near-level shelf added on to the Atlas verticalities with a prow sticking out towards the plains like the bows of a liner. Later we came to know it well (and climb Meltzen from there) for Yagour has sites of prehistoric rock art scattered among its red sandstone crags. On Meltzen we were surrounded closely by some of the highest Atlas summits and in a lifetime I have never seen them in such a uniformity of white majesty, floodlit against the inconceivably blue sky.

Regrouped, refreshed, we set off up our ridge which soon broke up nicely into pinnacles, giving good scrambling. (Janet's turn to be suffering.) Any skirting had us sinking thigh deep. After one awkward bit (we hadn't a rope) the going eased and led to a 'top' only for another to loom ahead. Off it, we were thigh deep again on the narrow crest. We had a pause to let everyone gather again. Strung out figures were good for photos as cloud was now boiling up from below - a good weather sign. Sacks were left before tackling the final ridge. We reached the summit at 13.30 just as the first wisps of clouds began teasing over the long sinuous line of our ascent. We had a naming of peaks: Toubkal from its 'wrong' side and first to vanish, mighty Anghrommer, Tashka n' Zat of our 'Ridge of Dreams', and a whole scrum to the east. Anne and Susan had altitude headaches so we didn't linger. The cloud swept over us.

Back-tracking was easy with the furrow we'd left and the cloud kindly hid the steep flanking slopes. It snowed during the traverse of the pinnacles. Beyond, we lost our tracks and among the dips and rises, and had no real indication of where we had first gained the ridge. After much pondering we set off down. I was fairly confident but the girls were anything but: we were descending mostly scree and scrag, not snow, as on the ascent. I'd a job convincing them that it was the same flank and the fierce African sun had simply removed much of the snow over the day. We teased away, hit a stream edged with mini-daffodils, skirted looming crags and, facing near rebellion, came on the recognised lower *azibs* and pulled up 'home', a very weary party by then, feet soaking and the world a wet mess. 17.00.

We had hoped to exit that day but with only a couple of hours of daylight left another bivvy loomed. We'd hardly eaten all day and gorged on everything remaining and could, and did, down endless brews. All were more than happy with their *grand course*. Susan decided to move in with Janet in the *azib*, while Anne, after crawling into various nooks in search of a howff, joined them. Which left me! I found a wee overhang where the ground was dry (droppings) and was ensconced at 18.30 as dark fell. Meltwater was dripping off the rock overhead and coming slowly nearer but, before dripping onto me, turned to a row of harmless icicles. The girls fared less well. Susan snored so was fine, but Anne and Janet, with swollen hands and faces from the sun and glare, did not sleep much. And their combined fug in the tiny *azib* resulted in a steady dripping onto them and their sleeping bags, drips which were basically a yellowish dilution of sheep and goat droppings and urine. Over breakfast brews, once they had sorted themselves out and exited their howff, I stood upwind of the trio.

The descent was a rewinding of our way up, all in clag, but still that serendipitous joy of coming back to vivid green fields and the shock of blossom. Nearing the Café Azagza we found a recovered and relieved Bob who had had a bivvy too as the kitbag with everything left had been locked in the café and the young lad had gone for a night in Marrakech! As was only 10.30 we had coffee and fresh bread smothered in apricot jam and lazed about in the now hot sun. The café roof was covered with the girls' drying sleeping bags and we'd all had a good wash in the river. A bus landed us in Marrakech for 17.00 and a *petit taxi* took us straight to a favoured *pâtisserie* for gateaux and milk sheiks (*sic*). They thought they deserved it. Our wine at supper was labelled 'grand ordinaire'.

There was a coda to this outing. Our girls aroused quite an interest among the youth of Setti Fadma and various offers were made to me for them: for Anne, older, they suggested ten camels, for plump Janet (they like them so) twenty camels and for Susan, who in any society would be thought an eyeful, I could have fifty camels. Years on I once heard this tale retold and Susan had become 500 camels. Talk of inflation! For years too I enjoyed having them star in my slide show of Morocco and telling of the various offers. Until one performance at Elgin. After the Elgin show a fine-looking lady approached me, said how she had enjoyed the presentation and added that she was grateful Susan was the one up for fifty camels. 'I'm her mum!'

HERE AND THERE

The long white roads ... are a temptation. What quests they propose! They take us away to the thin air of the future or to the underworld of the past.

Edward Thomas

Mo-i-Rana had been a magical name to us for several weeks of climbing and motoring northwards. It is the major town just south of the polar circle and from there we would launch our visit to the grim-sounding Svartisen (The Black Ice), the largest icefield in Arctic Norway. A third of Norway still lay beyond, the genuine 'land of the Midnight Sun', the North Cape, the border with Russia.

Mo was an uninteresting steel town but the friendly tourist office had maps and information to help our scanty home-grown information. We drove out to a campsite and packed in hope.

Svartisen is split in two by the Vesterdalen, a deep-cut valley, from which we would try for the top.

A succession of dirt roads took us into the back of beyond and when the last tract petered out at a farm we, perforce, walked. The farmer could speak no English so we left a note

238

on the van. The day was grey and cloudy and the route gave a good imitation of a steamy tropical forest. We had a haul of five miles up to a lake, desperately hard work and I can't recall ever sweating so much yet no skin could be left bare or it was pounced on by mosquitoes.

The Glomsdalsvatnet outflow suddenly vanished into the ground, the first evidence we had of this being a famous limestone area for cavers. (One system has been followed for more than 2000 metres.) And cavers don't have to suffer mosquitoes!

After rounding the lake we lost the path in the jungle and had a flounder before finding it again. It went brutally up from a *saeter* to round the prow that guarded the end of the Vesterdalen. The valley had two levels, so to speak, with the river down in the basement and a long ledge giving a sort of balcony for our purgatorial promenade.

This lead to a lochan and a furnished hut, the Pikhaugh-ytta, which made the perfect base - and it was safe from insects. We slept that night all of 300 yards inside the Arctic Circle, one ambition fulfilled.

It was an up-at-3, off-at-4, start to a day which was to yield a 16-hour escapade, but we duly returned with the scalp of Snotinden, the highest point on the ice-cap. All we had to go on from the guidebook was this bald statement: 'On the main glacier lies Snetind (now Snotinden) 1599m, which is the highest peak. It has been climbed, but there are no reports.'

Our ignorance yielded some adventurous bliss. Luckily we had bought a newer 1:50,000 map in Mo. Our older 1:100,000 did not show a lake, more than a mile wide, which lay in the middle of the valley and was its dominant feature.

It was quite impassable on its west side as cliffs fell into its waters and a glacier snout pushed down to deposit icebergs on its blue waters, so we had to round it on the east and somehow break up onto the snow dome of that western ice-cap where Snotinden perched like a toorie on a bunnet. The going looked desperate, and dangerous, with defences of cliffs and hanging glaciers and even before that there were the rivers.

A mile from the hut a whole series of streams came down into the valley. One had a fine waterfall and all gave tricky crossings. We then battled down birch and willow slopes (an arctic equivalent of *maquis*) to the bouldery edge of the big lake, the Bjornefossvatnet, and round where the Vesterdal waters poured into it in a braiding of four separate rivers.

We managed to hop across one river, forded a second, but the next two were serious and called for the rope. We were very glad to have practised the specialised techniques of river crossings beforehand - on that Christmas Day, in the River Carron below Gerry's hostel at Achnashellach (p.79).

That Scottish deluge had produced a waist-deep spate which was useful and exciting for working out the systems. A continuous loop is used so, whichever man is crossing, he is held above *and* below and can be fielded quickly. We stripped off and had a good tussle with River 3 but Number 4 only needed a handrail rigged up. An iceberg was grounded offshore and had been so undercut by waves that it looked like a blue mushroom. We scampered up the moraine deposits beside the Bjornefoss in an effort to warm ourselves again - the river, after all, was just melted ice.

The hard uphill work began after that, giving what is perhaps the best of mountain fun, the choosing of a line up unknown territory. Our route 'went' which was the main thing. We cairned much of it as we dodged along rakes or up granite steps. We ate our lunch below the final slabs across from a cold, blue snout of hanging glacier and actually saw a chunk break off and crash down the cliffs into the valley. A long traverse took us onto a rock ridge that curved up onto the ice-caps. We had won through.

A snow dome led us safely above the glacier we had been dodging. Its summit was a *nunatak* (a rocky islet in a sea of ice) and from it we looked out over the snowfields of the ice-cap - a dozen miles across at least. With the signs of a front coming in from the sea we pushed on over an intermediate *nunatak* to the bigger snow dome of Snotinden.

It was well crevassed and even our lively Ian was silenced when he put a foot through the snow above what appeared to be limitless depths. The summit was a shock for there were boxes of buildings and piles of aerials, batteries, and suchlike for some new construction. Nobody was there and we assumed it had been carried in by air. Our devious route had taken eight hours.

It took as long to return even without going astray down all the slabs, ridges, rakes, and gullies. We cut down more directly to the river above the *foss* and where boulders split the flow had another full-scale roped river-crossing. Stuart managed to go under but his clothes were well wrapped inside his rucker. The river was waist deep and flowed with impressive force. Dave didn't think this game would do his cold much good. We dispatched Ian off ahead to start supper and followed as fast as weary legs allowed.

The slopes down to the lake were heavily scented with blossom. We hoped we could cross all those side-streams where the merged into the river but it was too dangerous and we had to haul up the jungly, insect-ambushing slopes. Feet were wet and tongues dry when we stumbled back to the 'Piggy-hutta'. Someone (or was it the trolls?) had been in and tidied the hut during the day - even to cleaning our dixies. The weather was reverting rapidly and we fell into bed with no thoughts for the future except sleep.

We took 12 hours of it, and Dave managed to go a full 24 hours without leaving the hut. I read *Kenilworth*, all 444 pages, before nightfall, as self defence against the bridge school. Snotinden was climbed on the only reasonable day in several weeks. Now and then you do actually hit the right place at the right time, with the right friends.

We spent several summers in Norway using my camper van and tents as base and paying close attention to the barometer. When conditions were bad we drove on, when there were signs of improvement we stopped and climbed whatever mountains were available, cherry-picking many of the country's finest peaks, whether rock peaks like the Romsdalshorn or snow challenges like this. Lyngen would prove our furthest north though later in life I would reach Tromsø with glimpses of Sami life and sea-eagles by the dozen - and travel on to Spitzbergen. Norway was everything of Scotland - writ large: the peaks were rockier, the jungles junglier, the lochs were great fjords, our brief snows were ice-caps - and our wee midges were replaced by the bigger biting mosquitoes.

SHOCKING ICELAND

Two weeks in Iceland in 1984 gave me a journey to a world still in the throes of creation, a scene both grim but starkly beautiful, with great plains of black sands, red rocks, yellow ridges, caldera five miles across, dead volcanic plugs, walls of basalt columns, caves and pinnacles, glaciers and geysers, ground too hot to walk on, active volcanoes, huge waterfalls, vast ice-caps, unimaginable gorges - every feature you might think of and much more to ambush imagination.

We 'toured' for two weeks of camping and walking in buses which had wheels higher than I could reach in order to cope with ragged lava reefs or raging rivers. One was a kitchen and opened up to become such. We dined well though some folk were not so sure of regular *fruit* soups. In July it was scarcely dark at night so, early and late, besides the official walks, I was off exploring, seeing flowers and birds in greater abundance than ever dreamed of. On the first night my tent door faced the geyser Stokkur which exploded periodically from a greeny-blue bubble dome in a pool. Whimbrel, snipe, golden plovers called. There was no *cold* water on that site. The next day's wild camp was near a mountain with summer skiing where you returned to plunge into hot springs. Hot water was everywhere. We made the most of it.

We visited caves, found by a British school's trip in 1936, where a decade later (1975) notices were posted warning not to swim there any more. We, another decade on, were not tempted: the water was now boiling. A farmer nearby had recently lost his complete potato crop: it had suddenly been cooked where it was in the ground. In one geothermal area under Krafla they opened a power station just as the mountain began to erupt. The power station is floated on concrete rafts in case of earth movements and all the joints were made flexible: high-pressure steam from the bowels of the earth is not something to be let loose in the workplace.

All our camp spots were fantastic: at one the background noises were of the varicolored muds bubbling up or steam hissing periodically, at another my bird companions were snow buntings, at another a crag with merlins and croaking ptarmigan. At one site we had to strike and move to avoid being flooded and our big-wheeled buses were employed to rescue cars marooned in an inundated ford. My favourite was at Landmannalangar where there were clear springs and streams of every temperature - and natural hot mud baths. I don't often stay in water for an hour. I looked like a prune when I came out.

The best swim of all was at a large exactly circular, caldera, with 50 metre scree slopes running down to yellowy waters, the site, a bit like a flooded clay pit. It was called Viti (Hell) and gave a hilarious international skinny dipping. And no midges.

Our literature warned about midges but we had none. A farmer however told me they came in several generational waves and we were neatly between bad spells. He pointed out just how bad - yet useful - they could be. The cows grazing his lush pastures had their udders in trusses and I asked why. 'That was the midges'. Each recurring swarm, rich in nitrogen would die and enrich the soil, so the grass grew and grew and the cows grazed and grazed and produced plenty of milk. But their distended udders tended to stot off the ground - so were given support. For one place in the world at least, midges have a *use*.

I hired a cycle for the free last day in Reykjavik and visited all the natural history museums. Never in my life have I been so overwhelmed with such a superabundance of alpine-type flowers and what we regard as rare northern birds. I laughed aloud when one notice beside a stuffed *Passer domesticus* proclaimed it a 'rarity'. But it was the naked landscape that most shocked: every aspect of earth's creative powers were on display, overwhelmingly powerful, in one's face (and often, literally, underfoot!) and, often, very much active. And yet this was a world people live in and which prospers. Talk about natural adaption! No wonder the people we met were sturdily independent, hospitable, amusing and able to deal with fate. I'm told the following was true.

At the National Day celebrations at Reykjavik the bishop was offering a prayer, 'Thanks for no big earthquake this year, no dreadful floods . . .' (At which moment he was splattered on top of his head by a passing gull.) ' ... and thank you, God, that our cows don't fly.'

Strangely waterfalls were scarcely mentioned in the above note for our local climbing club rag; for me they were the finest signature of Iceland. I did write home about them: 'The waterfalls are an Icelandic speciality: immensely powerful, creamy and grey with scoured silt, and falling over into deep, narrow gashes of gorges where you can stand within spray distance on trembling edges of wonder and fear. They milestoned our wanderings from Oxrarfoss at Thingvellir onwards. Gullfoss sees a wide, wide river tumble over a natural weir of rocks then pour like a broad kilt along the cleft of gorge, overarched by a rainbow on our visit. Dettifoss is the most powerful fall of water in Europe, frightening in its power, 120,000 tons of silt is washed down every day. Godafoss had a wider-than high symmetry, like a book opened out. Aldeyjarfoss was a squeezed force, a tremendous smack into a turmoil of water that sprayed up like a geyser, at the end of another 'box canyon' whose walls were ranks of columnar basalt. Best was Ofaerufoss, a whole descending series of falling sheets with a natural arch spanning their show. We walked for an hour before coming on its serendipitous splendour. But it's shown on the stamp which you'll see on this letter.'

By the Bitter Lakes

Liberty is the right to discipline ourselves in order not to be disciplined by others.

Clemenceau

Because I had had years in the school's CCF (RAF section) I was called up to do my National Service in the RAF. Possibly for the same reason I never completed square bashing but was flown out to the Suez Canal Zone some weeks early. I had been encouraged to be a POM (potential officer material) but many CCF visits to RAF stations had shown me what that would mean: general dogsbody, and an alien mess loud with flying/career types. No thank you. As it was I look back on my RAF service with gratitude; the working hours were easy, we were paid overseas allowances to live in places where the cost of living was a fraction of the UK, the climate cheerier than at home (even in Egypt's warmer side of hot), there were other cultures, wildlife and experiences to thrill, good friendships (some lifelong) to be made, plenty of sporting, social and religious occasions, in fact I'd the longest paid holiday of my life. I also put myself to school again and studied hard. The RAF was my equivalent of university, to which there had been no hope of going on leaving school, and to which, afterwards, there was no desire. I perforce trained, on the job, in Egypt, as a telephonist.

During square bashing at RAF Hednesford, on Cannock Chase, many evenings were spent in Birmingham where the Carl Rosa Opera Company season was in full swing, (I managed *Il Travatore*, *Butterfly*, *Faust* and *Barber of Seville*), so it tickled my fancy to be sent to the Suez Canal whose opening in 1869 was celebrated with Verdi's *Aïda*. I'd be stationed in the Zone through 1954. There were then 10 RAF and 34 army bases and two dockyards up and down the 100 miles of canal. Our forces were beginning to move out as per agreement but then Nasser arbitrarily nationalised the Canal in 1956 and the British-French-Israeli fiasco of invasion and withdrawal followed. I was based at RAF Deversoir which was where the Suez Canal entered the northern end of the Great Bitter Lake. An endlessly curious spectacle was seeing stately liners ghosting along as if land-borne, towering over the palm trees that lined an invisible canal. Now and then there were troop ships with our soldiers being sent out to Malaya, a nastier posting I was glad to have missed.

'A French Legion troop ship bound for Indo-China passed

the other day and before our eyes a fellow dived overboard in full kit. When the ship passed there were four in the water, one, English, had got roped in at Marseilles while drunk, so he said. Our police rescued them from the locals who were told to 'Imshi!' [Not an isolated incident. The lucky ones fell into our military hands.]'

We didn't realise it at the time but we were witnessing the beginning of the end of Britain as super power. We would not be policing the world much longer. Between the end of WW2 and the mid-Fifties British forces had been deployed in policing and garrisoning, giving humanitarian aid or fighting serious-enough wars in Germany, Austria, Trieste, Greece, Cyprus, Malta, Gibraltar, Libya, Egypt, Sudan, Somaliland, Ethiopia, Eritrea, Palestine, Jordan, Iraq, Aden, Kuwait, Bahrain, India, Ceylon, Malaya, Singapore, Indonesia, North Borneo, Hong Kong, Japan, Christmas Island, British Guyana, Belize, Guatemala, Barbados, Jamaica, Bermuda, Gold Coast, Cameroon, Togo, Zanzibar and Kenya. This 'peacetime' demand created Britain's biggest-ever worldwide military duty, sucking in two million men. In the 'graveyard' of the Canal Zone in 1951 there had been fourteen RAF squadrons (152 aircraft) and something like 60,000 army personnel were based in the Zone. The retreat only became clear in retrospect. The government made sure of hiding the reality of the Zone years. More than twice the numbers killed in the Falklands War died in controlling the Zone. A medal was only, grudgingly, made available - *fifty years afterwards*.

Our Signal Section personnel lived in Nissen huts half sunk in the sand and, between huts, were the tents of the army signals personnel. (When we buggered things up they repaired them.) A water *chatti* stood at the door: a porous Ali Baba jar of water wrapped in wet canvas that kept us supplied with cold, safe water. Inside we fought a continuous war against all manner of biting creepy crawlies. (Ah, the smell of squashed bedbugs.) Bedsteads may have had legs in saucers of water or DDT powder but that was no protection against the airborne divisions falling from the rafters. There were hordes of flies everywhere too. And ants. Showers had a primitive bucket and chain system: pull the chain to tip out some water. Standing naked below this system on one occasion I pulled the chain and received a shower of cockroaches. Our clothes became sweat-stained and rotted in the heat (125°F at times) but nights could be cold. Everyone thought being issued with greatcoats for Egypt was a gaffe. It wasn't. Sandstorms were another nasty experience. Camp food was continuously and unnecessarily bad and many were the food parcels sent from home - along with books, always books. We all stood guard duties. I suffered endlessly from boils. We felt like wartime POWs. Towns were long out-of-bounds so there were no trips to Cairo and the Pyramids. Nasty things happened. People turned up in the Sweet Water Canal. And I thrived.

Work could be demanding at times but was interesting enough. I once sent home a description of working our PBX (Private Branch Exchange) switchboard. 'I rather like its simple logic. An 'eye' closes. Plug in with 'Number please', then, for an internal call, the companion plug is pushed in and you press the ring key. As you are doing this you are already saying 'Number please' to the next call. You could end juggling a dozen calls at once or have every cord in use. Call over, the plugs are pulled out and their cords shoot back into place. A great exercise in coordination. Calls from outside came in on a row of little flaps which fell open as the current triggered a latch. Certain outside lines were directly connected to other stations. At busy periods two boards would be in use, both hands of both operators working frantically and words flowing without pause. At two o'clock in the morning there was no need to sit at the board all the time. An alarm could be switched on which would ring when any call came up. I once had an unhappy morning with senior officers, accused of sleeping on night duty and not answering an important operational in-coming call. The time had been noted and, luckily, the Orderly Officer had been in the exchange at that time (for chai and a chat no doubt) and could verify I was wide awake. The flap had not dropped, we found, a discovery which should have been made by the other station on a routine check. Everything was logged, everything was covered by set procedures. You just got on with the work. The 'panics' were welcomed for much of the work - like anybody's anywhere - was just routine but still required concentration.'

We were often short-staffed, and we were forever changing shifts and also having guard duties. There were times when sleep was all one wanted yet lying in the billet was sometimes like sleeping in a Turkish bath. If most people on the base heard The Last Post as a 'Goodnight' it was meaningless for us. Irregularity became the regular.

'Last night was killing, all alone, though I got a wee sleep by letting the dog-handler cope with routine calls (not many at night of course). He likes coming in and has a delightful dog. He manages extra rations so I cook up for the three of us. There was a wonderful electric storm with flickering sheet lightning among the fantasy clouds, all in complete silence.'

'Just had the Orderly Officer in for tea and a chat, mostly about literature so am about to grab some hours trying to sleep across two chairs which will move apart with repetitive consequences. Be back on the board for waking the place up. The CO's wife is a bossy horror so I crossed her line with a nasty Warrant Officer's and enjoyed hearing them swearing at each other to get off the line, then screaming 'Operator! Operator!' A smarmy, 'Oh I'm so sorry, madam. I'll see what I can do' - then make the line crackle so she was going berserk.'

Calls to the UK had to be slotted in and booked by arrangement in those primitive days of telecommunications and, such calls being expensive, the operator listened in to UK calls, to see nothing cut them off or to deal with anything that did. We heard it all: the bad, the glad and the sad. An airman or soldier phoning home was likely to do so only for important family reasons: the joyous arrival of a baby, an engagement and, too often, losing a parent, wife, or girl-friend. I hated listening in to those calls.

'I've given up watercolour painting. Touch the paper and it dries instantly. No breakfast today. Just couldn't touch it. Even the bread was foostie. Made a mug of soup instead then, after cleaning for CO's inspection, on duty for morning and evening shifts. The board is dripping wet and giving shocks. From heavy dew. Has cut off outside lines and half the extensions are PG (Permanent glow, indicating out of order). Rectified itself as the sun rose higher. The dew drove cockroaches and beetles into the billet last night. In the wee small hours I felt a creepy crawly on my chest and leapt for the light. A four inch beetle. Everyone promptly rolled down their mosquito nets.'

'I went on guard Friday night and had the officers' mess to patrol. I met a very nice bloke and we stood and had a good blether. He was just back from Cyprus so we had plenty to talk about. There were two wee ginger cats which followed me everywhere, full of fun and purring fit to burst. My second shift, 0200 to 0400 was wearisome. Glad when the sun began gnawing away at the shadows. I slept 0400 - 0600, had breakfast and reported to the guardroom. Escort duty.

The driver told me we'd be back and forth to Abu Sultan - for sand!'

One of the posts for guard duty was sited out in the desert, far from camp, and was intensely unpopular so I regularly swopped with mates to be sent there. Night had no fears for me and I grabbed every chance of hours *alone* under the unbelievable desert stars in a rare quietness only broken by distant dogs barking at their own shadows. The guard sat in a hole, eyes level with the desert surface to spot any movement against the sky - which would then be reported - and inspected. Now and then shots were fired into camp and on one famous occasion one of our Circle's army tents was stolen (from above its sleeping occupants) and vanished over the perimeter barbed wire fence and tangles. The occupants were put on a charge for losing military equipment. My other delight in that lonely spot was music: I'd get onto a *mukka* on the switchboard and be plugged in to Radio Moscow which broadcast 24 hours non-stop classical music. There was also a Music Circle which met down by the lake - pure romance with the waters lapping the shore, an evening breeze rustling among the palm fronds, and that jewelled or moon-washed sky overhead.

I also liked being on searchlight duty as the light attracted a wonderful and colourful range of insects.

'Saw a praying mantis yesterday: four inches long, green with white spots, a vicious insect which wouldn't move over to let me sit down, just, put back its feelers and waved at me with its horny claws … The other day the Orderly Officer came out of the guardroom to check on me as I'd been sitting for ages in the sun and he was wondering at my sanity. I was just watching a dung beetle. He was not at all interested. There are iridescent beetles but they tend to give off a pong when handled … The Lido was noisy with black-headed gulls just like Crail, there are always kites overhead and a whirl of white egrets passed ... Had a swim as usual this afternoon after doing a large washing. You may notice a few smudges on the first page of this - that is from my nose running water. It does that whenever I have been under water a lot. We swim way out where it is deep and dive down, down, down, till chests ache and the lining of my nose hurts. But we can see the vivid variety of fish and, my favourites, the dainty sea horses.'

Swimming was almost a daily activity, mentioned regularly, 'What a swim I had today. It was really blowy but, strangely, no dust. The white horses were galloping down the Canal. After an hour of splashing about I set off on the 'measured mile'. It usually takes about 20 minutes. Today it took an hour of really tough battling to finish. Going out was into the waves and you could hardly see for the spray. Leaving the buoy for the return was against the current. I was exhausted by the finish but it was fun.'

Weather of course was a constant topic of letter conversation.

'The weather is creeping to 100°F and I am pouring sweat. We have a Station Parade on Thursday for the Queen's Official Birthday for which I washed and ironed a uniform yesterday. Washing here is fine – it takes five minutes to dry a vest and only ten for a sheet or a uniform. The pegs you sent are a boon, stops my dhobi dancing off into the date palms. Had a terrific sand gust yesterday; it burst open the doors and went through the billet like a train in a tunnel. It will take several days to clear out the sand.'

Seeing a solitary cloud once was reported home - along with a cartoon of the event. Life was strange with months passing without rain, until one autumn day brought a pitter patter on the roof. 'We were out in a flash and were soon dancing about in the first rain in memory. A scene from Charlie Chaplin for it lasted two minutes and merely left a pretty pattern of dots on the sand ... I am writing this just after lunch in the billet. You may notice sploshes on the page again. This time it's the sweat dripping off my forehead. We have all reached the stage where we do not bother to try and keep a dry skin. The actual action of mopping only makes you run more. After lunch I took a couple of salt tablets as I am on guard again tonight. On collecting the parcel I noticed that a corner was wet and smelt a bit beery. On undoing it I felt like crying or laughing. What a mess: the syrup tin had been bashed on the side and the lid had popped off. You can imagine the mess. Do diplomatically ask Aunt Jessie not to send chocolate. It arrives in liquid form, equally messy.'

Restrictions on visits to Suez, Ismalia and Port Said were lifted but not much benefit to me. We were short-handed and had no spare time. 'Today our Cpl. Supervisor is going home so I'm off nights to take over A Watch. Strange to sleep a *night* in bed. Woke to a desert-tasting fog so thick one could almost swim in it. Even the weather has a feel of running down ... Conditions deteriorate steadily. The Sailing Club has closed. We have five visitors in our Nissen hut billet who are dismantling the Air Traffic Control Tower and Ops building. This week the photo intelligence go. Then the Regiment. We telephonists stay till the end and the Gypos are welcome to the temperamental old PBX.'

We rubbed along fine in the confines of our billet. Life would have been intolerable otherwise. As we all were in Signals and worked irregular hours the billet was usually a quiet place. 'Many hours are passed on 'Egyptian PT' - lying flaked out on a bed damp with sweating - and there is a constant grumbling on anything and everything. I am amazed how much time is spent by so many doing nothing.

They are bored. One works at making a wireless set, one is a competent artist (he's drawn a fine pencil portrait of me), one was once in a choir that competed against the Vienna Boys Choir at a festival, one was (still is) a la-de-da actor, and one spent a happy evening telling me all the ways to break into houses or cars.'

'Two days ago a mukka phoned in to ask off escorts as feeling sick. I came off night bind. Apparently he grew worse, vomiting and messing everything but would not report sick. When I came to I rang for an ambulance. Next day I was asked about his previous behaviour as he was now running amok in the wards without any clothes on. He's been taken to hospital in Fayid and next-of-kin informed. We felt a bit bad but the three of us were all sleeping off night binds so it was evening before we noticed just how bad he was.'

I felt this miasma of boredom was partly from their civvy life being so uninteresting, few had sporting commitments or mental challenges, few had travel experience, nobody read books, and so just lacked the will to make the best of the situation. There were plenty of opportunities beyond *Stella* in the NAAFI, poker in the billet or going to the pictures. I wasn't averse to the pictures - in a cinema open to the sky. With hindsight I reckon it was a particularly rich period for films. From reading through my letters I went to see The Pickwick Papers, The Cruel Sea, The Yellow Balloon, Sparticus, Stagecoach, The Glen Miller Story, Les Miserables, Prisoner of Zenda, Calamity Jane, Moulin Rouge, A Day to Remember, The Holly and the Ivy, Hobson's Choice, The Good Die Young, Kind Hearts and Coronets, The Planter's Wife, Genevieve, Escape from Fort Bravo, Gentlemen Prefer Blondes, The Caine Mutiny, Eight O' Clock Walk and The Million Pound Note.

I obviously took my 'reading' (and writing) seriously. With

a windfall of back pay I made a 'raid' on the closing-down
bookshop in Fayid, our nearest town, returning with Macaul-
ay's *History of England*, plays of Oscar Wilde, and Chekhov,
the *Kalevala*, a book on Buddhism, one on the Aztecs, *Aesop's
Fables*, Thomas à Kempis, and novels by Dumas, Flaubert
and Dostoyevsky. No wonder an ammunition box of books
was sent home on leaving. I had bookshelves by my bed made
from orange boxes. I once overheard myself described as 'the
book bloke'. My billet mates always demanded I read out 'the
funny bits' when I sniggered on my pit. Very few ever take up
my invitation to 'borrow any book any time'.

One of my major commitments was becoming involved
with Christian activities, with services in Deversoir, rallies
and conventions at the Mission to Mediterranean Garrisons
in Fayid or enjoying some social life at the Church of Scotland's Dumbarton House. This led to the course in Jerusalem,
mentioned elsewhere, and also my conducting services, both
for C of E or O Ds. There can't be many Leading Aircraftsmen
who have had the opportunity of preaching to their senior
officers! (I probably had the largest-ever congregation at
Deversoir as all my mates in the Signals Section came along
to support me.) I'd several of these services at Fayid as well
as Dev. Padres were becoming in short supply like everything
else. Most curious of all was a ceremony, in mid-November,
of 'undedicating' the station church and I wrote home giving
a full description of this with helpful illustrations.

This was very much a C of E ceremonial but the ecumen-
ical Scot was invited to carry the Bible in the procession. In
front went the Crucifer then, in pairs, two Taperers; Font
bowl and Bell; Prayer Book and Bible; Altar Cross, Cruet
and Altar Book; The Dev. C of E chaplain with chalice, etc;
the O D staff chaplain and C of E staff chaplain; the Dev. O
D chaplain and the C O. There was much singing and then

every object was undedicated, including the pulpit and altar. I found it quite moving. We slowly went out, the doors were shut and we processed round the building to the singing of Onward Christian Soldiers.

'In Orders today the O C said that as far as the RAF is concerned we will nearly all be spread out in the Command, which means one of Gibraltar, Malta, Cyprus, Turkey, Amman, Aden, North Africa, or Iraq. Much as I would like to return and see you all again, I hope I'll not be posted back to England. Who knows, I might even end up by living with aunt Nell in Kyrenia. Not a hope for Germany [brother doing his years there in REME], though having said so I will probably go there now!'

On my last night at Deversoir I gave the billet a shock. They came back from the NAAFI to find the teetotal Brown sitting on his bed - drunk. I'd in fact collected lots of empty beer bottles which I scattered about and one full one which I poured down my front so the place reeked. My mates were greeted in slurred tones. 'Ma goad, it's Broon, drunk!' I couldn't not snigger, which made it worse. 'Really, I thought better of him. Listen to that language.' They began to panic: I was off at 0600 in the morning. 'Here, gie's a haun wi him'. I fought against being put to bed and a glorious mêlée ensued. Eventually they realised they'd been had. Quite a few of *them* were the worse for wear the next morning. I flew to Aden, with its even hotter conditions, then on to RAF Eastleigh, outside Nairobi, for the equally eventful second year of National Service.

PERUVIAN PLACES

Into the 1970s expeditions to Peru were rare and tourism almost non-existent so I was lucky to spend summer 1971 there, seeing many of the great historic sites and making a big circular trek round the Cordillera Blanca, ascending, at last, a peak over 6000 metres. The following are just three glimpses from that time.

1.

Arequipa sat like an oasis in a desert when seen from the air. We liked the place, even with Sunday being as lively as a Stornoway Sabbath. The buildings are all a volcanic rock, *sillar*, like Camembert cheese in texture, old churches with carved doorways and secretive courtyards round the Plaza des Armas. Things improved in the evening: we shopped in a lively market, ate locally, and enjoyed the *passeo*. The worst deluge in years had cut road and rail access so, luckily, we had flown from Lima. Bolivia was having one of its regular revolutions so we were advised to stay this side of Lake Titicaca. (The British Ambassador in Uruguay was kidnapped by terrorists in January.) We did cruise out to see the reed boats and sad floating islands.

After exploring the lake and the ruins at Sillustani we had a bus ride to Juliaca. We met Beryl and Bruce there, and a trio who took us to their Hotel Benique, where we had an enjoyable spicy *lomo chorillaña*. After a siesta we had our 'ending' shopping spree: fantastic alpaca scarves, rugs, brass figures of laden llamas [on my window sill as I write], all being sold by brightly-dressed, over-dressed, well-proportioned peasant women in exotic hats. Part of the market, alas, was given over to selling the worst of Chinese/Western junk to the locals. Next day we ran into the Feddens and Patrick Leigh Fermor and met two of a big climbing expedition who had dispersed following their success in the Andes.

This sudden 'conglomerate' of Brits was due to our all being mountaineering, entomologists and other groups making up membership of the Andean Society, formed through the efforts of Beryl Griffiths, who organised the chartering of a flight to Peru, chartering the only cheap option in those days. [I'm still in touch with Beryl 45 years on.]

From Arequipa we spent a morning at the Monasterio de Santa Catalina, 'an incredible place, for all the world like the Alhambra in its ramifications. To the world all white *sillar* walls, inside it is a town in itself with streets, courts, churches, baths, kitchens... Wealthy girls have their own quarters and the communal resources of the nuns, now occupying only a small part. Each courtyard was a different colour, there were paintings everywhere, even a 'Zurbaran Room', the wash place was simply a row of huge earthenware jars cut in half, the kitchens were black and reeked of smoke, shafts of light piercing the gloom from holes in the roof, and wrought-iron chandeliers hung in the cafeteria. The garden was a blaze of bougainvillea and agelessly peaceful, so returning to the twentieth century was quite jarring. Most of our gang have been in Morocco often enough that when we first caught sight of the monastery several said, 'It's Morocco!' which in a roundabout way it was. Many of the Conquistadors came from the south of Spain or Extremadura, lands which had been Moorish for many hundreds of years (more centuries than there's been a Spain!) and whose architecture was Moorish. So it seemed logical to us that when they built this great edifice it had the look of what we knew in Andalucia or El Jadida. Morocco had also obtruded some days earlier. Peru, Portugal and Morocco are the great sardine producers of the world. We opened some tins of sardines bought locally and they were spicy, just as we knew in Morocco, which was commented on, and then on the bottom we found stamped, 'Fabrique au Maroc'. Talk of coals to Newcastle!

2.

We were in Coche 13 which we had to ourselves. The train left Cuzeo by a succession of zigzags, shunting back and forth while the town seemed to expand in its bowl below. We were soon higher than the big cross figure and change to loops and bends through to Arco, the high point at 3678m (12,000 feet). The smoky dawn light on the town became crisp sunlight over the wide spaciousness we travelled, in the distance snowy giants like Salquantay. Landscape, colouring, crops, beasts appeared as in all desert-into-mountain locations we knew. Passengers, we noted, came from the USA, France and Germany, many locals, the tailored, the poncho-ed, the beatniks, and we bearded climbers.

The valley seemed to have no exit till we suddenly swung right and plunged into a gorge. On to Pachar where we joined the wider Vilcanota/Urubamba valley. Pedlars lined the track. We crossed the road to the great Inca walls of Ollantaytambo [visited later] and thereafter made our lonely progress down, down, the river sometimes docile, sometimes rushing rapids, sometimes the valley opening up, sometimes the line merely squeezed between mountains and river. Here and there above us we glimpsed jagged peaks and snowy giants. Strange raptors and bright jungle birds were puzzles. The vegetation became progressively more jungly, soaring 2-3000 feet above us in spinach-greens, granite walls with red flowers clinging to niches, all the more exotic from not recognising what we saw: trees with red blossom, bamboo-like groves. After about 70 miles we went through a tunnel and passed a train which could have come straight out of a Western: bulbous chimney puffing out black smoke, cowcatcher in front, wild-looking passengers ... We glimpsed buildings on high. Our destination. The station was at 1998m (6,500ft), the ruins above at 2430m (8000ft). Fortunately there were minibuses and a truck to carry us up the 15 or so hairpins to reach this seldom-seen, long-hidden Inca marvel of Macchu Picchu. [In 2014 over one million people visited Macchu Picchu.]

3.

The Portachuelo de Yanganuco (4,767 metres) was the resounding name for our pass back over the Andes spine. We had woken to a frosty world which attractively decorated all vegetation in white hoar but set the tents stiff as boards. The cloud rolled in and it began to snow, the path was muddy and Pedro's voice echoed among the crags as we threaded a route through the tarns: following the dainty slots of the *burros'* footprints and the sprawling tyre-sole treadmarks of Fidel and Benedicto. Pedro, tall and dignified, we liked very much. The two *arrieros* were sad, incompetent youths with whom we could establish no relationship. An Indian family came down, singing one of their haunting refrains, garbed in brilliant colours as usual, and we noticed the mother had a dog instead of a baby tied to her back. The col was bleak but we saw Huascarán, high, and lifting its chunky twin summits above the clouds. The 6,768 metre North Summit is the highest point in Peru while, in the Americas, only Aconcagua and a few neighbours are higher. We walked with giants: Chacraraju, Pisco, Huandoy ranging along the north side of the Quebrada Yanganuco, while Chopicalqui and Huascarán hemmed in the south. Dusk, supper and rain came together. The drips from the roof of the tent tinkled on the plates sitting on the floor. We squatted in the squalor quite contentedly - till a larger patter of drips landed on the candles. The overnight occupiers waited till everything froze-dried before rolling out their bedding.

The path zigzagged down, contoured, then zigzagged again as we came 'down to a temperate valley ... smelling of vegetation ...' We found a hidden shelf under the peak of Pisco and set up our tents. 'Wake to frozen calm. Out to a staggering view of the great, castellated Huascarán: the South Peak a bridal train of snow, the North Peak a plastered keep of warm rock and white battlements. Chopicalqui lies edge on, improbably steep, while on this side of it the mists boil over our pass of yesterday. The snow is almost down to our level, so we just crossed in time. Later, the sun touched everything with gold ...'

We kept on by the old ways, a track which wended by the two larger lakes set in the valley. Past the first lake was a colossal stone avalanche, from the 1970 catastrophe. Under the debris lies the fatal camp site of fifteen climbers from Czechoslovakia. The second *laguna* was noisy with ducks, gulls and an osprey. Red-barked *quenual* trees gave a somewhat stagey touch but the gentleness vanished abruptly as the trail wound down, much too steeply to try and cut the corners while, overhead, rose sheer rock walls and prows of granite on a scale none of us had ever seen before. The Huascarán side was a succession of massive buttresses. After a final twist down, the country opened out before us, patched with fields of barley, a rich landscape of yellows, purples and browns.

We came on the debris of the great avalanche of the year before and stopped to eat simply to break the hold of its overwhelming impact. Hummingbirds, oropendolas and blue butterflies were daggers of life in that valley of death. We walked for miles with the wounded world of the *teremoto* beside us. Across the valley it looked as if open-cast mining had been operating up in the clouds on Huascarán and the rubbish of a century tipped down to obliterate cultivation and trails with sharp brutality. The Cordillera have a long history of earthquakes but that of 31st May 1970 was unprecedented. In the Callejón de Huaylas 70-80,000 died and a million were left homeless. Huaras, with 40,000 inhabitants, saw 20,000 killed. This was the biggest human disaster in the history of the Americas. And Huascarán too was shaken.

Our first glimpse of the mountain had been from Huaras, which was a mess of rubble and rebuilding, and Caras, along the Rio Santa, was cut off for days as helicopters could not fly through the dust and it was a month before any vehicle could break a way in. But, for us, the full horror was personified that day leaving the mountains.

High in the North Peak of Huascarán a granite buttress collapsed in the quake and fell into this valley. The forces and figures are hard to grasp: 10-15 million cubic feet of rock and several million cubic feet of ice fell, mixing together (and with the soil) to form a concrete-like mass travelling at 300 kilometres per hour. It fell 4,000 metres and travelled 14 kilometres before reaching the Rio Santa near Yungay, turned down past Caras to finally stop after a total distance of 65 kilometres. Yungay was wiped off the face of the earth: 18,000 people perished, only 240 survived. To try and grasp the scale imagine a mountain the height of six Ben Nevises, standing in for Ben More on Mull. Yungay would be Oban - to which disaster came in 3 minutes and the flow ended not far short of Glasgow.

Our walk down into Yungay was an emotional experience. An inestimable sadness seemed to haunt the dead, concrete-bare, slopes. Only a few straggling plants starred the wastes. Rough wooden crosses had been erected all over the place and we passed one or two black-dressed women here and there, kneeling before these markers of lost homes, lost families. They told their beads and the tears fell down their shocked faces. In passing we could only turn to them our own tearful eyes, a brief bond in the bleak misery of suffering. Yungay had been protected from previous avalanches by a 200 metre high hill ridge but this gigantic avalanche simply swept over it and down onto the town. The debris lies four metres deep over everything, 70 million tons of it. The few who survived were able to run up a hill to the cemetery. As we descended we could see how the flow lapped up to the statue of a Christ figure, arms outstretched, leaving just that tiny island of safety. The tops of four scrawny palm trees marked the town centre - the only living things to have survived the crushing sludge.

It was not the happy ending we had envisaged but it was an unforgettable one. The name Yungay can still bring a lump to my throat and I look back on one of the most moving experiences of my life. The world, sadly, is full of Yungays, all crying out to shame our soft, self-indulgent, affluent society.

PEGGY AND PEOPLE

I speak of Africa and Golden Joys.
Shakespeare

Peggy and I first met at the one-time Essaouira camp site half way along the seafront where we had our camping cars: my VW, her Land Rover. The site was shaded by mimosa trees and the yellow pompoms often dropped into our soup. I'd an interesting task to work on: adding all the Munros on to Bartholomew maps, so frequently had sheets spread all around. Peggy's curiosity eventually had her asking what I was doing and we became good friends. (Over the years she would tour with me in Morocco, Spain - where she lived - Scotland and Ireland.) Next to us was a rather grand GB mobile home where a lady sat at a typewriter for many hours a day, too formidable-looking for us to dare interrupt or ask what she was doing (writing a book it proved on the life of Burckhardt.*)

Eventually she invited us to tea, which proved a rather formal affair with a card table covered with a cloth and proper china. She chanced to sit looking out over the road to sands and sea and Mogador Island while Peggy and I faced into the bustling campsite. We felt a bit like children who had to be on our best behaviour. Our decorum was to be seriously tested. Thirty yards away a big black local mongrel had found a small lovesick poodle - with natural consequences. But the quickly satisfied pair were then unable to separate. The dog yowled, the bitch whined and the contortions they went through would have graced (or disgraced) a canine Kamasutra. The poodle owner was screaming, her husband poured a bucket of water over the writhing couple, while half the campsite danced around the agonising performance. Meanwhile we had to sit impassive and polite, sipping tea, nibbling Welsh cookies and contribute sociable chitchat.

A hotel now stands on that campsite and Esssaouira has spread out to become a city; extraordinary, as in Victorian times it stood in the middle of a desert with the walled town and port clinging to the dangerous coast. Francis Drake had a last rendezvous here before heading off on his circumnavigation. The constant *alizé* (wind) and wide Atlantic-fuelled rollers make it Surfing City today - so it escapes the concentrated beach-shy tourism of Agadir. The old walled city however has kept its charm: narrow streets and tall buildings, warm yellow stone arches and woodwork picked out in sky-blue, miles of sand running north and south. You can walk the battlements (the *skala*) with rows of brass cannon pointing seawards and the waves crashing onto the jagged reefs below. Under the battlements are the arched workshops of wood-workers who turn out inlaid work (marquetry) of great skill, very much an Essa speciality. The knotted roots of the local *thuya* give unusual spotted patterns.

Peggy and I had wandered round the busy fishing port where graceful boats are still being built by centuries-old methods and had then retreated to the main square for a lunch of fresh, grilled sardines served with bread hot from the oven. Later we sat over by the red walls to catch the after-noon sun and have coffee. Two boys came and stood beside us and, when a tourist family at the next table departed, leaving barely-started *cocas* behind, the boys gestured to us to pass them over. They then sat down beside us, smiled their thanks and slowly supped their drinks.

They were well dressed and groomed, obviously not beggars, and had an air of self-possession though somewhat enigmatic. As soon as we started a conversation we realised they were deaf and dumb, not that that inhibited them in any way. We had a hilarious hour together, a challenging hour too, swopping information and questions, questions, all through gestures and meaningful grunts and facial expressions. Peggy taught them to count up to a hundred, I entertained them by drawing objects which they pointed to, such as the bulbous teapots (a British introduction centuries ago) or even people. I then had them drawing and was inter-ested to see them produce the potato and matchstick figures kids would draw at home. I'd my camera with me so took photographs of them and Peggy and let them take photo-graphs of each other and us. In the gathering dusk we walked across the square to the hotel Peggy and I were staying in. At the arched *medina* entrance we shook hands after they had invited us to the beach next morning to see them playing football. (At weekend low tide times the beach is taken over by many serious teams and leagues playing the game.)

Our hotel was a new one which had tempted us to stay there. A couple of years before, book and antique store owner Josef Seabag was acting agent for the now foreign owners (Josef had lived in New York for fifteen years). Historically, Essaouira had a strong Jewish element, but this had declined through the C20. This house had not been lived in since early C20, but was still in the family possession. Josef had shown us round the house, the traditional five storeys with central space, balconies round each floor, an Esssaouira design that made for coolness and shade in the summer heat. We trod warily as much of the timber had almost turned to dry honeycomb. It was a strange time capsule. On one wall there was a copy of the well-known Jubilee portrait of Queen Victoria. The interior had been gutted and, keeping to traditional styles, was now a graceful hotel, the flat roof looking to the sunset ocean, and with gulls already nesting in the corners.

The next morning, we duly attended the football match of our two lads and several more of like disability. What disability? From a distance it could have been any group of youngsters enjoying their game. Silent it wasn't! Peggy and I departed that afternoon and I told them I'd bring prints of the photos we'd taken the following year, *Insh'Allah*. I did, but strangely, never encountered any of the boys again, nor during an autumn visit so the following spring I showed the photos to one of the square's touts who said they knew the boys; they were from the local deaf and dumb school. He'd get in touch. The following night I was at the postcard rack when suddenly hands were clutching my arms and the familiar grunts and noises were there. The photos caused great excitement, so much so that another teenage tout came over to see what was up. Reassured, he went in to the shop and brought out an envelope so the trophy photos could be carried away safely.

The touts knew me well enough (I probably kent their faithers) and we always greeted each other. They could sometimes be pestilential to tourists but they were just trying to make a little money, to exist. They'd nothing, often no home, no support, *real* nothing. They had enterprise however and determination to better themselves. I counted several as friends. In the Marrakech Gueliz (new town) I used to encounter a teenager who, all day, carried his severely disabled brother on his back, surviving on what they could beg among the cafés. Islam is strong on charitable acts (one of the pillars of their faith) and locals I noted gave more readily than tourists. We encountered each other often, became friends of a sort I suppose, meetings that were hard to bear, the younger smiling as speech was impossible. They were always together, but carrying the helpless brother must have become an ever-growing ordeal then, when we met on one occasion, they had a wheelchair - thanks to the American Peace Corps - and were so proud. They wiggled through between the tables of posh foreigners at this up-market café and I was greeted by kisses on each cheek and happily reciprocated. We received some startled looks.

Up at the Saturday *souk* in Asni, on the route over the Atlas and also part of the 'Toubkal Trail' I knew a tout who had no legs and buzzed about on the ground begging and trying to sell 'Berber silver' items. He was one of a tribe who had come over the Atlas and squatted on barren ground nearby and were slowly, doggedly, improving themselves, the teenagers becoming skilled purveyors of this basically cheap jewellery. At the time of Saddam's war when there were no flights and no tourists they faced really hard times. I recall the extraordinary affection I gained when passing through Asni at the time and had them all receive bowls of soup and bread from a stall. Next year I was there with Peggy and at once my legless friend invited us for mint tea, swinging himself up onto a chair and going through the complex ceremony with gracious skill. He too was now the proud owner of a wheelchair. 'Where was it?' 'Oh, I don't use it at the Saturday *souk*, I get far more money scrabbling about on the ground'. There are few towns in Morocco today where I am not greeted by name from some owner of a jewellery shop who originally was one of these 'pests' in Asni. Essaouira has several and I've difficulty walking an alley without being invited to stop for a chat and a cup of mint tea. Moroccan life has this graciousness which is so warming, the true Berber/Islamic culture which is a million miles from the abhorrence of the brainwashed extremists. (Christian extremism was just as bad in its time.) Peggy, in her eighties, was to experience this graciousness to the full at Asni. She was bitten by a mule.

Decades on I'm still asked about 'the mule lady'. Mules don't bite people. Peggy was carrying a bag of vegetables and we assume the beast made a snatch at that and accidentally caught her forearm. We were living with 'my' Mohammed and family up at Imlil and, like any locals, went down to shop at the weekly *souk*. All I could do was ask another Imlil lad to inform Mohammed we were heading to Marrakech and might not be home for a day or two. At the shared taxi rank the driver waved aside the 'only going when six people aboard' rule and sped down to Marrakech and took us right to the Hotel Ali in the *medina*, breaking the rule of keeping outside the city walls. 'The police would understand.' The hotel was teeming (a Moroccan and French holiday) and full but, Ellam, busy booking people in, changing money, doing a hundred and one things, calmly told us to use room 109 as those booked were only coming off a late flight. She'd phone for a doctor. He came in and said Peggy should go to the hospital and also have a course of rabies jags. Ellam put the hotel's car at our disposal and, finally, the hotel full, took us to her home for the night.

---

*Katharine Sim: *Desert Traveller, The Life of Jean Louis Burckhart.* Gollancz. 1969. Burckhart was the discoverer of Petra and Abu Simbel and also made a successful visit to holy Mecca.

LAST GASP ETHIOPIA

There aint no journey that don't charge you some.
Mark Twain: *Huckleberry Finn*

Ethiopia became more than a mythical sort of name when I was in the Junior School at Dollar at the end of World War Two. I'd come as a refugee from our Japanese defeat in the east and sat between two other likewise exiled by differing wars: a blonde Norwegian boy and one Alexander Desta, grandson of the Emperor Haile Selassie of Ethiopia - and an odd trio we must have looked when parading to church in our kilts.

Over the years my reading and listening to the radio kept the name Ethiopia fresh. I found and read Dervla Murphy's book, *In Ethiopia With a Mule* (Murray 1968), then the only English language account of the real life among the poor, proud peasantry. She travelled alone, was robbed by *shifta* (bandits), scratched and starved, fought and froze ...

a real female, Irish, Thesiger. (Wilfred Thesiger was born in Ethiopia of British diplomatic stock but as a young man made hair-raising journeys in the country, and went on to become one of the most famous travellers of the C20.)

In another book I came on this brief note mentioning, 'Commander Alexander Desta, a British-educated grandson of the Emperor and a man of great gifts, is the senior Ethiopian officer in this young [Air] Force'. My old classmate. I'd also read of Blashford Snell's madcap first descent of the Blue Nile through its gorges in 1968, a real *Boys' Own* adventure with plenty of near disasters and being shot at. (One Chris Bonington was expedition photographer but thereafter decided to keep to the less dangerous world of mountains.)

When Ethiopia floated to the top of a 'must see' list I signed up in 1973 to go on a tour of the country, travelling mainly by bus, sometimes flying, mostly camping and taking in much of the rich culture, sights and wildlife. A remarkable introduction it proved. That Ethiopia had summits even higher than my regular Atlas Mountains was a lure. The country is nearly all mountains but often of vast plateaux, dissected by mighty gorges and weathered into peaks of fantastical appearance.

Nobody really knows where the people originated: as black-skinned as can be yet unrelated to the rest of Africa. Some suggest an Arabian origin. There are the myths of Prester John and the more historical Queen of Sheba. In one roadside market among the pottery items were the figures of Solomon and the Queen of Sheba lying on a bed. For a few pence more you could have a small baby figure as well - the one who became Menelik, the claimed ancestor of all rulers since. Haile Selassie's full title was 'His Imperial Majesty, Conquering Lion of the Tribe of Judah, Elect of God, Emperor of Ethiopia'. At Axum the monks showed us ancient imperial crowns, royal robes and ceremonial parasols, and at others we saw manuscripts of immeasurable value - and paintings and frescos likewise - often in woeful state, smeared with pigeon droppings, and frail to failing. The country was desperately poor, in some areas we saw markets overflowing with grain while at the same time in another province starvation loomed. [In this year many hundreds of thousands did perish.] In the capital our hotel was next to a fine equipped modern hospital, the gift of an affluent western state, yet it stood empty. There were no trained medics to run it. We travelled with an armed guard because of *shifta*. Often chilling mutterings of '*farange*' (foreigners) came our way. Ineffectual government was writing out its own death warrant. One gain for us was the absence of massed tourism, despite some posters tempting with 'thirteen months of sunshine'. (Their calendar had 12 months of 30 days, one of 5 days!)

We journeyed north-south in a small bus, starting from Asmara in what was then a province, Eritrea, which was bubbling with secessionist revolt and ended up in the capital Addis Ababa. I'd a tent companion who seemed to spend the night thumping into me. In self-defence I was often early up and the one to get stoves on for breakfast. I quite enjoyed people-watching within our group because I'd no responsibilities. There were the skivers and the workers, the helpful and the obtuse, old and young-ish, the kitchen queens and those who were carefully kept off cooking duties after their first effort.

The north was very arid, the best cultivation up in the Simien Mountains. Ras Dashan 15,158ft (4620m) is Ethiopia's highest summit but was simply a swelling on the vast high plateau land, a patchwork of fields and grazing animals. Shepherd boys would strand on one leg, muffled up in their cloaks, arms linked over a stick on their shoulders to watch us pass. They wore woven hats like inverted flowerpots. No begging though one was rewarded for playing a primitive one-stringed instrument with a bow. I think the tip was to stop any chance of an encore. I've never seen such a fly-blown world. Toddlers would turn faces to us with flies massing, unchecked on their eyes and mouths. We carefully avoided well water, seeing how donkey and human churned-up glaur simply ran back into the well. Girls lowered buckets made from half an inner tube with a rope through it and the rope was a tube pared like an apple into a continuous strip. Bottled water was our mainstay. One bottle informed, 'The mineral water Dongollo is very efficient in any disturbances …' Roadside cafés were marked by having a cup upside down on top of a stick stuck in the ground.

The road was unsurfaced and quite a feat of engineering. We once drove twenty miles to cover three miles as the crow flies (or the flies crow). A hairpin bend on stilts appears on a postage stamp, and at it there was a warning, 'Caution. Viaduct ahead has started moving and may be hazardous to traffic'. There was a gap a foot wide to get on to it.

The landscape is the abiding memory, a landscape of almost oppressive spectacles, vast, far horizons, yet as our guide said, 'You cannot eat rock'. We constantly had to remind ourselves we were over 7000 feet for days on end. The Simien Mountains shoot up improbable-looking spires and towers with huge faces on which vultures nest. (I wonder if any rock-climber has eyed them up yet?) Other hills are flat-topped and cliff-girt, *ambas*, on which forts and monasteries were built, safe from attack. Many royal princes were marooned on such a perch 'in the interests of national security'.

We camped under one *amba*, Debre Damo, crowned

with an early Christian sanctuary. The only way in was to be hauled up by rope and, that day marking some festival, the action was continuous. The pilgrims came striding over the hills, powerful, gangly figures in flowing white *shamas* (robes) and carrying the heavy stick without which no adult male seems to feel safe.

We descended from the Simiens to Gondar, one of the world's notable 'lost cities', with pepper-pot castles influenced by Indian and Portuguese styles. The latter were the first Europeans to penetrate this fortress of a country. They were called in to balance the Ottoman threat. Christian and Moslem co-existed we noted. (Now?) Fasiladas, the founder of Gondar, expelled the Portuguese in 1632 and over the next two decades successive rulers built palaces, according to what wealth, power and longevity was granted. It was thought unlucky to live in any previous ruler's building. The wonder is so much remains. The last battering was from the British, wartime bombing to oust the occupying Italians (hence Alexander Desta at Dollar).

After the great days at Gondar the country disintegrated into warring factions - their Wars of the Roses. In the mid-nineteenth century the Emperor Tewodros (Theodore) had to face the realities of the west. He squabbled with Queen Victoria and imprisoned various diplomats, missionaries and artisans. Not being within reach of a gunboat a cumbersome army was sent under Sir Robert Napier who defeated the Emperor in Tigre province, sorted things out, and then reversed homewards. (Britain did not want to be involved.) In 1941 Ethiopia and Liberia were the only parts of Africa not under some kind of colonial rule.

From Gondar we visited the most astonishing historic site of all, at Lalibela, flying there in an old Dakota. Lalibela is hard to explain. Imagine walking along and suddenly being brought up short on the edge of a deep hole, sharp-edged like a quarry rim, inside of which, rather tight-fitting, is a church. Yes. In the hole. There because the church was not *built* but was hewn *in situ* out of the solid rock. And there are eleven of them, all the work of a ruler Lalibela who died in 1225. Lalibela and Axum are now World Heritage sites.

Britain first became aware of Ethiopia in the C18 from the writings of James Bruce of Kinnaird, a remarkable man in many ways besides being huge in stature; he was squire, businessman, scholar, scientist, linguist, artist, consul and ceaseless traveller. By sheer force of character he survived years in Ethiopia and his *Travels* included a mass of history, geography and ethnology on the country. Some of his reporting, though true, saw him laughed to scorn. (Who could believe tales of fresh meat being sliced from living animals which were then sent off to graze again?) His travels took him round Lake Tana to discover the source of the Blue Nile, but erudition was combined with his audacity. For centuries the Book of Enoch was a 'lost book' of the Apocrypha but Bruce brought back a copy in Ge'ez, an ancient Ethiopian language. And it was only translatable because an equivalent of the Rosetta stone was found, inscribed in three Ethiopian languages.

We flew over Lake Tana and also sailed out on it to visit remote island monasteries. Reed boats on it looked very similar to those I had seen on Lake Titicaca in the Andes, another big high-altitude lake. Lake Tana is 6000ft above sea level. From it flows the Abbai, the Blue Nile, most powerful of Africa's rivers. Between the Lake and the Sudan border lies 500 miles of canyon, bridged only at three places. The slim 'Portuguese Bridge' is an old pack bridge reminiscent of the Linn o' Dee - an impressive sight but only a prelude to that further along the path - the Tississat Falls. These rank with the finest in the world, finer I reckon than Victoria, to which there is a close resemblance, as both plunge over long lips into gorges. Here you can step back and see much of it in one panoramic gaze, which is impossible with the Victoria Falls.

Gorges of thousands of feet always impress. A hundred Stanage Edges one on top of another - and the happy home of rare baboons, and also climate on top of climate. This trip gave me the most exciting bird-watching ever, quite apart from the constant of vultures high in the sky. Vivid memories are of an Abyssinian ground hornbill struggling with a snake in its bill or a pair of white-naped ravens in flight passing a stick to and fro between them and a turaco perching on the tent. There were so many birds too small, just glimpsed, so impossible to recognise. Names were often a delight: paradise whydah, wattled ibis, auger buzzard, woolly-necked stork, blue-winged goose, slender-billed starling, mousebird, long crested hawk eagle, crowned crane, white-backed black tit, and many more. (I haven't made up any name.)

Addis Ababa, which translates as *New Flower*, was simply the practical return to civilsation so called. We did see the Emperor drive past with a guest, Archbishop Makarios, in his posh car. There wasn't much else posh and there was a distinct feeling of tenseness. Only a couple of months later various mutinies began among lower officer ranks.

Ethiopia had fascinated me on our November 1973 visit to an extent I wanted to return, and soon, to go afoot into some of the wild places and immerse myself in its peoples' cultures. I thought it might be fun to contact my old Dollar classmate who was now in charge of the country's navy: might just lead to something interesting on the Red Sea. During a lunch break at school a year later I roughed out a letter with the intention of typing it at the weekend. I never did. The radio announced there had been a coup in Ethiopia, the Emperor had been deposed (he was later murdered) and among the first sixty or so executed in the first wave of revolutionary violence (November 1974) was Admiral Alexander Desta. Decades of drought, famine (worst in 1984) and civil war would follow, the Marxist regime's stranglehold lasting till 1991. I was not to return.

THIS AND THAT

DURBAN CASTLE

During my year in the Canal Zone I joined a consortium who had built a catamaran out of whatever could be found, the hulls made by beating-out the drop tanks from the early Vampire fighters. These would be found out in the desert by the locals and sold on to us. Sailing on the salty Bitter Lakes was another great freedom which I relished. We were based where the canal entered the lake and found 'steam gives way to sail' something of a myth. The *Durban Castle* finally did for us.

The liner probably left the canal too fast but, whatever, the effect was to suck the water from under us so we hit bottom - and then were smashed by the returning walls of water. I had a cold so was dressed, sitting in the bows reading, rather than in swimming trunks manning the ropes. Swept away like a rag in a washing machine I came up still clasping my book: Philippe Diolé: *The Undersea Adventure*. (I still have the water-stained souvenir.) Our craft was beyond repairing and we were lucky not to have had anybody injured. Not long afterwards I was posted to Nairobi.

There was a sequel to this episode. Almost a year later some of us took leave for a holiday in Mombasa on the

Kenya coast. Nancy Graham, a civilian friend, was sailing to Blighty and we accompanied her aboard her ship to see her off. The liner was the *Durban Castle*.

A JERUSALEM LETTER

While stationed in Egypt's Canal Zone (RAF Deversoir) in 1954 I was able to go on a course in friendly Jerusalem. This is what I reported home after the visit - now one more place in the world I'd not care to return to as gods and greed have created such misery for millions.

We flew from Fayid to Mafraq in Jordan, changed into civvies in Amman and on to Jerusalem by bus for our week living in the Christ Church Hostel in the walled Old City near the Citadel. Called a Moral Leadership Course but really a solid series of fascinating theological lectures: two dozen of us, all ranks, even females (!) with chaplains Douglas Lewis and Leonard Bridgeman the lecturers. Only for ODs ('Other Denominations', ie, all who weren't 'C of E'). Patronising, eh? I've even conducted C of E services but when I said I'd like to attend communion I was told this would first have to be considered by the Bishop of the Lower Nile. I almost laughed. What a Gilbert and Sullivan title.

Luckily we were in Jerusalem at a period of relative calm. Divided since 1949 with a no-man's land separating Arab and Jewish areas. Most of the sites are in Jordan who, of course, gain from all the Christian tourists. We made great friends with the soldiers of the Arab Legion next door in the Citadel. [Then still commanded by the Englishman Glubb Pasha]. We were living high on Zion looking down on the city, over the domes of the Holy Sepulchre to the Kedron

Valley and the Mount of Olives. The Old City, walled and gated, is only about 1½ miles round.

One night after prayers several of us explored the old town's unlit streets then ran into the padres and Nicem, our official guide. We then formed a 'dragon' and wended out of the Damascus Gate and in and out and along streets like tunnels to everyone's amusement. Among the exotic shops and crowds we came on a place, The Gondola, where 30 ices and much Turkish coffee was consumed. Cost about a shilling each! We took the girls there too and a boy entertained us and scores of locals with conjuring tricks. We also had our rotund policeman friend, Moses, along. He has a helmet with a spike on top and tells fantastic yarns. We are made so welcome. The graciousness of Islam.

Another time a sixteen-year-old Abraham invited us into his shop. He's an orphan and runs the place with two bonnie sisters and a wee brother who gabbles in half a dozen languages, sometimes all at once. Abraham keeps the shop smart and even showed us the books. He dreams of visiting England (don't we all!). We had tea of course. He wasn't trying any selling, just enjoying *us* in his hard, lonely life. I left some coins under a cushion as a surprise - offering them would have been offensive.

There's an old ragged shoeshine outside our gate, from, dawn to golden dusk, who always greets us with a polite 'Good morning' even at night. What a shine he produces and we discussed if we couldn't smuggle him to the Zone and hire him out.

I made quite a few visits to the Church of the Holy Sepulchre, a rather ugly place propped up by scaffolding, dark and dirty. It is used by Armenians, Greek, RC, Abyssinians and others who compete in many ways - but not in cleanliness (next to Godliness!?). Entering, a man prostrated himself to kiss the stone on which supposedly they laid Jesus after he was taken down from the cross. The Chapel of Calvary glittered from hundreds of silver lamps and altars with flickering candles. A child stood clapping hands. Pretty. Pretty. I placed a few coppers in a tray and took two candles. (A monk at once pounced on my coins.) There were chapels on top of chapels, some with services on, sonorous chanting, and processions of various orders in everything from glittering robes to black-bearded, black-robed monks in flower-pot hats. Everyone was given a swing from the incense-burners, including the devout and curious bystanders. In the RC chapel a few monks and visitors knelt silently before an unusually clean, tidy altar. My candle held aloft, picked out delicate frescos of faded saints and scenes, almost lost from centuries of grime. The dancing shadows, voices chanting, all far underground, was quite creepy.

Descending steps to the very depths I came on a bent, shrivelled, muttering old woman so I took her arm to help her down the steps. She eventually slipped onto her knees, weeping and kissing the stones. The only light was my candle. The old lady was from Finland. More chapels, more noisy chanting, incense, half-seen paintings. When I stepped out my mind was in a whirl and I was quite relieved to be plain Presbyterian.

We made some journeys outside the city: to Samaria, Mount Gerizim, Nablus (Jacob's Well), Bethlehem which was interesting in a sentimental way: a star marking where Jesus was born, another where he lay in the manger. As if they could know. Everything is now below ground and a church built over*. In the city we found the Pool of Bethesda; also underground, reached by narrow stairs in the dark. The lad going down in front suddenly went splash, splash, splash, so it is still a well! The most spectacular buildings of all were the Mosque of El Aksa and the glittery, tile-covered Dome of the Rock, this being the second most holy place in Islam, where the Prophet rose to heaven.

The most fascinating activity I discovered was down in the busy street of the Chain. In the back of the shop of one, Nieem, we saw candles being made. Beeswax and paraffin wax. An iron hoop hangs down with hooks all round the rim from which threads are suspended. Deftly he turns the contraption while pouring wax down the wicks. By the time it has circled right round the wax has dried so on goes another layer. It took three hours Nieem said to make a set of half-inch diameter candles. The wax is melted in a wide dish heated by a Primus stove.

We flew back at about 6000ft most of the way: two hours over rugged mountains and wavy sands, (why on earth did Moses and Co spend *40 years* wandering about?) so were almost glad to cross the Red Sea and get 'home'. Back to earth, or should I say sand. No more changing for civilised meals and a table bright with fresh fruit. Just corned dog and POM.

---

*By coincidence, the day I dug out this letter (17.01.16) there was a small newspaper article mentioning the completion of two years' work to restore the Church of the Nativity to how it might have looked 600 years earlier. New windows let in light and had mosaics sparkling. The work was carried out by enthusiastic local Palestinians (and president Abbas) who, of course, are all Moslems. And this at a time when the whole Middle East is a bloodbath of sectarian hatreds. The item should have had front page headlines.

AN UNFULFILLED CO-INCIDENCE

My two years of National Service in the RAF included almost a year in Kenya (1955). There was a big Billy Graham-type Crusade in which I became much involved, taking leave and working in their office and at all the rallies, etc. Ah, the confidence of youth! There was already much in the way of Christian activity. Scores of boys from the posh Prince of Wales and Duke of York schools were in Crusader Classes run by an evangelical family with a big house and grounds in Nairobi (Bwana Jarvis's). They also kept open house for any servicemen who would become willing helpers. (One task I enjoyed on Tuesday nights was making dozens of meringues for the weekend - ensuring boys' tummies as well as souls were satisfied.) Our Church of Scotland minister, at St Andrew's Church in Nairobi, turned out to be the father of David Steel who'd become Scotland's prominent politician. (On one occasion services were cancelled as a lion was sprawled at the entrance porch of the church.) Other people also kept open house for servicemen and a small group of us particularly enjoyed our times with Iain Buist a British civil servant, and Wim Schott, a Netherlands banker (our 'Civilian Attachés'), friendships that endured till deaths began interfering forty years on. As a result we visited game parks, had holidays on the coast, met Ugandan royalty and travelled to the Mountains of the Moon - and afterwards we were given service medals seeing we were there because of the Mau Mau emergency, something that hardly affected me as a lowly telephonist at RAF Eastleigh.

Another who befriended servicemen was Laurie Campbell, (recently married) who taught at the Alliance High School, later becoming its head. This had been founded in 1926 by an alliance of Protestant missions, the first national secondary school in Kenya. (More than half the first Kenya cabinet were alumni.) The Campbell's home at Kikuyu became one of our 'home from homes'. His status in Kenya can be seen when, fifty years after Independence, a new dormitory at the school was given his name. Somehow he had squeezed in divinity courses at New College, Edinburgh and, retiring as headmaster of Kingswood School in Bath, became minister of the city's Trinity Methodist Church. (The Church of Scotland wouldn't take him: too old.) Much of this I learned from a full page obituary in the *Scotsman* in 2011 - after failing periodic attempts over the intervening years to try and trace Laurie to tell him of the story that follows.

In 1960 I became a teacher, at Braehead School in Fife, run by visionary R F Mackenzie. Appointed to do what would become Outdoor Education, we often had an uphill struggle to obtain suitable equipment. ('Twenty cricket bats, fine . . .Tents, two primus stoves, no, not on our lists,') - so we made extensive use of youth hostels, Glencoe especially, where the warden soon became Auntie Ingrid to scores of boys. (Girls, *tut, tut,* came later.) The charitable Horsa Trust had given Braehead a minibus, and typical of the authorities, when we asked them for a needed replacement (other schools were by then receiving them) we were told, 'No, you already have one'. That old bus took us to places the length and breadth of Scotland but most frequently to Glencoe.

One of the teachers who drove the bus up and back several times was a Laurie Campbell. The co-incidence of name didn't strike me at the time but, even today, photographer Laurie Campbell's name didn't for long enough make me think of the teacher either. Braehead's Laurie Campbell was head of the English department and appeared good at the job and popular. 'A bit of a bullshitter' was staff-room opinion. I must admit on the long drives to and from the wilds I heard many yarns about what he'd seen and done abroad and thought much the same.

Returning to Braehead from one spell in the Highlands I found that our Laurie Campbell had been arrested! Typewriters had been reported going AWOL both at Braehead and at his previous post so the police investigated. They found a lot more than just missing typewriters - unbeknown to each other he also had two wives and his name was not Laurie Campbell.

The man's story was of escaping from the Congo horrors with just what he stood in: no belongings, no documents, no money. But an excellent CV apparently, so with all the data he could provide, he soon had another passport and entered the teaching profession. The identity he had assumed was Laurie Campbell's in Kenya. As a squaddy stationed there he had taken the opportunity to rifle through his host's papers and use them for his Congo subterfuge later on. One of the very real regrets in my life was that I didn't click with the name and on one drive (when he'd spun stories about his life) blurt out, 'Oh, I knew a Laurie Campbell in Kenya'.

ESSAOUIRA MYTHS

Essaouira on the Atlantic coast west of Marrakech has been one of my 'most favourite places in the world' ever since coming on it in 1965. Like any favourite place I came to know it well, both in its present form and its historical past. Many of the guidebooks mentioned it was the work of a French slave and though Theodore Cornut was French and the builder of the great sea defences of St Malo the truth was he was simply tempted away from working at Gibraltar for Britain by greater riches offered by Sultan Mohammed Ben Abdallah to create the magic of what we call Essaouira today (try *Essa-we-rah*). He was no slave. There were other Essa puzzles in guidebooks.

All of them mentioned monkey puzzle trees growing along the seafront but I had one growing in my garden at home and the species had long been a fascination. A Scottish doctor-cum-naturalist, Archibald Menzies, on board Vancouver's *Discovery* was once a guest at a dinner with the Governor of Chile in 1795 when he noted some strange nuts in a bowl. Being curious he put several in his pocket, and germinated them on board ship. Eventually these ended in Kew, and were named *Araucaria araucaria* - the monkey puzzle. In a desultory sort of way, over years, I tried to find out just what the similar but different trees were that grew in Essaouira. The answer came in a serendipitous way. At that time I collected stamps showing birds and ordered a set of stamps from the Norfolk Islands that portrayed that Pacific outpost's flora and fauna. And one of the stamps showed the Essa trees: *Araucaria heterophylla*, (Norfolk Island Pine). As a contributor to *The Rough Guide* I also passed on that information for correction. (Some years on I let out a laugh when reading one of Dorothy Dunnett's Dolly Johnson novels where she - oh dear! - had *cedars* growing along the seafront!)

Another matter had long-disquietened me. The guidebooks all mentioned that Disraeli, the Victorian Prime Minister's family, came from Essaouira, some of them giving pages of biographical detail. The politician Hore-Belisha's family did certainly originate in Essaouira. But Disraeli? His father was a wealthy man-about-town who dabbled a bit in literature but, on digging into full biographies, the family's origins were shown to be Genoa. Nothing at all to do with Essaouira. I found it baffling that whole *pages* of misinformation existed but can more easily understand it now with some recent researches and observations. (I may say *The Rough Guide* soon removed the Disraeli myth, and the rest soon followed.)

However, to this day, Essaouira's alleys are loud with the

(no doubt illegal) CDs of Jimi Hendrix and touts will vie to lead the curious to where he stayed (no doubt above a brother's marquetry shop) and regale them with stories about all that Hendrix got up to in his many visits to the town, or out at Diabet where indeed at one time there were hippy goings-on (and a multiple beach murder) before the police cleared such elements. (At that time one of our climbing party was refused entry at Tangier Port because of his long hair - and only arrived by flying to Marrakech.) The Hendrix stories were becoming outrageous. He founded a sort of hippy community out at Diabet and his famous song 'Castles in the Sand' was inspired by the sultan's ruined pavilion in the dunes - except the song was written before he visited Morocco. I had to read several Hendrix biographies (in the Music Library in Edinburgh) before finding any mention of Morocco; he simply spent 'a week touring the country'. Any visit to Essa must have been brief yet these myths have grown in a few decades and, again, the guidebooks were full of nonsense. *The Rough Guide* was at first unconvinced when told the screeds on Hendrix were as fictitious as the Disraeli ones. Recently, in Essaouira, I was accosted by an American lady of a certain age (and size) who demanded of me, seeing I knew the place, to tell her 'Where dear Jimi was buried'. She was most offended when I suggested Seattle. [He is buried at Greenwood Cemetry, Renton, to the south of Seattle.]

BUENO

Don't ask me where I stopped for the night; the spot was happily in the middle of nowhere after driving 350 kilometres southwards through Spain in the morning, exploring Salamanca, then driving on to turn off the main road somewhere, then off that road onto a minor one into cool, hilly country to finish along a tiny track up a wooded valley, maquis-scented, and noisy from the mountain torrent. I crossed over an ancient hump-backed bridge that made me think of Tam o' Shanter. I found a flat prow to park my camper-van on for the night. Peace one could almost breathe.

After cooking supper I sat out on a folding chair for coffee and started a bottle of wine, just enjoying the quiet solitude, when a great *baa-ing* grew near, and for several minutes a straggling, noisy, dusty flock of sheep passed, followed by the shepherd, an old man with a wrinkled face and droopy moustache who looked as if he'd stepped out of a Western, a Mexican bandit stereotype. He stopped before me, swopped his stick to his other hand, and held out a paw for shaking. A toothy grin. *Buenas tardes*. That far I could manage in Spanish but goodness knows what dialect he did speak in that lost corner of old Spain. He found 'Hamish' difficult to pronounce and I found his name impossible.

Lack of language in no way inhibited conversation. Where was I going? I told him I was heading to Algeciras to visit Morocco and he recounted that his soldiering days were spent at Melilla and he'd visited Marrakech. *Bueno*. Was I staying right here for the night? In the van? *Frío*. I'd freeze. So I showed him my Black's *Icelandic* sleeping bag. He had an appraising feel of it. *Bueno*. Yes, he'd appreciate a glass of wine. Drouthy work all day up in the mountains. He was seventy six years young. The 600 sheep had been brought up to the mountains after Easter. A hard life, *si* but ah, *bueno, bueno* and he gave a proprietary sweeping gesture round his world. Suddenly he joked that he was a bad shepherd. Where were his sheep? We could hear them, if distantly, and the last rays of the sun were sparking on the dust of their passing down by the ancient bridge. *Adiós*. We shook hands again and he strode off with that tireless gait that tells of walking many miles and many years.

AN ENCHANTMENT

Dusk had fallen this winter day with bruised colours as I wandered by the shore of deep-set Loch Etive. The frost had been intense and the less salty head of the loch had frozen. The shore stones were icy and the grass crystallised with hoar, so progress afoot was slow but as a result I was gifted the sight of a little wonder.

The ebb tide in receding had left the ice supported by rocks but hollow underneath, here and there the ice sagging or collapsing under its own weight. The tide had then come in again and, as I watched, began to work on the marooned ice gently lifting the disintegrating features off the stones, setting them free so they floated, first one or two, then scores, then hundreds.

In that strange last glow of light they looked translucent, magical shapes, like models of tall ships with all sails set. Slowly the current began to shift them from the shore and they became an imagined world of mythical swans, gracefully gliding, some asleep, others wings half raised, others dibbling, out on to the rocking of the sea, silent as ghosts.

I stood enchanted. If they had suddenly taken flight I would not have been surprised. As it was, they slowly, slowly went off into the deepening dark till I could see them no more.

ACKNOWLEDGEMENTS

Selected pieces have appeared in the *Scotsman* and *Glasgow Herald* (for whom I wrote features regularly in the Eighties and Nineties), in the *Scots Magazine* (my first there fifty years ago), *The Great Outdoors* and other lost outdoor titles, the *Scottish Mountaineering Club Journal*, *Alpine Journal*, *Scottish Mountaineer*, *MMM* and the historic *Blackwoods*. Current work has appeared in the commercial-free, no adverts, quality quarterly of writing about mountains by mountaineers, *Loose Scree*. Thanks to them all. I'm also indebted to my local Burntisland library, the Central Library in Edinburgh and the National Library of Scotland, which houses my 'archive'. My biggest debt is to Sheila Gallimore who has produced such perfect work from my often difficult pastiches and Robert Davidson of Sandstone Press who has now sent it out into the world.

Burntisland 2016

www.sandstonepress.com

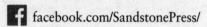 facebook.com/SandstonePress/

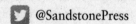 @SandstonePress